Viet Nam – The Unheard Voices

For Howard
and Margaret
What a wonderful
trip ... Thanks
for being here!
love
Don

29-1-
95

VIET NAM –
The Unheard Voices

By DON LUCE and
JOHN SOMMER

Foreword by
EDWARD M. KENNEDY

Cornell Paperbacks
Cornell University Press
Ithaca and London

First published 1969 by Cornell University Press.
Published in the United Kingdom by Cornell University Press Ltd., 2–4 Brook Street, London W1Y 1AA.

First printing, Cornell Paperbacks, 1970
Second printing 1972

International Standard Book Number 0-8014-9103-7
Library of Congress Catalog Card Number 69-18361

PRINTED IN THE UNITED STATES OF AMERICA
BY VAIL-BALLOU PRESS INC.

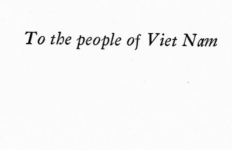

To the people of Viet Nam

CONTENTS

FOREWORD

Don Luce and John Sommer are two extraordinary young men. They were not involved in the Viet Nam war as we know it, although they and their colleagues personally lived through this tragedy—and still do. They were not on the side of a great power or a nationalistic movement, although they, too, have fought for others—and still do. Luce and Sommer became a part of Viet Nam. But most importantly, they and a few others became a part of the people, listened to them, spoke for them, worked for them, loved and understood them, at a time when a thoughtless war was rolling over them.

I met Don Luce when he testified so eloquently before the Senate Judiciary Subcommittee on Refugees in 1965. By 1967, he no longer could tolerate the suffering that our good intentions brought to the people of Viet Nam. So he left, returned to this country and spoke of things that America had lost sight of, and of a war that we were losing, the computers and statistics to the contrary. Now he has gone back.

John Sommer traveled with me through Viet Nam in 1968. With his knowledge of the country and its language he helped me to speak with the Vietnamese refugee, the farmer, and those women and children so horribly injured by war. In Sommer's quiet manner I found great strength, but more than that, I found a dedication in the truest sense to Viet Nam and her future.

Viet Nam—The Unheard Voices is a different story. Had the voices to which the authors refer been heard, or at least not dismissed, Viet Nam might have been different. Yet, neither Luce nor Sommer is anxious to focus on villains. They claim no prescience for themselves in the early days. But they do make the case that most now recognize: ". . . the fault is more ours . . . for it was our duty to understand before we intervened in such great force."

It is my hope that the war in Viet Nam will soon end and American soldiers will soon be able to leave that land. But it is also my hope that we leave with a moral—this adventure in Southeast Asia is not sad or regrettable simply because it failed. Fighting men died on both sides, and hundreds of thousands of civilians died on both sides, because in haste we relied primarily on the tools of war to attack social problems and to win political allegiance for an unstable government in a distant place. That did not do in this case. It will not do in the future.

EDWARD M. KENNEDY

Washington, D.C.
January 1969

PREFACE

When we first volunteered to serve in Viet Nam—one of us in 1958, the other in 1963—that little country was virtually unknown to most Americans, including ourselves. We went there largely through happenstance. An organization called International Voluntary Services (IVS) was sending young volunteers, most of them recent college graduates, to help in various countries of Asia, Africa, and the Middle East.

Founded as a private, nonprofit organization in 1953, IVS was led by persons drawn from various religious denominations, from the academic world, and from groups interested in rural development. These men were committed to the idea that dedicated young people could make a contribution to both international understanding and economic development by living with the people of newly independent nations and assisting them in common programs of agriculture, education, and general community action.

Several years later, as the American Peace Corps was being established, largely on the IVS model, IVS was evolving in various directions. From an organization concerned primarily with agriculture and other rural programs, it was expanding its scope to include teams in education (primarily for the teaching of English and science), youth activities (mainly in social-action programs), and urban or community development. From an exclusively American organization, it was internationalizing to include in its ranks volunteers from Britain, Canada, France, Haiti, India, Israel, Japan, Korea, the Netherlands, the Philippines, and Taiwan. Having served in fourteen countries and being currently encouraged to work in others, IVS now numbers about two hundred members, with some eighty of these in Viet Nam.

IVS had first come to Viet Nam in 1957, during the relatively peaceful period after what is now called the First Indochina War. Few would have expected then that an even more brutal war would break out. When we decided to cast our lot with IVS in Viet Nam, we were simply seeking an experience in which we could both help others and learn ourselves.

Like all IVS volunteers, we were required to serve for a minimum of two years abroad, and we were given an orientation that placed considerable emphasis on training in the local language. We received a living allowance adequate to cover our expenses overseas, plus an additional $80 a month that was deposited in our banks at home. Financing for IVS projects may come from either private or government sources, under contract with the host country. The money for our program was funded through the United States Agency for International Development (AID) and the South Vietnamese government, though for some specific projects we received support from private agencies as well.

Our jobs in Viet Nam, we soon found out, were to increase sweet potato production and to assist in the opening of primary schools in the villages. Politics, in fact, seemed quite irrelevant, and the challenges and rewards of our work were such that we decided to stay well beyond the initial two years of our contracts. Because we were trained to speak Vietnamese and lived among the people of the country, we increasingly came to know and admire them. We ourselves became far more committed than we had ever anticipated.

Over the years, however, the sufferings of the Vietnamese increased as warfare returned to the country. As the range of our own experiences also broadened, we began to see unnecessary mistakes being made by our American government in response to the new conditions. Our early humanitarian motives for wishing to serve in Viet Nam were being thwarted. Some of these frustrations we could chalk up to experience and practical education for ourselves. Others we could not. It became inevitable that our commitment to Viet Nam would take on political overtones. Finally, as we saw too many opportunities for reforms being passed by, and as the situation became increasingly desperate, we realized that we as individuals could no longer continue in our same roles in South Viet Nam. We knew that we could not long stay away from that country and that we would somehow return there. But in the fall of 1967 we left, determined to share our experiences with the American people.

This, then, is a story about Viet Nam. It is a true story, told for a purpose. If it is too late to correct mistaken policies of the past, our fervent hope is to avoid similar mistakes in the future. For this is not a story intended merely to bemoan the sufferings of war. Our purpose is to demonstrate that understanding people is the key to successful policy, that failure to understand them and respond to their needs is to fail in one's goals, and finally, that a great America cannot win hearts and minds by technology and material means alone. A concern for the human spirit is not a luxury; it is an essential.

We have attempted here to reflect the feelings of our Vietnamese friends and colleagues as they were expressed to us during our years of living and working in Viet Nam. We do not claim any foolproof solutions to the problems—or more accurately, dilemmas —of Viet Nam, and we have enjoyed the benefits of hindsight. We still feel that Americans can and should play a large and helpful role in the affairs of peoples of developing countries, though we would prefer to see this role fulfilled in an international framework. It is not the fact, then, but the quality of the American role abroad that concerns us. That Asians are not Americans is recognized perhaps in an intellectual sense, but not yet in an intuitive one. We still have much to learn about other countries and other peoples.

Government policies, perforce, are made by people other than those who are affected by them. In Viet Nam, our job, in a sense, was to bridge the gap between the makers of policy and the people affected. But the voices of the Vietnamese people—and our own as well—were not often heard. Now we raise them again, in hopes that those who have erred can learn from past mistakes, and that those who have suffered and given of their lives will not have done so entirely in vain. The Vietnamese people have much to teach all of us.

We owe the reader two small explanations. First, to facilitate the style of writing we have used the first person plural throughout, even when a particular anecdote or conversation has involved only one of us. The book, though presented in this form, is a composite of our largely separate and individual experiences in Viet Nam. Second, we have used fictitious names for certain Vietnamese friends and colleagues out of consideration for their safety.

We wish to offer our deepest appreciation to all those who have made this book possible. We thank the Project on International Relations of East Asia, of the Center of International Studies at Cornell University, for wholehearted support, both professional and logistic. We are also indebted to our colleagues in the Viet Nam Education Project and its sponsors in the United Methodist Church for their interest and encouragement.

In a more general sense, but in no way a less significant one, we want to thank all our friends and colleagues of International Voluntary Services: the founders, directors, and staff, who gave us the opportunity to serve and who made possible our entire overseas experience; and our comrades in Viet Nam, those with whom we have served over the years, who have shared our frustrations and joys, and who have enriched, each in his own way, the contents of the present volume. Last, but hardly least, we wish to emphasize our boundless debt to hundreds of Vietnamese friends and coworkers. From them we have learned not only about Viet Nam, but also about ourselves. Any mistakes in this volume are our own, but the book itself, we would like to think, is theirs.

D. L.

J. S.

January 1969

Viet Nam – The Unheard Voices

Our enemy is not a man;
if we kill the man, with whom do we live? . . .
Our enemy is inside each one of us.

—PHAM DUY, a folksinger of Viet Nam

[1]

CAUGHT IN THE MIDDLE

IVS Volunteers in Viet Nam

Dogs barked and children peeked around the corners of their houses. It wasn't often that a jeep drove into Ha Lan in 1958. No one in the village owned a car, although quite a few of the men had learned to drive in the French army. It was even less often that Ong Tay (Mr. Westerner) came. But it was exciting. The motor fascinated the children and they fought over who would ride in the front seat from the priest's house back to the village gates.

"The wild pigs are in the corn again," Father Nam, the priest, complained.

"We'll tell Mr. Paul," we promised, knowing that Paul had gone hunting in that area several times.

"Mr. Foul never hits them." Father Nam, like most Vietnamese, had trouble pronouncing Paul's name.

We smiled and followed Father Nam into his tiny home. An old table flanked by wooden benches dominated the center of the room. The dirt floor had a polished look from the thousands of bare feet that had come to bring news of births, deaths, weddings, and all other matters concerning the state of affairs in Ha Lan.

"Drink tea," Father Nam ordered as we sat down at the table. This used up his entire English vocabulary, and somehow we were envious that *we* had not taught him the two words. It was only after an hour of drinking tea and discussing in Vietnamese the problems of the Highland village that Father Nam asked why we had come.

"At the agricultural experiment station," we explained, "we have tested sweet potato varieties from several different countries. We have found two varieties that produce more than any local variety we can find. Perhaps you would like to try them." We showed him the two bags of potatoes. "This one is from Japan and this one is from Taiwan."

Father Nam studied them carefully, then asked one of the young women to cook three potatoes of each of the new varieties and three of his own potatoes.

Several cups of tea later, Chi Tu brought three plates of potatoes. Using both hands to be polite, she put the plates on the table. Excitement mounted as the priest methodically cut the potatoes into bite-sized pieces. He crossed himself and tasted each variety; then, waiting for the suspense to build up, he spoke solemnly: "Needs salt."

We all laughed. One comes to appreciate the gentle Vietnamese humor and flair for the dramatic, and Father Nam did not allow this mood to break. He summoned two of the older boys, Em Loc and Em Tan, quickly tied napkins over their eyes, and passed the three plates around for their judgment. Japanese 101 was the winner, with the local variety a close second. Em Loc spat third-place Taiwan 47 onto the floor to the amusement of everyone except his mother, who cuffed him behind the ears.

"The farmers will plant one row of your Japanese variety," Father Nam announced. We smiled. It remained only to set a date for distribution of the new sweet potato cuttings and to designate one person in the village who would be responsible for seeing that each farmer got his share.

Encouraging farmers to plant improved varieties of sweet potato is a typical assignment for the volunteers in International Voluntary Services. It is also a relatively simple one. Vietnamese farmers are receptive to innovation, particularly when little risk is involved. With new varieties, which can be planted in one or two experimental rows beside the old variety, farmers are not taking much of a gamble. Even more important, they don't usually have to follow any new practices, invest a lot of extra money, or change their pattern of life. Introduction of new varieties is thus one of the simplest ways of promoting economic development at both village and national levels.

Economic development has always been one of the principal goals of IVS volunteers in Viet Nam. Because of this, even as late as 1963 and 1964 it often seemed as though the war itself hardly existed. The problems we faced were mostly technical: What was the best way to dig a canal? How should teachers be trained for village school assignments? How could one maintain classroom discipline with eighty students in an English class? Such questions would arise in almost any modernization effort in almost any developing country. Of course we also had problems with unresponsive bureaucrats and with corruption, but in these respects too we knew that Viet Nam was not unique, and we could work in spite of them.

Around 1963, one volunteer agriculturalist was looking for a way to help the people of Minh Hoa, a large village located in a rice-growing area near the Gulf of Siam. The soil there was poor due to a high acid content, and salt-water intrusion during the dry season made it necessary for the villagers to go several kilometers to find fresh water. Furthermore, although the village headquarters was a center for many local businesses, there was no road or canal to connect it with the nearby hamlets. The people of Minh Hoa thus decided to dig a canal. From the experiences of other villages, they knew that a canal would facilitate drainage, thereby reducing the acidity of the soil and allowing increased rice production. They also hoped that the canal would provide fresh drinking water during the dry season. But perhaps most important, the canal as a transportation route would make it easier for them to market their goods and to visit their relatives.

The village chief in Minh Hoa was an exceptional person. During the war against the French, he had been a province chief with the Viet Minh. The rigors of Viet Minh life and the guerrilla's typical identification with the rural people made him ideally suited for his present job. He always maintained a sense of direction and order, while at the same time understanding and empathizing with the villagers.

Les, the young volunteer, had first learned of the village chief through the hydraulics service in Rach Gia, the provincial capital. An engineer there had told him of the village's desire for a self-help project, and Les visited the chief at his small thatch office.

"We would like to dig a canal," the chief told Les. "We need means of transportation and a way to drain the acidity from the soil. I am told that you understand the government's self-help project. Perhaps you could take our request back to Rach Gia. You see, this is the dry season. The farmers have now finished their rice harvest and there is little to do until the rains. They could use their labor to dig the canal. But we need food from the government because canal-digging is very hard work. Tonight we will have a village meeting. Can you come?"

Les nodded enthusiastically. After discussing how they could obtain foodstuffs for carrying out a self-help project, the chief took Les on a tour of the village. "The canal will start here and go six kilometers to the river," he explained. "The hydraulics service in Rach Gia has promised to help with the technical aspects."

Les had dinner at the chief's home—rice, a soup made from pork and some greens, and roasted river fish—and afterward they walked over to the village meeting house. A crowd had already gathered and men were arguing with one another, each intent on making his point understood by speaking a little louder than the rest. The village chief seated Les to one side and then went to the table at the front of the room. There was an immediate hush.

"I have studied your request for a canal very carefully," he began. "It will be possible, but it will require a lot of hard work on everyone's part. Tonight we can discuss some of the details. But first I would like to introduce the foreigner who is sitting over there." The village chief nodded toward the young American, and the villagers all stood and clapped. This is what they had done when the French were there, and respectful applause now came as a matter of course. Les half stood and then sat down, his face red with embarrassment. He saw no reason for the clapping and tried to make himself less conspicuous by slouching down in his chair.

"The young American is here to help us. He has explained the government's program of self-help to me, and we can obtain food if we dig the canal." Les wanted to object to this. He hadn't promised that they would get food. He had just explained how the program worked. But to interrupt would cause the village chief to lose face. The chief had passed to him the responsibility for getting the food.

By this time one of the men was standing, waiting for recognition. The chief saw him and gave permission for the man to speak.

"It has been a very bad season; the rice was very poor. We cannot dig without rice to feed ourselves."

"Yes," said another man, "and we need rice, not bulgur wheat like the government usually gives out. Bulgur makes us sick and—"

"You can always sell the bulgur for pig feed on the market and buy rice," the village chief cut in.

"Then we must get a lot of bulgur because its price is low and the price of rice is high," the second man replied.

"I live more than one kilometer from where the canal will be built," a third man complained. "Why should I dig?"

"Because," answered the chief, "you will benefit in the long run. It will still be easier for you to send your rice to market. The village will be more wealthy and your children will be able to go to a better school. If we are to have a canal, everyone must cooperate. Now I am going to ask you to make an important decision. We have had six meetings and if we are to have a canal we must stop talking and start digging. I ask that you give me full authority to make work assignments on the canal." This request caused a shuffling of feet, and neighbors looked at each other to see if there would be general agreement. But the village chief was popular, and the villagers realized that this was the best way to proceed. They agreed.

"Good," smiled the chief. "It is six thousand meters [four miles] from here to the river. There are one thousand families in the village. Each family will dig six meters of canal. The canal must be five meters wide and one and a half meters deep. Next week the hydraulics service from Rach Gia will come and mark out the path of the canal. Each six meters will be numbered. The numbers will be written on slips of paper and put in a hat. Then they will be drawn out and put beside the name of each family on the hamlet list."

Discussion went on into the night. There were a hundred details to be decided, but the basic organization had been established. Les returned to Rach Gia the next day and talked with Vietnamese provincial officials who then went to Minh Hoa and made arrangements for provision of food in the form of cooking oil and bulgur wheat. (Bulgur wheat is a cereal product of high nutritional quality. Being a surplus commodity in the United States, it has been exported in huge amounts to Viet Nam. Unfortunately, however, few Vietnamese like to eat it, preferring rice instead. Attempts to demonstrate imaginative recipes for bulgur cookies and other delicacies have usually been unsuccessful, but at least the pigs like the wheat.)

Les visited Minh Hoa often, sometimes to help a family dig its six meters and sometimes to talk with the village chief. The chance to talk over problems with someone from outside seemed to clarify issues and to help the chief arrive at solutions. One problem was that the land was not exactly level, and some families had to dig more than one and a half meters deep. They were very unhappy about this, especially since others had to dig only one meter. Finally it was decided that the village chief would talk with provincial officials in Rach Gia about getting extra bulgur wheat for those farmers who had to dig deeper than the average.

Another problem was the heat, which made the workers thirsty. Young girls hurried back and forth with tiny buckets, but fresh water was far away and they could carry only a little. The villagers began to wonder whether the canal was so important after all.

Clearly something had to be done. The chief and his family, laboring over their own six-meter stretch, were also hot and irritated. Would such a small problem destroy the whole project? Suddenly the chief had an idea, and he tossed his shovel aside.

"We will take an oxcart and haul water in the large American cans [fifty-five-gallon drums] the government gave us," he said. "Old Tao [whose arm was lost in the war against the French] has been complaining because he cannot dig. Now he can take part. Yes, we can continue digging the canal!"

Two hours later, old Tao, beaming over his new responsibility, began the first of many oxcart trips up and down the canal bank. The diggers cheered as he came into sight, and Tao's smile broadened.

As problems came up, new meetings were organized or the village chief himself worked out solutions. Les's role was a subtle one: facilitating relations between village and provincial authorities and lending moral support to the people involved in the project. It was the subtlety that the villagers appreciated most. They did not need or want an exalted adviser or someone who would do the job for them. These people, and especially the Minh Hoa village chief, were too proud for that. They were grateful simply for a volunteer who would come and help them in this way.

It was early morning on a day in 1966, and the situation was changing in Viet Nam. An old woman with wrinkled skin and toothless mouth was washing clothes by the well at Trai Hai, a resettlement area for the people who used to live in Kinh Dinh. When we asked some small children playing nearby how old the woman was, they said, "Oh, she is very old." In traditional Viet Nam, age is dignity. Our addressing her as "old woman" was thus a sign of respect.

"What are you doing, old woman?" we asked.

"I'm washing clothes," she said.

"They look like American clothes," we continued, noting that they were military green and in large sizes.

"Yes," she replied, but unenthusiastically, as if not wishing to discuss the matter further.

"Where did you live before, old woman?"

"Kinh Dinh."

"Where is that? Is it far?"

"Very far. It's over there." The old woman lifted her head from the clothes just long enough to nod in a northerly direction.

"What was it like there?" we continued.

"So much fighting . . ."

"But *before;* what was it like before?"

The old woman lifted her head, put down the shirt she had been pounding against the cement apron of the new well, and showed a glimmer of recalled joy through her wrinkles and her saddened brows. "Oh, *before!* Our life was good. There was peace. We had our rice fields, our buffalo, our chickens and pigs. Every year, when the season of afternoon rains was just beginning, we would plant the rice—all the women would line up in rows to plant the seedlings. When the sun was high above our heads—and very hot!—we would eat our lunch in the shade of the coconut trees and gossip among ourselves about all the village love affairs. We had to work very hard, but we were never afraid of anything then. At harvest time, we all worked together—there was a lot of work—but after the harvest we had celebrations, the whole family together. Oh, that was fun!" Her eyes lit up as she chatted on about her children and how, when they were young, they had splashed about in the river. The cycle of life was punctuated by weddings and funerals and holidays on which ancestors were revered, special kinds of cakes were baked, special costumes were worn. The pattern of one's days was predictable, hallowed by tradition. Life was secure.

"Why did you leave, old woman?"

"Things changed," she replied, turning despondent again. "Strange people began to pass through our village and talk with us about revolution and changing the government. We did not know about such things, but some of the young people listened. Then sometimes there was shooting at night, and in the morning it was dangerous to go into our fields because of shells that had not yet gone off. Huge war machines drove through the rice fields. It became difficult to transport our rice into the market because the road was often destroyed. Soldiers came to our village, asking many questions and sometimes taking off the young men. Life became very difficult."

"But when did you finally decide to leave?"

The old woman looked up with determination. "Our lives became sick with misery. Perhaps you cannot imagine what it was really like. Noisy airplanes flew overhead, dropping fire and bombs very near to us. Sometimes they dropped leaflets telling us to leave, but we did not want to leave our grandfathers' land. More of our people were taken off, and we were threatened by many sides. The women had to do the work of the men. Some of the people had their crops turn brown from the sky medicine. It was hard to sleep at night. My son was arrested by the authorities; they said he had some bad leaflets. Our family was divided and very sad. We became too poor, and it was hard to take proper care of our ancestors' tombs, especially after my son was taken away. We had no choice; we had to leave. We brought all we could here to the town. Oh, we were so tired, so tired." She returned to her clothes, then suddenly looked up again and asked "Why are you here, Mr. Foreigner?"

"We're here to help," we said. "We would like to dig a well or clean out those dirty drainage ditches."

"Oh," she said uncertainly. Then, finished with her washing, she picked up her clothes and made her way arduously up the embankment from the well toward her house. We helped her carry the basket of clothes to the top. She was surprised at the gesture, but did not thank us.

This kind of apathy was the most common characteristic of many of Trai Hai's people. They had never even bothered to name their settlement. Trai Hai, meaning literally "Camp Number Two," was the designation given by the local government refugee-service chief. Whenever the question of naming the camp arose, as it had from time to time during the year, the people responded, "Why bother? We'll be going back to our own village soon."

"Vui vui len, vui vui len." The girls sang the joyful rice-planting song—the words mean "happy, happy grow," but their flavor is untranslatable—as they placed the palm leaves on the bamboo frame to make the conical hats. The rhythm of the song seemed to fit what they were doing, and besides, it was rice-planting time in Phu Yen.

The girls were from a group of twenty-five refugees between thirteen and seventeen years old who had attended a 1967 training course on how to make conical hats. A woman who was very skillful at hat-making had come from another village and spent several days with the girls. It took a day to make a hat and each hat gave them fifty piasters ($0.40) profit. The program had been developed by Tom, a young IVS refugee worker, and it had all the characteristics that a volunteer comes to admire in a project. It was not a giveaway program, it taught new skills, and it reached people who really needed help. Tom was concerned over the large number of girls in the refugee camps who, in need of money, were going to work in the local brothels. He felt that making conical hats offered them a more honorable and permanent source of income.

The girls liked it, too. It gave them a chance to be together and gossip and to have the independent feeling of a wage earner.

"What will happen when the war is over?" one of the younger girls asked as they finished singing.

"Oh, the men will all come home and there'll be lots of husbands." The girls all giggled at the thought.

"Well, I won't be wife number two," an older girl stated em-

phatically, referring to the old custom, still in practice, of some men
having two wives.

"Humph, you'll be lucky if you get married at all," another girl
quipped, and she dodged the bamboo switch that the older girl
directed at her in mock anger.

The joking and singing continued until the sun began to set. Then
the girls gathered their palm leaves, bamboo, and half-finished hats,
and walked down the line of tin houses of the Chop Chai settlement.
The smells and stuffiness of the camp contrasted sharply with the
shady spot by the small stream where they went on sunny days to
weave the hats. They huddled around the tables that their families
had been fortunate enough to bring from the old village. A bowl of
soup made from leaves the mother had picked and a bowl of rice
were in the center of each table. The families dunked the leaves in
fish sauce and thought, but seldom spoke, of the fish they wished
they had.

For two months the girls made the conical hats. Each week the
IVS volunteer bundled the hats and sent them away to be sold by a
private group of Americans. The money came back and rice was
bought for the girls. Everything seemed to be going well.

Then one night several rounds of gunfire hit the nearby American
artillery camp, creating mass confusion. The American officers
feared they were under a general attack, and to defend themselves
they directed a return attack on Chop Chai with armored personnel-
carriers mounted with .50-caliber machine guns. The bullets sliced
through the tiny tin shacks and the heat twisted and even melted the
metal sheets. The frightened refugees crawled into their carefully
dug foxholes. A few ran out into the night.

The next morning Tom went to Chop Chai to see what he could
do. The refugees were still milling around in a daze. Twelve had
been killed, including some of the hatmakers. More than twenty
others had been wounded. An angry woman approached Tom, crying, "We hate the Americans," and soon a small crowd gathered
around him, demanding to know why their village had been destroyed.

When he drove back to town he talked to a soldier about the
attack. "Well," the soldier said, "we thought the bullets came from

Chop Chai. Actually, they came from another direction, as we found out later when we studied the situation. But you know how it is when you're scared and there are bullets flying around. The major said we'd help the villagers to rebuild. We are awful sorry about this. I wish there was a way to keep from making mistakes."

Tom walked away. Understanding what had happened did not make him feel better. He went to see the major.

"It was a regrettable error. We're sorry. But it is none of your goddam business. Stay out of military affairs." The major had too many problems to spend time with an eighty-dollar-a-month volunteer, to him the equivalent of a private.

The refugees moved a third time. The conical-hat program never got started again. Somehow it didn't seem to matter anymore.

The accelerating tempo of war and the increasing hostility of many Vietnamese people toward Americans began to affect the work of IVS seriously after mid-1965. In the early years, security conditions peculiar to Viet Nam sometimes limited our travel into the countryside, but never critically. Americans at home, or even in Saigon, were often amazed at the extent to which volunteers could carry on work even when newspaper headlines were dwelling on the battles that seemed to rage everywhere. In the final months of the Ngo Dinh Diem regime, to be sure, psychological tensions were very high. Some Vietnamese were hesitant to associate too much with any Americans, both because of the U.S. policy of upholding the increasingly hated regime and because of the regime's own suspicions of Americans. Then, after Diem was overthrown in the 1963 *coup d'état*, government ministries were in a state of disorder, causing volunteers' projects to be frequently delayed or canceled. But the worst was still to come.

By 1964 and early 1965, many volunteers, though instructed to keep out of political controversies, became more concerned over the trend of the war. As the Viet Cong acted more and more boldly, and occasionally even engaged in small firefights in the towns, a number of IVSers privately felt that more pressure should be brought to bear by the United States. We should start bombing the North, some suggested, thinking it was foolish to let the Viet Cong enjoy privileged sanctuary. If the Vietnamese Army could not lead its troops to fight, said others, then U.S. commanders should be placed in charge. Such suggestions, born out of desperation, were to prove embarrassing when we found out how wrong they were. At the time, however, an answer to a worsening situation had to be found. As individuals committed to the development of Viet Nam, we did not like to see our work destroyed. Our volunteer motto, to be sure, was "to work ourselves out of a job"; but we wanted to do this by instilling in our Vietnamese colleagues the ability to carry on, not by being forced out prematurely.

With escalation by both sides and the introduction of large American troop units in 1965, the role of the volunteer became gravely compromised. Late in that year, Pete Hunting, a good friend and outstanding IVS team leader for the Mekong Delta area, was riddled with bullets in a Viet Cong ambush along the road. Our earlier, almost blithe nonchalance about the war was deeply shaken by his death. Vietnamese friends were equally distressed. Since we were always much influenced by the attitudes of the Vietnamese with whom we lived and worked, we noted their shifts carefully. Some, of course, stiffened in their hatred of the Viet Cong. Others came to resent the Americans. In 1958, villagers had invited us in for tea and asked about life in the United States or jokingly offered to find us wives. Upon seeing us in 1967, these same villagers got up from their front steps, walked into their homes, and closed the door. Vietnamese who in 1958 had noted that Americans were unlike the French who had colonized Viet Nam, in 1967 added their voices to those who compared the Americans with the French. Vietnamese with whom we had gone to fun-filled work camps at Dalat, Can Tho, Ban Me Thuot, Bien Hoa, and Vung Tau were in 1967 saying that "the only way to help us now is to give us peace."

At the same time that the Vietnamese turned away from us, the U.S. Mission wanted us to cooperate more closely with American officials. But such associations made our role more difficult. The massive and increasingly resented American presence made it nearly impossible for volunteers to preserve a separate identity in the eyes of the Vietnamese. Even those Vietnamese who did appreciate the essentially neutral role of the IVS volunteer were afraid that close association would compromise them in their relations with other Vietnamese. Being sympathetic to their problems, in this case, did not make matters any easier for us.

But the American Mission appreciated IVS, and there were many frustrated and friendly government bureaucrats who were happy to while away the hours with the comparatively young and very unbureaucratic volunteers. Since we could speak Vietnamese and had friends at almost every level of the society, our participation on "the American team," as it came to be known, was widely solicited. This could be to our advantage, too, since we relied on U.S. government representatives for everything from transportation to project materials to moral support. But, at the same time, our associations with American power made us less appealing to Vietnamese who had learned to mistrust it and to fear it. In a 1966 efficiency move, the Office of Civilian Operations (OCO) was formed by the American Mission to incorporate all branches of the provincial civilian effort: JUSPAO * (information and psychological warfare), USAID † (economic assistance), and the CIA ‡ (intelligence). This marriage of the information service, the economic aid program, and secret intelligence activities made many Vietnamese suspect even more any American who associated with "official" Americans. It also, unfortunately, curtailed the effectiveness of the many Americans in organizations like AID who were simply trying to bring economic improvements to Viet Nam.

In one province, a student group was anxious to obtain cement so that their organization could hold a work camp to lay the floor for an elementary school nearby. The only place to get the cement was from the OCO office, yet the students were afraid that by going there they would compromise the reputation of their group. They believed that the American provincial representative was a CIA agent, and to avoid becoming involved with the CIA they asked an IVS teacher to get the cement for them. But one of the volunteer's students, upon hearing the story through the student grapevine, immediately went to the IVS member and advised him not to get

* Joint United States Public Affairs Office.
† United States Agency for International Development.
‡ Central Intelligence Agency.

the cement. He feared that any IVS participation would brand IVS as CIA, too. This incident hurt the image of the American economic aid program and embittered the IVS member toward the "official American policy." Still worse, an elementary school continued with a damp dirt floor, and the Vietnamese students decided to hold a seminar instead of a work camp. The seminar's topic was "The Effects of the American Presence in Viet Nam." When OCO was later combined with the military into MACCORDS,* primarily for purposes of the pacification program, the move alienated the Vietnamese still further from the Americans. It also frustrated American civilians.

It was for these reasons that when American government officials praised IVS as being an integral part of the American effort in Viet Nam, we took it as a left-handed compliment. It seemed more and more left-handed as the American effort fell under increasing attack from our Vietnamese friends. Still, American VIP's would search out volunteers in order to learn from them or to pay recognition: Vice-President Hubert H. Humphrey, Ambassadors Henry Cabot Lodge, Maxwell Taylor, and W. Averell Harriman, Secretary of Agriculture Orville Freeman, and numerous Senators and Congressmen. Interestingly, it was usually the Senators and Congressmen who asked the questions, while the men from the administration only came to pay recognition. In either case, we were naturally honored, though all the attention added to the fear of some Vietnamese that we might be connected with the mysterious and ever suspect CIA.

It was an accumulation of all these problems and dilemmas that served as the backdrop to a critical meeting of IVS members held in Saigon over the Fourth of July weekend, 1967. The question in everybody's mind was whether we should continue our work in Viet Nam.

The living room of the IVS house was hot and stuffy as seventy volunteers crowded together. (There were some who did not choose to attend, mainly because they were unwilling to leave their

* Military Assistance Command, Civil Operations and Revolutionary Development Support.

jobs even for those three days.) One of us—then the IVS director for Viet Nam—had been asked to describe the latest confrontation with the U.S. Mission. The Dean of Hue University's Faculty of Letters, he began, had requested the services of an IVS English teacher. In response, IVS had assigned a talented volunteer with a master's degree and previous college teaching experience to that position. Soon afterward, the U.S. Mission, smarting from the university's involvement in the anti-American Struggle Movement in 1966, registered a protest, stating that "all assistance to Hue University was to be discontinued with the exception of some humanitarian aid to the hospital." All other American groups were forbidden to be associated with the university. The American government felt that IVS, given its contractual relationship, had a duty to follow U.S. policies. And the U.S. Mission policy toward Hue was threefold: first, Hue University was a nonuniversity since it "lacked a serious program of instruction"; second, there were problems regarding professors, rebellious students, and uncooperative rectors; and third, the United States government could not give assistance to a noninstitution. IVS, on the other hand, felt that its role was to respond to the needs of the Vietnamese as they themselves saw them, in this case as interpreted by the Dean of the Faculty of Letters. Most volunteers felt that as long as students continued coming to class the IVS teacher should stay and teach at Hue University. Several gave vent to their frustrations.

"Whether we like it or not, we're considered part of the American war effort rather than individuals just here to help," an English teacher complained. "We look like Americans. Most of us are Americans. And after two years, we'll return to America. We are just part of this huge American happening."

Several hands shot up, but before the moderator could call on anybody one of the refugee workers was already talking. "What bothers me is that by helping the refugees, we are just easing the conscience of the military when they make more refugees."

"Do you think General Westmoreland pays any attention to whether there's an IVSer around before the refugees are created?" countered another.

"Well, what about the case of Jon?" Jon had overheard American soldiers radioing in from an operation to ask whether there was anyone who could take care of fifty VC suspects. When headquarters told them that La Hai had a refugee man who could handle the problem, the soldiers announced that they would then go ahead and burn the whole hamlet and bring in 350 people.

"Our job is to help people. If we spend all our time arguing about whether U.S. policy in Viet Nam is good or bad, we'll end up having only a stimulating intellectual exercise for ourselves. Is that why we're here?" The volunteer who spoke looked around the room, challenging someone to argue with him.

"I would like to say that there is a role for the IVS English teacher," said a teacher from Ban Me Thuot. "Viet Nam has little technical information in Vietnamese. The students can best get this material in English. Advanced study is best done in English. Besides, we are not just teaching language skills. We are teachers bringing new ideas. Look back into your own life. Who besides your parents influenced you more than—"

"And what happens to our students?" a delta volunteer interrupted. "They become interpreters for the Americans!"

"In whatever we do," said another volunteer, "we must always consider whether we are truly helping the Vietnamese people. They, after all, are our reason for being here. We want them to know that there are good Americans along with the bad."

"Whether the Vietnamese remember us or not doesn't matter," replied a girl who worked in Central Viet Nam. "The important thing is to leave behind some skills that will be useful to them. We shouldn't think so much about our own ego-gratification."

The discussion went on. Some IVSers said that their American identification was helpful. They could serve as intermediaries in getting supplies for projects useful to the Vietnamese, and the fact of having white skin helped to spur projects through Vietnamese government bureaucracies. "We are effective," they argued, "precisely because we are Americans in an increasingly American-oriented country."

Others, though not wishing to seem unpatriotic, simply did not believe in the wisdom of American policy. They wanted to disassociate themselves from it. "O.K., if you want to disassociate," someone challenged them, "why don't you give up your PX cards and why don't you stop going to the USO for ice cream? And you shouldn't hitch rides on military airplanes either, or send your letters through the Army Post Office." Some volunteers, in fact, felt so strongly that they did turn in their PX cards, though it meant they would have to pay more for films and toothpaste on the Vietnamese black market, which is where the Vietnamese shopped. The meeting demonstrated clearly that the volunteers not only differed among themselves, but also sensed basic dilemmas within themselves as individuals. In the entire meeting, only one resolution earned the wholehearted agreement of all the participants: a call for further internationalization of IVS so that Americans would no longer form the overwhelming majority. This seemed like one way to ease the political burden of being American.

The IVS leadership had prided itself on being the only predominantly American organization in Viet Nam to have a wholly Vietnamese advisory board. The Vietnamese were also pleased that they should be given a forum for advising Americans, since for them advising always seemed to be a one-way street. We had invited members of this board to attend the Fourth of July meetings and to give their opinions on how volunteers could best help the Vietnamese. We had asked them to be frank, and they were.

"You should not worry so much about having a political role," said one young teacher on the board. "Of course you are political, simply because you are in Viet Nam. Nothing is without politics in my country." Then he became more philosophical: "It is the function of IVS to work toward the improvement of social conditions, is it not? Well, that is a political activity. Politics and social participation are not independent processes." The volunteers listened with interest.

"The Vietnamese make no distinction between your organization and the U.S. government," he went on. "This is too complicated, and, as a result, U.S. policy casts a direct shadow on whatever you do or say. Whether these U.S. policies are good or bad, you cannot escape association with them. I advise you to tell the American people what your government is doing in Viet Nam, with the hope that a change will bring a better plan than the present one. You

must also continue your free dialogue with the young people of
Viet Nam. If you leave, you will leave unfinished the beginnings
made by your predecessors. If you stay, you will suffer this political
identification, but you can continue your tradition of contribution."

Any volunteers who were surprised by the remarks attributing
political significance to their economic assistance were soothed
when another board member got up and noted that Americans in
general were having surprisingly little effect on Vietnamese culture.
He seemed pleased, in fact, when he could recite various examples
of how his people, in spite of the massive foreign influx, could hold
on to so many of their own ways. "We have our own way of
thinking, our own logic," he said. "You may try hard, but Asia will
remain a mystery." He smiled, then continued. "You and we look at
Viet Nam in different ways. You see it through two sets of eyes,
Saigon's and Washington's. We Vietnamese hold only one view:
Viet Nam's. We sometimes wonder why you Americans like to
come to Viet Nam, anyway. Can you conceive of foreign nations
sending advisers to your country? We Vietnamese are sensitive
about maintaining our national identity. When you try to assist us,
it is important to remember that we value your friendliness over
your advice. The way you act is very important." The board member had finished speaking, but some of us were not sure what he
had really meant to say. He seemed troubled, as if purposely avoiding the key conclusion he had meant to draw. Finally someone asked
him point-blank:

"In view of Vietnamese sensitivities and the critical war situation,
can a volunteer still be of real help to the Vietnamese people? And
what is the best way to help now?"

The board member stood up again, shaking his head knowingly.
This time he was going to respond directly to the question. "You
know," he said, "if you really want to help the Vietnamese people,
then you must help us find peace."

No longer soothing, his words served to stir the uneasy into action. For several, they tipped the scale and led them to agree with
the board member's advice to "go back to America and explain what
the war has done to our people. Peace can only be found in America." Many volunteers continued to feel that they could still serve

the Vietnamese people by remaining at their posts. Others of us felt that someone must speak out, that the answer to the refugee problem, for example, was not to distribute more bulgur wheat, but to stop creating refugees; that the only way to succeed in Viet Nam was to minimize the American effort, because the more U.S. troops that came to Viet Nam and the longer they stayed, the more harm they would do both to Vietnamese society and to the very goals the United States wished to pursue.

After numerous postponements by the American Embassy, a meeting of leaders of several similarly troubled voluntary agencies was finally arranged with Ambassador Ellsworth Bunker to discuss these problems. The Ambassador was cordial and correct, but the session produced no satisfaction for us in our concerns. It would not be proper to speak out publicly on these matters, he said. The role of volunteers is to help in economic, not political matters. The refugee problem, he said, was a political matter. Yet, from our experience with refugees, we felt that it was at least as much an economic and social problem, and it was very serious. We felt that we had to speak out, and we decided to write a letter to President Johnson. At the same time, however, we wanted to be fair both to the two governments that supported us and to other IVS volunteers who wished to stay in Viet Nam.

For several weeks in the late summer of 1967, lights burned late in the upstairs office at the IVS headquarters. A small group of the deeply concerned were trying to decide how best to help the Vietnamese in the pursuit of peace. Meanwhile, others of us started drafting a letter to the President. Writing in terms of our own experiences, we said:

We are finding it increasingly difficult to pursue quietly our main objective: helping the people in Vietnam. In assisting one family or individual to make a better living or get a better education, it has become evident that our small successes only blind us to how little or negative the effect is in the face of present realities in Vietnam. Thus, to stay in Vietnam and remain silent is to fail to respond to the first need of the Vietnamese people—peace.*

* The full text of this letter is given in the appendix.

Forty-nine volunteers, spread throughout the country, signed the letter. Four of us determined to resign so that we could speak out freely on what we saw and felt. Fears of a premature leak to the press corps compelled us to send the news to Washington as quickly as possible. We were advised that the correct procedure was to deliver the letter to the Ambassador's office for teletype transmission by the Embassy. The procedure, however, turned out to be more complicated than we had anticipated.

Late in the afternoon of September 19, 1967, we handed the letter to the U.S. Mission Coordinator. After reading it, he asked us to come back two days later to meet with Ambassador Bunker. We explained that we merely wished to transmit the letter as quickly as possible and that we planned to release it to the press before the news leaked out in any other way. A certain feeling of tenseness also contributed to our desire to send off the letter without what seemed to us unnecessary delays. The Mission Coordinator left his office for forty-five minutes while he talked with the Ambassador alone. On returning, he repeated the request to come back two days later, explaining that Ambassador Bunker had to leave to meet someone at the airport. The Mission Coordinator again asked that we reconsider the wisdom of sending the letter, pointing out that it was not ethical to publicly protest American and Vietnamese policy while we were guests in Viet Nam. He added that such irresponsibility would make it impossible for us to get jobs in the Foreign Service. He said that the IVS transportation priorities would be upgraded. (We had complained two weeks earlier about our flight priority being lower than that of a colonel's mistress.) In frustration, we tried to explain that our protest was not about technicalities, but about the massive creation of refugees, the free-strike zones, the defoliation. . . . But he interrupted, saying he did not want to discuss U.S. policy with us, that that was not an IVS concern. We gave him the letter and left in frustration and anger, asking that its contents be forwarded by the teletype to President Johnson. Five hours later, we made the letter public to the *New York Times*. The next morning, Ambassador Bunker agreed to see us. He was cordial, but termed our handling of the resignations and the letter "unethical and discourteous." He showed little interest in discussing the reasons for our actions.

On our return to the United States, we found that members of Congress were concerned and that they wanted to discuss with us the problems of Viet Nam. One of us was asked to testify before the Senate Subcommittee on Refugees. Other Senators and Representatives asked us to talk with them privately or in small groups. In all, we met with more than seventy-five members of the Senate and the House. They were concerned about how the United States could get out of Viet Nam in a responsible way and how our government could bring an end to the war and prevent further suffering by the Vietnamese people.

Some Congressmen felt that we should discuss our experiences in Viet Nam with President Johnson. To see the President, it would be necessary to be "checked out" by one of the President's close associates. This was attempted through two different channels. One of these failed to work out, as each appointment was canceled at the last moment. The second channel did lead to an interview with a very high White House aide. After the interview, however, it was made clear that to discuss the widespread resentment against the Saigon government, the growing anti-American feelings in Viet Nam, the effects of defoliants on the crops of Vietnamese farmers, and the problems caused by the creation of refugees would be wasting the President's time. The President's adviser was interested in providing the President with information that would support present administration thinking.

There were also some who thought we should meet with Vice-President Humphrey. Mr. Humphrey had been an enthusiastic supporter of IVS and had visited us in Saigon in 1966. In fact, it was at the animal husbandry station next to our headquarters that he had given his Minnesota hog-call, delighting both his entourage and the press. But now the Vice-President seemed to be unreceptive to our views. We learned that he had called our resignations "one of the greatest disservices to the American effort in Viet Nam." Two U.S. government officials, to whom he had made the remark, disagreed. They felt that discussing the issues openly could be most constructive. Unfortunately, as happened so often, they felt it would not be wise to say this to the Vice-President directly.

On the State Department side, one young officer felt that we should meet with some of the higher officials there. Appointments were made, and we arrived at his office at the specified time. Embarrassed, he explained that one man we were to see had been summoned to a meeting, and the other was "busy writing a report." He gave us some magazines to read and went off to find someone else who would listen. After two hours, however, he admitted defeat.

Several days later, after Senator Edward Kennedy chided a high official for his reluctance to hear us out, we had more success in getting to see State Department officials. Yet we could not suppress our feelings of frustration as the experiences we cited seemed to make little impression. Policy had gained a momentum of its own, and conflicting views had to be strongly countered. Secretary of State Dean Rusk, for example, felt obliged to say that our statements reflected the opinions of only a small minority of Vietnamese, that the vast majority were all for continuing the military effort. Assistant Secretary of State William Bundy expressed the view that those of us who had resigned from IVS could not see the Viet Nam issue in its proper perspective. But, privately, the fact that volunteers so close to the Vietnamese and so close to the implementation of American policy had spoken out in despair could not help but disturb officials at many levels. Lower echelon officers, if they were willing to speak out at all, admitted sympathy with our position and said they too had been ignored higher up. Even Navy counter-insurgency instructors in California, who had used the "IVS approach" as a model for social and economic development, were asking whether anything could now succeed in Viet Nam.

The most appreciative reaction came from the Vietnamese themselves. Before we had left Saigon, friends who had somehow drifted away came back to see us. "Now we know that there are Americans who are really concerned about us as people, not just as political chessmen," said one. "You have said what we have wanted to say, yet would be put in jail for saying," confided another. A Vietnamese secretary working for the American Aid Mission had read the letter and said wistfully, "I wish I could sign." A Vietnamese teacher in the Mekong Delta told his IVS coworker, "Now we know you aren't with the CIA." A group of taxi drivers in Saigon, who had read about the resignations in the local newspapers, invited us to a meeting to convey what they felt should be told to the American people on our return. An old friend applauded our decision, but said a regretful farewell: "The problem is, the people we want to have stay, leave; and the people we want to have leave, stay." But perhaps the most eloquent testimony to the problems at hand was written later by a Vietnamese friend who had just begun studies in the United States:

I think that your actions will have an influence on both American youth and Vietnamese youth, and that your actions will create a deep feeling of love and trust among the Vietnamese youth. . . . The right place to find out a solution for Viet Nam is not in Saigon, . . . neither in American officials there, nor in the Vietnamese authority there. *It is here, in America*, with the awakening of a deep, true love for human beings, a realistic view of the world relationship today, in the mind of the American people and the American government. Only by that awakening and realization can the U.S. gain back love, confidence, and friendship with the Vietnamese people and the world. And you can only do that here, in America.

This, then, is our purpose: to tell the story of Viet Nam to our fellow Americans.

[2]

"WHAT A PITY FOR A CAMELLIA FLOWER!"

Vietnamese Society over the Years

For many Vietnamese, the imperial city of Hue is the symbol of their past, the repository of their great traditions and culture. It is not an ancient city, but its very name conjures images of poetic vistas, gracious palaces, fragrant blossoms, and timeless remnants of a glorious history. Standing atop the Emperor's Ngo Mon Gate, one can see the mighty Citadel walls, the winding lotus-covered moat, and the Throne Room and its wide courtyard balanced by two ponds and surrounded by frangipani. Beyond these walls, and several miles up the stately Perfume River, elaborate royal tombs of the Nguyen dynasty trace the story of this earlier Viet Nam: Gia Long, Minh Mang, Thieu Tri, Tu Duc, Dong Khanh, and Khai Dinh are buried here. Bao Dai, the last of the line, is still living—on the French Riviera. It was the Emperor Gia Long, founder of the dynasty, who began construction of the Imperial Palace in Hue on the propitious ninth day of May, 1804. Many of the buildings have since been destroyed in the intervening years of war and revolution, the most recent damage being incurred during the Tet (New Year's) holidays in 1968. But physical destruction cannot extinguish the spiritual light radiating from Hue throughout the land. Hue's history is too profoundly enshrined in the minds of the people, its charm and romantic grace too deeply loved in their hearts.

Barely three miles upriver from the Imperial City is Linh Mu pagoda, a quiet, blissful spot dominated by a seven-tiered tower. Linh Mu has served as the seat of the head Buddhist monk for all of Central Viet Nam. On a veranda, enclosed in glass, is a gilded statue of the "laughing Buddha" who represents happiness and prosperity. When the Venerable Don Hau was head monk, he would point to this statue and smile, because it looked very much like him. Linh Mu pagoda is not the most beautiful of Hue's many treasure spots, but it is the most historic. Legend has it that an elderly goddess appeared there and chose it as the site for the capital city of the Vietnamese people. The pagoda was constructed in her honor by Nguyen Hoang, the governor of Thuan Hoa, in 1601.

Viet Nam's history reads like a catalogue of expansionary wars, of internal revolts and subsequent efforts at reunification, and of foreign intrusions and withdrawals. For these same Vietnamese who were to suffer at the hands of Chinese and French colonialists had themselves expanded from a small group called the Viets, located in the southern China border regions, into a vigorous and aggressive nation. According to legend, it was the union of a dragon and a goddess that gave birth to the first hundred ancestors of all Vietnamese. They would grow and expand southward, though not yet as far as the present site of Hue. Their new land became known as the Kingdom of Nam Viet, "nam" meaning "south." In 111 B.C., however, foreign intervention compromised the new territory, and the people of Nam Viet were conquered by the Chinese, who later renamed the country An Nam—the pacified south.

The Chinese controlled the land almost continuously for the next thousand years, demanding tribute from the vassal Vietnamese. It was during this time that elements of Chinese civilization and culture came to permeate Vietnamese society, a heritage for which many Vietnamese are still profoundly grateful. But where the Vietnamese were receptive to new forms of culture and technology, they were not receptive to Chinese political domination. Even against overwhelming odds, they rebelled. The names of heroes and heroines of this long period are not forgotten even today, lending themselves to epic poems, to national holidays, and to city streets. The most prominent of these heroic figures, perhaps, are the Hai Ba Trung, the two Trung sisters who in A.D. 40 mounted elephants and led 80,000 of their compatriots against a Chinese governor and his reign of terror. The Chinese returned in full strength three years later, forcing the Trung sisters to suicide by throwing themselves into the river. Others continued to fight their cause, however, and the Chinese yoke was finally removed in A.D. 939. Periodically, to be sure, the Chinese tried to subjugate the Vietnamese again. Le Loi led the Vietnamese in a counterattack in the fifteenth century, and Nguyen Hue later surprised carousing Chinese soldiers with a New Year's attack on occupied Hanoi. These struggles against Chinese oppressors have never been forgotten by the history-conscious Vietnamese.

The Chinese have not been the only ones to arouse Vietnamese nationalism. Three times in the thirteenth century, the Mongol hordes of Kublai Khan were repelled by numerically inferior Vietnamese forces, on the last occasion largely through Marshal Tran Hung Dao's guerrilla warfare tactics.

Beginning in the fourteenth century, and with their northern borders relatively secure, the Vietnamese again turned their attention southward. They conquered the once-great kingdom of Champa that occupied much of what is now Central Viet Nam, and then proceeded into the Mekong River Delta and fought the Khmers, now called Cambodians. Oddly enough, the fertile Mekong Delta was sparsely populated until Vietnamese pioneers moved south in families or by entire villages to settle it. Now the delta is heavily populated, and the sole reminder of these colonial years are a few hundred thousand Cambodians still living there. Along the central coast, most Chams have entered the larger society, and only a handful remain unassimilated, continuing to eke out a living in the shadow of crumbling Cham towers.

It was during this period of expansion that Vietnamese civilization, under the fifteenth-century Le dynasty, attained a remarkable brilliance and sophistication: an elaborate legal code, a complex religion, a hierarchical civil service system, and flourishing arts and commerce. All this, however, did not lead to political unity. With fewer dangers threatening from outside, the Vietnamese soon took to fighting among themselves. By the early seventeenth century, North and South were effectively divided between two powerful ruling families, the Trinh and the Nguyen. For almost two centuries this internal division and struggling continued, and no attempt at reunification succeeded until that of the Emperor Gia Long, who founded his throne at Hue in 1802. It was Gia Long who for the first time ruled over a single Viet Nam extending from the Chinese border in the north to the Ca Mau Peninsula in the south.

But unification, though it would last more or less until the Geneva Accords of 1954, hardly brought an end to problems. From the West new intruders had been showing themselves, first in the interests of commerce and converts, but later in demand of territory. One of the first was the French Father Alexandre de Rhodes, who in the seventeenth century developed the "Quoc-ngu," the Romanized alphabet which ultimately replaced the traditional Chinese characters in the written Vietnamese language. Other early arrivals brought arms and were well received by various Vietnamese factions that wished to strengthen their hand against competitors. In later years, however, the Court at Hue took a dimmer view of the foreigners and decried "the perverse religion of the European." In the nineteenth century, fearing erosion of their national traditions, the intensely nationalistic Vietnamese took revenge by murdering some 100,000 of their fellow countrymen who had been converted to Catholicism. It was a complex combination of these affronts to French efforts and the need to compete economically with the other European colonial powers that led to the actual French takeover of all Indochina, beginning with the forced cession of three eastern Cochinchinese provinces in 1862.

Like the Chinese, the French contributed much to Viet Nam, both culturally and physically. They built or improved much of the infrastructure for future economic development, such as roads and railroads, canals and dikes, not to mention schools, hospitals, scientific institutions, and the elegant buildings of the larger cities and towns. It is true that the French did all this with a view to their own profit, extracted chiefly from the rubber plantations and through commerce, but some gains could be felt by the Vietnamese too. Nevertheless, it is rare for a colonized people to feel gratitude toward their colonial masters. Receptivity to cultural and technological contributions, yes; to political control and personal subjugation, absolutely not. Again, the names of city streets recall the heroes of resistance: such names as Phan Dinh Phung and Phan Boi Chau. The name of another such hero may not be uttered on the streets of South Viet Nam, and its use is discouraged in the North because of the man's humility. That man is Ho Chi Minh.

When independence had been won from the French, but while disunity was rife in the South, frustrated Vietnamese often attributed all their problems to the period of French domination: The French, they asserted, used divide-and-rule tactics in order to weaken Viet Nam. That was why the people found it so hard to unite against the Communists. There was some truth to this accusation, but in all objectivity it would have to be admitted that the Vietnamese have been a divided people throughout most of their history. "Their favorite national pastime," wrote Bernard Fall, seemed to be "bitter quarrels among themselves . . . , and between Northerners and Southerners in particular." This is a sad commentary, and no one is more exasperated by its truth than the Vietnamese. To them, history seems to have taught three things: one is this sense of frustration over disunity; another is the belief that they have been singled out for special suffering in this world; and the third and by far most important is the feeling that, in spite of everything, the Vietnamese people *will* overcome adversity.

"Now my country has changed so very much," a friend wrote to us after the 1968 attack on Hue. "Many buildings, houses, schools, hospitals, are in rubble, in ashes, in ruins. Now I think that the Vietnamese people are the unhappiest people in the world. We have endured this war for so long. Yet, I keep working. We must keep working to help our suffering compatriots and to rebuild our Viet Nam."

Just as the Vietnamese share a common history, replete with divisions though it may be, so do they also share a common culture. To be sure, they have adopted much from the cultures of their conquerors, particularly from the Chinese. Yet, even the Vietnamese who proudly cites his debts to the great power to the north will stoutly maintain his own awareness of what it means to be *Vietnamese*. Thus, while the basis of social organization in both cultures is the family, and while the patriarchal Confucian ethic is central to both, the Vietnamese differ from their former mentors in that in Viet Nam women enjoy considerable authority. Vietnamese religion also tends to be more eclectic than Chinese, consisting as it does of a combination of Confucianism, Buddhism, Taoism (with its cosmological outlook and animism), and in some cases Christianity. Some of the characteristics which distinguish Vietnamese culture can be explained by history. Some scholars, for example, believe that the relative authority of women in Vietnamese society entered the culture through contacts with the matriarchal Chams. Certain religious influences, particularly Theravada Buddhism, have entered Vietnamese society in a similar way, for what later became South Viet Nam was a traditional crossroads of commerce and religious proselytizing between China and India. It is because of this geographic location between the Indian subcontinent and the expanses of China, and the fusion of cultures transmitted by merchants and monks traveling in both directions, that the area became the melting pot eventually known as Indochina. The Vietnamese have generally remained quite open to adopting what they consider the best traits of other cultures. Still, because of the special and long history of involvement with the Chinese, Viet Nam is the only country in Southeast Asia to be influenced by China far more than by India.

The foundation of Vietnamese society, as of Chinese, is the family. This fact is widely cited in the textbooks and is recognized by most Americans. Yet its importance and significance are usually underestimated. Family ties explain many social phenomena in Viet Nam. One of these is bureaucratic corruption (see Chapter 5). Another is the apparent immorality of that whole sector of society turned topsy-turvy, of young girls and women who all too readily become prostitutes, of children who become beggars or thieves. Family ties help explain why the creation of refugees is likely to convert these people into Viet Cong (see Chapter 8), and why government administrators or soldiers sometimes seem unconcerned about "the war effort." Many of the everyday habits of Vietnamese, which sometimes lead Americans to shake their heads in wonder or even anger, are explained by an understanding of Vietnamese family ties.

The devotion of a Vietnamese to his family is practically unlimited, and the sentiment he feels toward his father is one of near reverence. This devotion toward a paterfamilias is, of course, the essence of Confucian doctrine, and it is extended in a religious sense to what amounts to ancestor worship. In every home is a family altar where sticks of incense are lit on family anniversaries and holidays, and where offerings are made and prayers are said in memory of those who have passed away. The deceased cannot be forgotten, for their spirits are believed to affect the daily lives of their descendants. It is true that modernization and Western influences in the cities, and to some extent the rigors of war, have diluted the ritualistic elements of this worship, but the customary family ties remain strong among even the most westernized of the elite.

As Americans, we were constantly confronted by manifestations of these strong family ties. Vietnamese children, for example, refer to their fathers as "serious," or "worthy," or "hard-working." They see their fathers as persons from whom they must gain permission to complete their education or to do this or that, not as an assumed source of material gifts. Many express their concern over their father's unhappiness or ill health, and very few ever express negative feelings toward their parents, even in momentary fits of anger. Vietnamese children are generally oriented toward family expectations, rather than toward their rights and duties vis-à-vis the society as a whole. Their main concern is to fulfill their role as a member of the family. There are reasons for this general outlook. Most Vietnamese children are aware that their parents have had difficult lives, and they feel that they have contributed to some extent to their burden. Having incurred a debt, they feel that they owe something in return. Their parents have given them life and shared their usually modest resources. The child's duty as he gets older, then, is to accept responsibility for his parents. This is the Vietnamese system of both social security and social organization. By extension, it calls for revering the parents of one's parents, or one's ancestors, and for assuming responsibility for the ancestral altars and tombs. Because of these tombs, the same piety that characterizes the relations of a Vietnamese to his family also characterizes his attachment to the ancestral lands. To be forced off these lands by war is a deeply upsetting experience. For, seen in the larger perspective, the rhythm of everyday life assumes a kind of deeply ingrained religious significance.

These cultural traditions explain why Miss Thuy, a government civil servant, sends a part of her earnings every month to her father —even though her father is a wealthy man and doesn't need it. Other civil servants, seemingly derelict in their duties because they have taken extended holidays to visit their families, may feel that they are fulfilling responsibilities more important than those of the civil service. When we bravely told our Vietnamese friends that we did not miss our families, that we were not homesick, they had great difficulty in believing us. It seemed most unnatural to them. The closeness of the family also explains why Vietnamese seem to have so many brothers and sisters. It takes a patient Vietnamese-speaking American to determine who is really a brother or sister and who is a cousin.

On the other hand, Vietnamese couples do have numerous children. Even though they are, by Western standards, too poor for this, they have very compelling reasons for accumulating large families. One is this very element of social security—a large family insures that parents will be well cared for in their old age. Another is the advantage in terms of enhancing the family name and reputation. Every family must also be assured of at least one male offspring who can carry on the ancestor cult and maintain the tombs. There are more directly pragmatic reasons, too: large families mean more helpers around the house or farm. Finally, because the death rate has always been high, earlier because of poor health facilities and now because of the war, parents feel they must, in a sense, "overcompensate" in their family planning.

Sometimes there seems almost to be a competition among Vietnamese men to see who has produced the largest number of children. One deputy province chief bemoaned the fact that he had only eight children, whereas his boss, the province chief, had twelve. "Why don't you just go ahead and have four more?" we suggested in a half-joking attempt to cheer him up. "That's all very well," the deputy chief replied sadly, "but by that time the province chief will have twenty." Flippant remarks touching on family ties were harshly received by Vietnamese colleagues, no matter how jokingly intended. One such quip earned an American volunteer a lasting lesson. "Well, Mr. Thong, if you have so many children that you

can't take care of them all," he had said, smiling, "why don't you
just get rid of one or two?" "That shows how much you know
about Vietnamese society," Mr. Thong replied. "No matter how
desperate we are, we could never break up the family." At other
times, Vietnamese friends or acquaintances seemed to complain
about the difficulties of raising such large families. Women sometimes urged us to adopt their children, though they did this only
when they seemed assured the offspring would be treated well and
given more advantages than they could otherwise receive.

The Vietnamese government also made mistakes in its judgments
of family life. During the regime of President Ngo Dinh Diem, the
infamous Madame Nhu, Diem's sister-in-law, took it upon herself to
redraft the family legal code. Divorce was outlawed and men were
limited to one wife. Although her intention was to stabilize and
strengthen family life by this law, the result was upsetting and she
was accused of extending Catholic morality into a predominantly
Confucian-Buddhist culture. Divorce or having "second wives" may
be an important way out for Vietnamese who find themselves in a
marital situation that, for physical reasons, cannot be consummated
with natural offspring. And offspring are vital for continuation of
the family line and for upkeep of the ancestral tombs. "Of the three
crimes of filial impiety," said the Chinese philosopher Mencius many
centuries ago, "the fact of not having children is the greatest." A
Saigon newspaper of the day published a letter to the editor asking
how the dilemma posed by Madame Nhu's action might be resolved: "Are we to disobey our whole tradition and religious codes,
or are we to obey the government's new law?" The newspaper,
naturally under government control, published an interesting reply:
"The concept of filial piety has changed, whether one likes it or not.
If by some misfortune you are unable to perpetuate your line, your
ancestors will pardon you. But if you disobey the government Family Code, surely your ancestors cannot be content."

In a way, it is surprising that the ravages of war have not affected
Vietnamese society more than they have. On the surface, and judging from conversations with individual Vietnamese, the war seems
to have left practically no facet of life untouched or unmarred. Yet,

the pillars of Vietnamese cultural values persist, their strength proved further by the awful stresses. American visitors are sometimes repelled by certain practices that they take to be natural to the Vietnamese people. Corruption is one such practice, and though it should not be condoned, it is, to a large extent, one method by which individuals adjust to the uncertainties of economic life in a war-torn country. Another mutation in the society is the fantastic proliferation of prostitution, of the "bar society," and of the other nefarious activities which seem to glut and degrade the once fashionable city streets or areas surrounding foreign military camps. Prostitution is hardly new to the world, and if its rampant presence seems to cheapen the country in which it thrives, the motivations behind it must be understood. If one asks a bar-girl or prostitute why she entered her profession, the answer is frequently, "To help my family," or "To aid my parents in old age," or "To send my little brothers and sisters to school." Theirs is a pathetic story, because the way they have chosen is not always the most desirable for them. If their American military clients could speak with them in Vietnamese and know the extent of their suffering, and at the same time the frequent nobility of the desire to help their families, they would undoubtedly see their bedroom mates in a different light. Not all pursue their professions with such altruistic intentions, of course, but the fact is that many do.

Parents do not necessarily look down on their daughters' efforts to help the family in this way. They wish there were better ways, perhaps, but surely none is so profitable. There is a certain desperation in the whole thing, and among some a deep cynicism. One young schoolteacher friend announced that his wife was expecting their first baby. "Congratulations," we said, adding our hope that it would be a boy, for a boy is generally a desirable first offspring for the traditional reason of wanting to perpetuate the family name. "Oh no," he replied, only half-jokingly. "I hope it will be a girl; then she can help the family by working in a bar and making lots of money."

Giving oneself up to prostitution in order to help one's own family is a sacrifice exalted in Vietnamese literature. The noble and beautiful heroine of the nineteenth-century *Kim Van Kieu*, Viet

Nam's greatest literary masterpiece, sold herself in order to earn enough money to help her father and brother survive difficult circumstances. "What a pity for a camellia flower!" moaned the poet, Nguyen Du. But the heroine, Thuy Kieu, saw in her deed the nobility of aiding her family. "It is better that I should sacrifice myself alone," she said. "It matters little if a flower falls if the tree can keep its leaves green."

It is difficult with the Vietnamese, as it is perhaps with any people, to differentiate between their way of life, their social values, and their religion. The family as the pillar of society represents all three, embodying the Confucian ethic as an underlying characteristic common to all people. Another such common characteristic is the broad Vietnamese cosmology. Based in part on Taoist ideas, it comprises belief in spirits, in astrology, and in a "Mandate of Heaven." Many "modern" Vietnamese, of course, do not share all aspects of this cosmology, and even more will deny sharing it. Nevertheless, such beliefs are widespread, particularly in the rural areas. The Mandate of Heaven, for example, determines the worthiness of an emperor or other governing power by his ability to mediate between Heaven and people on earth. In the late 1950's, Ngo Dinh Diem was thought to enjoy this Mandate of Heaven, his authority being largely acknowledged and opposition being limited. In the early 1960's, however, as dissension increased, and as he seemed to be misusing his power, he lost the Mandate. The people and Heaven frowned upon him, and he ultimately fell. No subsequent government, the Vietnamese believe, has earned the Mandate of Heaven, and that is why South Viet Nam is so out of kilter with the heavens.

There are many examples of the influences of astrology on Vietnamese life. On a higher level, the new Vietnamese constitution was made to center around the lucky number nine. Written by 117 deputies, it was composed of 117 articles, included a 117-word preamble, and was issued on April 1, 1967 (4–1–67). In each case the sum of the component digits (of 117 or 18) was nine. On the everyday level, wedding dates are always chosen in consultation with an astrologer, and we knew a provincial education-service chief who determined the rare days on which he would visit village schools by consulting his astrologer's calendar. Province-wide teachers' meetings were scheduled for auspicious days, too. "You would do well to abide by the signs yourself," he cautioned us. "Just because you come from a technological society does not mean you know everything about life and the ways of the universe."

On a still lower level, this cosmology is represented by spirits or goddesses such as the one who in late 1963 took up residence on the top of the highest mountain in the area around Dalat. The popular name of the mountain is Nui Ba, the Woman Mountain, so-called because of its double peaks which resemble a woman's breasts. For weeks, throngs of Vietnamese of all ranks climbed to the main summit of Nui Ba, which rises to an altitude of more than 6,000 feet and requires a full day for the round trip. In a flat clearing just before the last steep climb, they stuck thousands of incense sticks into the moss of the forest trees and set up makeshift altars there. At the summit itself, the pilgrims filled their containers with holy water which they believed the goddess had left there, and then they descended. We met a sophisticated-looking midwife who had just made the climb and asked her about it. "It's all true," she replied. "The holy water cures all kinds of sickness. My cousin saw himself how the blind and the mute were cured. Everyone who takes the goddess' water is cured by it."

Related to the cosmological hierarchy is the social hierarchy of man. There are four levels to the Vietnamese social order: first there are the *si*, the scholars or men of letters; next come the *nong*, the farmers; third are the *cong*, or workers; and fourth are the *thuong*, the businessmen and merchants. Occasionally a fifth is added: the *binh*, or soldiers, whose position is somewhat ambiguous. For although they are considered a rather lowly breed, many, and particularly those who led troops against foreign invaders, have become heroes to the people. Vietnamese history honors most the men of letters, and the kings who doubled as poets are especially revered. The entire mandarin system—which formed the basis of traditional civil service—paid honor to the fruits of learning, for to be appointed a mandarin one had to pass stringent qualifying examinations.

Now, however, all this has changed, and even been reversed. Now government is by the military in cooperation with businessmen—that is, by those who profit most from the war and from corruption. Its leaders are young in a culture that still associates wisdom with age. High on the ladder of wealth today are the prostitutes and bargirls, and more generally the whole segment of society that serves the foreigners. In traditional terms the foreigners, too, are lowly soldiers. "Nhat di, nhi tuong," goes the new Vietnamese expression—first the prostitutes, second the generals. To the cynical, this represents the current hierarchy. The scholars and intellectuals, respected in years past, are now alienated, forgotten men, and it is the farmers and workers who suffer most from the direct effects of the war. It will be of great interest to see how the Vietnamese social order will sort itself out after the war is over, to see whether it will reinstitute its traditional levels or whether a new hierarchy will evolve.

Although events have thrown the social order into disarray, some of the underlying assumptions remain. Chief among these is the value attached to education, the traditional vehicle for social mobility and stature in the Confucian order. Parents, who quite naturally desire the best opportunities for their children, work hard in order to send their offspring to the best schools available. One of the more gratifying sights for us was of the supremely proud faces of bearded old village notables attending the inauguration of a school in whose establishment we had played some part. And on the rough plank walls of an unimposing barbershop on the outskirts of Saigon, our barber had taken the pains to hang only one small picture—that of his children's school.

It was in response to the high Vietnamese regard for education that IVS first established an English-teaching team in 1962. Previously only agriculturalists had been sent, but they found themselves constantly begged by the people in their communities to teach them English. We teachers were sometimes embarrassed, however, to note that in spite of our youth and just-out-of-college appearance, we were exalted by Vietnamese as "Ong Thay"—Mr. Teacher. Vietnamese students are particularly respectful toward their teachers, and the youngest often take off their hats and bow as "Ong Thay" goes past. Outside the high schools, in our extra evening classes for friends and colleagues in the community, being a teacher could occasionally even compromise our desire to be "one of the gang" with those near our own ages. "I'm sorry," said one friend and former student, "but we must remain on a relatively formal footing together. After all, I still consider you as my teacher."

There are never enough public-school facilities in Viet Nam to handle the masses of children to be educated. The drafting of large numbers of teachers into the army has aggravated a situation in which each class already averaged sixty pupils. A tough examination system still exists in order to scale down the number of pupils to something approximating the number of openings available. Education is thus competitive, and cases of bribing officials among those who have the means, or of suicide among those who do not pass, are not uncommon. For those who do not succeed academically—and this applies from primary school all the way up the line—there is the thriving private-school business. Although not as good, generally speaking, as the public schools, private schools are in such demand in urban areas that there may be one on every block. They are often very profitable too, since no parent would skimp on his child's education.

Students of all ages enjoy a deference unknown to their American counterparts, though not unlike that known in Europe. It is not surprising, therefore, that their influence on national politics has been considerably greater than in the United States. To the Vietnamese, they are still the privileged and the leadership class. This position does not always serve them to advantage, however, especially in this modern revolutionary age when demands are being made to narrow the gap between rural and urban populations. Here the *nature* of their education is the critical factor. Vietnamese sometimes point out that traditional education under the mandarin system was eminently suited to those who would govern the rural Viet Nam of the past. With the combination of a new French veneer and a society in revolution, the setting has changed. The educated still enjoy great prestige, but the educational content, they say, is now outdated. The mark of the educated man is no longer a mere talent to recite poetry. It is rather the ability to solve problems of economic development and to cope with modern technology.

Throughout their history, we have seen, the Vietnamese have united together most effectively when called upon to throw out invaders on their soil. For the Vietnamese are bound together as one people and one enveloping culture. Each person has his own niche in the greater whole. North, Center, and South, they share traditions and beliefs in common: a Confucian social perspective, with its cult of ancestors and respect for family and education; and a particular view of life and the universe, with its sometime belief in spirits and astrology. Of course, organized religion is important too, and we shall later note the impact of Buddhism and Catholicism (see Chapter 6).

But Buddhism and Catholicism, as well as the newer religions of Hoa Hao and Cao Dai, have also proved divisive during certain periods of Vietnamese history. For all their shared attributes of culture, the Vietnamese have been plagued, as their history shows, by several serious impediments to national unity. Probably the greatest of these is the fact of regional differences and regional loyalties among Vietnamese.

To some one million northerners who came south after the 1954 Geneva Accords, life in the new land seemed different and in some respects alien. One of our students, a young lady, described it well in a composition exercise:

For me, no place on this earth is more attractive, more pleasant than my native country. My country is not only an interesting place to live in, but it is also a friend, a dear and close one who shares joys and sorrows. I have there all my relatives to whom I am bound by affection. My beloved ancestors slept their eternal sleep under the ground. My country keeps so many childish memories. Never shall I forget those winter evenings when I joked with my friends or those summer nights under a smiling moon and myriad twinkling stars.

This mental treasure increases year after year and cements slowly but solidly this eternal attachment between me and my ascendants.

In 1954, Saigon was for me the prosperous, luxurious, and fairest city of Viet-Nam, but I never imagined that one day I could land in it.

According to the settlement of Geneva (July 20, 1954) Northern people in Viet-Nam had two choices: stay in the North or go settling in the South. All families were perplexed and hardly knew how to decide, to act. There was separation in all of them because some of the members intended to stay, regretting to leave their property, their souvenirs; the others who were afraid of V.C., to go away.

My family was in that general situation. On one side, I wanted to stay with my parents and on the other I was afraid that the V.C. would oblige all the rest of the Hanoi girls to get married with their invalid militaries or send us to a "Correction Camp." . . . My parents missed me very much but they didn't want to see me unhappy, so they let me choose the way.

I remember that I took a long time to make up my mind, so I left Hanoi on the 4th of October, the last day in a last plane of Air Viet-Nam and the last ticket, too.

As the day of departure approached I got more and more excited. Some days I intended to tear up the ticket and stay home. At last the day arrived: my parents, sisters, brother, friends and relatives went to the Air Viet-Nam agency to see me off. . . . When the plane flew off, I felt so lonely and upset. . . . I was too tired from so many great emotions, exciting experiences and because of the airsickness and the altitude which made me dizzy. . . .

Now I am happy in the South of Viet-Nam, but though Hanoi is out of sight, it is never out of mind.

It is true that Vietnamese from the North are different from those of the South. The differences go beyond sheer sentimentality and the inevitable feeling any Vietnamese has for his own "que huong," his homeland. They involve more than varying food preferences and language peculiarities. There are, indeed, marked character differences between northerners and southerners. For example, people from the North are often more high strung and active than the relaxed people of the relatively new lands in the South. Somehow the hardest workers and the most progressive innovators seem to be the ones who came from the North after the Geneva Accords. Even their accent reflects this trait to some extent: the speech of northerners has a staccato quality that contrasts sharply with the soft slurring tones of the southerners. There are reasons for these character differences, which many of the more candid Vietnamese will discuss.

The simplest reason is that those who left the North were, relatively speaking, the most progressive ones, those who had accumulated some wealth already which they feared would be lost to the Communist regime there, and those who had the courage to pull up their roots and start again elsewhere. But aside from this, the climate in North Viet Nam's Red River Delta is very hard. The winters are cold. Flood years alternate with drought years, and the farmer must match his wits against nature. Dikes must be built to regulate the water, and making a living is arduous and challenging. The climate, in a sense, hones the body and mind to their sharpest. By contrast, the Mekong River Delta of the South is always warm and rarely floods. There are no years of real drought and the farmer's life is comparatively easy. The soil is fertile, and the rice grows well with a minimum of emergency precautions. And so, the explanation concludes, the northerner is more alert and more aggressive than the relaxed and fun-loving southerner.

The geography of Viet Nam is often represented by a woman balancing a bamboo yoke on her right shoulder, on either end of which is suspended a basket for carrying rice. The rice baskets represent the two deltas of the North and South, the regions called Tonkin and Cochinchina by the French. The pole in between is the narrow coastal strip of An Nam, or, as the Vietnamese call it, Central Viet Nam. Half of this area is now administered by the government in Hanoi, but the Saigon government was able to hold onto the old capital of Hue. The people of Central Viet Nam have their own customs, traditions, dialect, and foods, which differ again from those of both the South and the North. Central Vietnamese invariably point out that all the greatest national leaders, of both South and North, were born or at least educated in the Center: Ngo Dinh Diem, Ho Chi Minh, Pham Van Dong, and Vo Nguyen Giap, for example, all attended the same high school, Quoc Hoc, in Hue. (We would remind IVS English teachers, frustrated over their classroom discipline problems at Quoc Hoc, of the prestigious background of their school. But even though the school still attracts talented boys, it must be hard for the teachers to visualize *their* students achieving such fame.)

Political activists in Viet Nam still tend to be Central Vietnamese. It is no coincidence that every antigovernment movement from 1963 to the present, for example, originated in Hue before spreading to Saigon. Hue's own calm and stately appearance hides the political machinations going on under the surface. Why are people from Central Viet Nam likely to be more politically interested than those elsewhere? Vietnamese from there believe that their political involvement is a function of the poverty of the region. It is true that the land is probably the poorest in the country, and the people are crowded onto a thin strip between the mountains and the South China Sea. But no one could explain very precisely whether poverty drove people to seek improvement through politics, or whether natural politicians simply made more progress among a have-not population looking for something better. In the case of Hue itself, the influence of the imperial past certainly has something to do with her people's political consciousness. Although recent years have seen considerable mobility of the population, Hue is still full of names that indicate varying degrees of direct descendancy from the royal family. The Queen Mother still lives in Hue, and so do various nieces and nephews of Emperor Bao Dai. Among the other oldest and most respected families, each member knows from exactly which emperor he is descended. Those bearing the name Buu or Vinh are among the most closely related to royalty, and they point to it with understandable pride. It may or may not be coincidence that of the two top Buddhist student leaders in the 1964–1966 period, the family name of one was Buu and that of the other was Vinh.

The different characteristics and even mentalities of North, Central, and South Vietnamese go far toward explaining their suspicions of one another. To the other two, the northerner often seems aggressive and power-hungry, the southerner lazy and uncommitted, and the Central Vietnamese haughty and provincial. This by no means implies any rigidity of conception, for the feeling of being Vietnamese still overshadows these regional rivalries; but in weak

moments, jealousies flare up and cabinet crises ensue, club member-
ships are limited, and revolts may even break out, with each group
fully believing that "the others do not understand us."

Understanding, in fact, is the key to the whole matter. It is important not only in terms of regional differences between individuals, but also in terms of the outlook of the Vietnamese government
toward its people. It has been partly through failures in understanding that governments have been unresponsive, leading to dissatisfaction among the population. For the Vietnamese, life itself has
changed too abruptly in recent years. The affairs of earth have been
thrown out of harmony with the heavens. A new equilibrium is
needed, and the Mandate of Heaven must be restored to a worthy
ruler. Only then can the descendants of the early Viets live in peace
and stability.

[3]

REPRESENTING THE PEOPLE

Saigon Politics

The boom of a cannon reverberated in the early morning air, rattling windows on the broad Thong Nhut Boulevard in downtown Saigon. It was October 26, 1963, the eighth anniversary of President Ngo Dinh Diem's Republic of South Viet Nam. But the bleachers along the boulevard were barely a third full for the National Day ceremonies. Although most of Saigon's elite class had been invited, many of them had anticipated trouble and were afraid to attend. As for the common people of the city, barbed wire strung for blocks around kept them from approaching the parade route.

All passes had been carefully checked, but the security police were jumpy and we had the feeling that spies, counterspies, and counter-counterspies were planted everywhere. The cannon continued to boom. We wondered whether the long-expected *coup d'état* might not be under way.

As it turned out, however, the cannon was only saluting President Diem as he departed from Gia Long Palace (where he had been living since his regular palace was bombed in a coup attempt in 1962) on his way to the National Day ceremonies. Moments later, preceded by a phalanx of motorcycles and military jeeps with sirens screaming, he appeared: a small, pudgy, pleasant-looking man who waddled from his glistening Mercedes into position to review the colors. Four bands played the national anthem and the special song of praise entitled "Long Live President Ngo." The President then reviewed the troops from another glistening car, this one a convertible, and after that the parade began.

Standing in front of us were two German journalists with a Viet-

namese interpreter. The latter, noting that one of us could understand German, began identifying the various troop units parading in
front of us. "Those are Ngo Dinh Nhu's shock troops—the special
guard, the ones who raided the Buddhist pagodas a few weeks ago.
And there are Madame Nhu's women's solidarity troops." They all
looked trim and polished as they marched down the boulevard.
"There certainly are a lot of troops marching," we noted. "Yes,"
the interpreter agreed, still speaking German, "and that means that
no one is out fighting the Viet Cong. A terrible situation . . ." He
proceeded to discuss the faults of the Diem regime. An American
newsman standing nearby announced that all the weapons carried
by the parade participants had been assiduously unloaded before the
procession began, so fearful was President Diem of an attempt on
his life or his regime. As we acknowledged his remark in English,
another man standing in front of us turned his head, obviously
listening and straining to catch every word.

"No, don't say anything in English or French or Vietnamese," the
interpreter warned in German. "That man is a spy. All the spies are
trained in English, French, and of course Vietnamese. But none of
them knows German. As long as we speak like this, we're safe. Look
how he's struggling to understand us!"

As volunteers, we were affected by all these tensions only indirectly, particularly those of us who were far from Saigon and working in the provinces. Generally speaking, we were more observers
than participants in the affairs of the Vietnamese government.
While we could seldom avoid a feeling of anguish at seeing the
psychological stresses of our Vietnamese colleagues and friends, we
were directly affected only when the chaos of internal politics actually touched on our own projects and work. The day after this
particular National Day parade, for example, an IVS girl came back
from church and reported at the lunch table what she had just seen
downtown: government police hosing away the ashes of a Buddhist
monk who had burned himself to death in the square. This, of
course, was enough to shock everyone. But at other times our natural reactions to momentous political events were so mundane as to
seem ridiculous in retrospect.

Six days after the parade, we were driving back home to Dalat after a full day out in the hamlets. It was a few minutes before six o'clock, and we had gauged our return so that we would barely have time to change clothes before going to teach English at the Vietnamese-American Association. Near the control post on the outskirts of town, however, a long line of cars, buses, and trucks was stopped—apparently as the result of an accident on the road. Swearing to ourselves because the delay would make us late for class, we tried to pass the waiting line. But our Land Rover was soon halted by armed soldiers. We could hear other drivers talking about President Diem being "out." Among them were some Frenchmen on holiday who had spent the afternoon at one of the waterfalls which helped make Dalat so popular with sufficiently wealthy vacationers. They had heard that a *coup d'état* was in progress, and that there was fighting going on in the city. This would not have been surprising, since the effervescent mayor of Dalat was very pro-Diem.

We were still disgruntled at having rushed so, only to miss our class now anyway, but one of the French girls giddily announced that this was her first *coup d'état*. Among the others, jokes were exchanged over the possibility of having to spend the night on the road. "What are you worrying about?" one of the men asked us. "With a revolution in progress, you are hardly very likely to have a class tonight." He was right, of course. When the report of fighting turned out to be untrue and we were allowed to enter the city some forty minutes later, hardly a Vietnamese was in sight on the streets. They were all home listening to the radio play martial music, the broadcast of which later became an automatic signal that a military coup was in progress. Except for some excited soldiers, the only man we saw, in fact, was a lone gas-station attendant (the station was closed) who stood by the Shell pumps as we passed. He saluted briskly and grinned from ear to ear.

The IVS house in Dalat was embarrassingly large and opulent, but in Dalat the villa style was rather common and this one was loaned to us without rent. Of more interest than our house, however, was the villa next door, which was one of Madame Ngo Dinh Nhu's vacation retreats. She rarely stayed there, and when she did it was only long enough to order a change in the construction or *décor*. The roof of the swimming-pool pavilion, for example, underwent

numerous changes of tile, one having just been completed about the
time of the coup. That night, however, her house was dark and
silent. Her children, who according to rumor were staying there
while she was traveling in the United States, had allegedly fled into
the forest nearby. We could not help recalling the Christmas before
when Madame Nhu herself had come over to our yard for a hot-dog
roast with a group of IVS people. But that was before she began
talking of the "barbecue shows" of Buddhists. ("I would clap hands
at seeing another monk barbecue show," she had said in a letter to
the *New York Times*, "for one cannot be responsible for the mad-
ness of others." She was referring, of course, to the Buddhist self-
immolations.)

At our house, Chi Ba, the cook, was excited, though she wasn't
quite sure why, nor did she fully realize what was going on. She did
announce, however, that she was glad if something had happened to
Madame Nhu, and she repeated some common gossip about Madame
Nhu's bedroom life. Bao, an interpreter for AID, was taking the
matter more seriously. He had come to our house because he didn't
want to spend the night alone. We guessed rightly that the object of
his worry was his wife of just three weeks. She was visiting her
family in coup-embattled Saigon at the time. The radio news offered
little consolation for him, since the martial music was interrupted
only occasionally for announcements, most of which merely urged
the population to remain calm and to obey the new military rulers.

At the market place next morning, in spite of a light rain, there
were unusually large numbers of people milling about. Throngs of
soldiers, armed with bayoneted rifles, were preparing for an eleven
o'clock public meeting in the central square. As we made our pur-
chases, the saleswomen beamed with happiness over the new events.
"Vui lam, vui lam," they kept repeating—"we're very glad, we're
very glad." Yet they remained cautious too, for Diem's death had
not yet been revealed. Although the radio did not hesitate to de-
nounce him and his family rule, the people in the market were more
circumspect. "We don't know," they said when asked about him.
But an hour later, at the public meeting, Diem's and Nhu's deaths
were announced, and the crowds were exuberant. More cheers
greeted the remarks of the confident local military leaders when

they, like Chi Ba, denounced Madame Nhu as a chicken with scratching claws. Vietnamese in the crowd leaned over and spontaneously shared their feelings with Americans they did not know. "President Diem very bad," they said. Then they turned away, jockeying for position in order to see the men making speeches. The applause and exhilaration of the population were overwhelming. Even the bayonet-carrying soldiers could not conceal their smiles as the man who had replaced the once-jolly mayor promised the new government's program: unity against the Viet Cong, freedom of religion and speech, and progress toward a just and more prosperous society.

Actually, President Diem had not always been considered "very bad." In the early years, his success and popularity surprised every observer. When he first came to power, with decisive U.S. government support, opposition to him was ferocious in South Viet Nam. At the time of partition in 1954, it was widely accepted that in a free election in both North and South Viet Nam (with roughly equal populations), Ho Chi Minh would have won 80 per cent of the popular vote against Diem. In 1955, a story made the rounds comparing the position taken by the United States in supporting a South Vietnamese government under Diem with the case of the prisoner condemned to death by a Turkish sultan. The prisoner was given a year's reprieve when he offered to teach the sultan's horse to talk. When his comrades asked him why he had made such an incredible bet, the prisoner said, "Anything can happen in a year. I may die a peaceful death. Or the sultan may die and I will go free. Or, who knows, I may even teach the animal to speak." By 1958 it seemed indeed as if the horse had learned to speak. The army had fallen in behind Ngo Dinh Diem, the gangster bands of the Binh Xuyen were defeated, the armed religious sects of the Cao Dai and Hoa Hao were under the control of the government, and most of Diem's political enemies had been effectively suppressed. In addition he had the strong support of the refugees, those who had "voted with their feet" and come south after the Geneva Accords placed North Viet Nam under Communist rule. The American policy of support thus seemed justified.

It was not long, however, before Diem's rule grew too strong and his consolidation of power turned indiscriminate and arbitrary. As with subsequent governments, Diem did not know how to keep control while still permitting responsible dissent. Criticism became heresy and threats (usually called Communists) appeared behind every bush. National elections were rigged to assure massive Diemist majorities in the Saigon Assembly, and we knew at least one opposition candidate who left the country in protest against the regime's vote manipulation and harassment of her campaign. In the summer of 1956, Diem abolished the elected village councils, destroying a traditional form of democracy in Viet Nam, and replaced them with village officers appointed by the province chiefs with Ministry of Interior approval. The autonomy that the villages had once enjoyed, even under the French, was gone; the villages were now run by officials whose loyalties were to Diem's central government and not to the villages.

Still, most Vietnamese were reluctant to criticize the President, since he was, after all, the equivalent of the emperor and inspired, as such, a certain respect. Moreover, there was always the fear of the secret police. The criticisms that were made were cautious ones and were directed at his advisers and family. "The advisers of President Diem, especially Councilor Nhu, don't tell him what is going on," friends would tell us. "Diem is a bachelor and he doesn't understand the hardships created by the Family Law," said others. "It is the fault of that wicked Madame Nhu." It was ironic, perhaps, that Diem was so widely criticized for this overreliance on members of his own family in conducting the affairs of state. After all, family loyalty was the basis of Vietnamese society, and as hostility mounted against his regime, it was understandable that Diem would rely increasingly on people he could trust. If it was, on the one hand, easy to understand why the Vietnamese people felt alienated from the regime, it was also important to realize Diem's difficulty in compromising and in removing his brothers and his sister-in-law from positions of power. As a Vietnamese, family loyalty came first. Yet it was family loyalty that turned out to be Diem's "tragic flaw." In a sequence reminiscent of ancient Greek drama it caused the collapse of the whole House of Ngo.

When the regime fell, pro-American feeling rose to an all-time high. Vietnamese naturally credited the United States, and especially U.S. Ambassador Henry Cabot Lodge, with ridding them of the Diem family's tyranny. The U.S. had, indeed, cut back certain aid items to pressure Diem toward reforms. Yet Lodge himself heatedly denied any complicity in the coup. On a brief visit he once made to the IVS headquarters in Saigon, we innocently recalled having seen him with President Diem at the inauguration of a U.S.-financed atomic reactor at Dalat in October, 1963. In those last days, when it was publicly known that relations between the President and the Ambassador were strained, we had noted with interest that they seemed quite genial toward one another. At the reminder of that day, however, Lodge flared up. "I remember that very well," he said. "President Diem was just beginning to come around; he was just beginning to show some responsiveness to our suggestions—and then they killed him!" The Ambassador said this last part with great bitterness, emphasizing the "they." What struck us as ironic was that the one aspect of American policy which almost all Vietnamese thoroughly appreciated—the creating of conditions whereby Diem could be overthrown—was denied so vehemently by the U.S. government in the person of Ambassador Lodge!

The overthrow of the Diem regime was widely heralded at first as a revolution. From then on, National Day would be celebrated on November 1, the day of the coup, rather than on October 26. Streets were renamed Revolution Boulevard. The new leaders called their junta the Revolutionary Council. Would this "revolution" bring about improvement? We waited and waited, but on the whole it did not. Some commentators would call the 1963 *coup d'état* and its aftermath the "*lost* revolution," but Vietnamese, after a few months, ceased to refer to it as a revolution at all. Everything was the same.

"The same" meant essentially a government unresponsive to the needs and desires of the governed. The South Vietnamese government has certainly not been the only unresponsive one the world has known, as American apologists for the war often point out. What has made its problem more serious, however, is the competition

which grew increasingly fierce as the years went on—the competition of the National Liberation Front.* Although few Vietnamese
believed that either government by the Liberation Front or government on the order of North Viet Nam's would be truly democratic,
fewer still placed much stock in the high-principled rhetoric emanating from Saigon. This was their dilemma: they were caught in
the middle with no attractive alternative.

No Vietnamese demanded that American-style democracy be
fostered in Viet Nam. Most intellectuals, in this sense, agreed that
conditions were far too different in the two countries to permit of
such a transplantation. In a developing country with a relatively low
educational level such as Viet Nam, most of them felt that strong
leadership was needed. Some would even advocate a dictatorship, on
the condition that the dictator be a benevolent one. Certainly a
popular assembly would be important also, in order to express the
desires and demands of the common people, but less stock was
placed in this kind of institution than in the quality of the leader.
Vietnamese knew that their lack of viable political parties or organization would reduce the political effectiveness of such an assembly
unless its development were actively promoted by the national
leader.

What Vietnamese expected, then, was a good leader, one who
could be entrusted with the Mandate of Heaven and one whose rule
would be marked by stability and perhaps progress. Traditionally,
of course, the national government had not sported the trappings of
modern democracy. The emperor ruled through his mandarins, and
citizens had duties toward these men just as they had duties to a god
who was one notch above the emperor. The government owed
nothing to the people except protection and a minimum of intervention in their daily lives.

As Western ideas became known, however, the people—or more
precisely the intellectuals—came to expect more. Government, according to the teachings of French and American writers, should be

---

* Pending further discussion in Chapter 13, we are using the terms Viet
Cong (VC) and National Liberation Front (NLF) virtually interchangeably.
While the latter term is a more accurate one, the former was most frequently
used—at least until recent months—by the Americans and Vietnamese we are
describing in this book.

"of the people, by the people, and for the people." To the Vietnamese laymen who may have heard of these new concepts, particularly as they were copied in the Diem constitution, this meant that their government should be responsive. It meant the government should strive for social justice by easing the burdens of the poor who suffered at the expense of the rich. It seemed to mean that peasants should not be exploited by landlords, that the poor should have equal rights before the police and in the courts, and that the government should help the people to improve their lives. If these ideas had never been given much consideration before, they certainly were when the Viet Minh fanned out through the countryside during and after the war against the colonialist French. Yet the governments that followed Diem's showed little understanding of what was required to respond to these new demands. And even if they had understood, the necessary conditions of stability were lacking.

When the reins of power were assumed by the popular and genial General Duong Van "Big" Minh, in conjunction (cooperation would not have been the right word, as it turned out) with two other generals who had been instrumental in the *coup d'état,* there was an outburst of hope. The new regime made gestures of reconciliation toward previously anti-Diem religious groups such as the Cao Dai and the Hoa Hao, and of course the Buddhists. It released thousands of prisoners. The whole atmosphere reflected a sudden lifting of tensions, and dancing and the singing of sentimental songs, once banned by Madame Nhu, reappeared immediately. Yet this period of hope soon turned to disappointment. The coup gave rise to even more indecisiveness than was evident in the last trembling days of the Diemist bureaucrats. The salaries of rural workers and the implementation of new programs were even further delayed by confusion. There were massive changes in personnel, and it seemed as though almost everyone in government had to start from scratch learning a new job. All of us, to be sure, had expected some period of confusion as the government reorganized. We expected to see our work bog down in bureaucratic delays as personnel were changed around and as new programs replaced old ones. We did not know, but we hoped, that things would improve. Then, in January of 1964, when Minh had been in office less than three months, we heard the news that a little-known general, Nguyen Khanh, had pulled another coup in Saigon.

The idea of Khanh's taking power in place of a previously ineffectual triumvirate under Minh was not altogether displeasing. On the other hand, we shared the opinion of many: if coups and countercoups should become a way of life, the constant series of personnel and power changes throughout the country could, in practice, minimize the possibility of any positive government action at all. Khanh did, it seemed, consolidate a good deal of power behind him, and it was presumably in acknowledgment of this fact that the Americans embraced him so warmly. At the unusual hour of three o'clock in the morning, as Khanh staged the coup, he was actually seen in the company of three American advisers. Yet, few Vietnamese trusted or liked Khanh; they considered him an opportunist.

One American who embraced him with a fraternal devotion was U.S. Secretary of Defense Robert S. McNamara. Beginning in this period a long series of visits to Viet Nam, each of which wedded the unpopular Saigon regime ever more closely to the Americans in Vietnamese eyes, McNamara would troop with Khanh about the countryside. To him, Khanh represented Viet Nam. As the two men would raise their arms high in a joint victory gesture, McNamara would shout, in a humorous attempt at the Vietnamese language, "Viet Nam Muon Nam"—Long live Viet Nam. Unfortunately, and unbeknown to McNamara since he could not hear the ripples of laughter he generated, the Secretary's pronunciation gave a different meaning to his intended triumphant message—"the southern duck wants to lie down."

Khanh's rule was marked by a unique sense of melodrama. To the Vietnamese with whom we worked and associated every day, he was a ruthless power-seeker. His black goatee made him appear at once evil and comic. If we remarked on having seen him drive by in his black Mercedes, Vietnamese would ask with a resigned chuckle, "Did you see his beard?" This, perhaps, was an insignificant reaction on their part; yet such reactions told much (to those who listened) about how the Vietnamese felt about their government. At one point he shaved the goatee off, proclaiming the "new Khanh." But the new Khanh was no different from the old.

Khanh's melodramatic flair was best demonstrated by his various reactions to criticism and attempted coups. When he engineered a bill giving himself dictatorial powers, for example, hostile students in Saigon marched on the Palace in mass demonstration against his "despotic act" (see Chapter 12). Khanh was courageous enough to appear before them in person. Then, feeling humiliated by their opposition to his action, he flew off to Dalat in his private plane and pouted. Every time something went wrong in Saigon, he would take off for Dalat, or occasionally for the seaside resort of Vung Tau, confusing journalists by circulating among the various palaces placed at his disposal. (In Dalat alone there were three.) When a plane was heard taking off from Dalat's Camly Airfield late in the night, people in the town knew that the situation had quieted down in Saigon. Khanh was on his way back again.

During the period of Khanh's ascendancy, lasting about a year, it was not always clear who was really in power. Various others would be announced as having taken over, but shortly afterward the resilient Khanh always popped up again. For two days in August, 1964, for example, a ruling triumvirate of generals was announced, and then came a week of interregnum under economist Nguyen Xuan Oanh. (As deputy prime minister, Harvard-trained Oanh would again take the fore, at least technically, for a twenty-day period in early 1965.) It was during this period that we lost all track of what was going on in Saigon's political netherworld. Vietnamese complained more and more about the devious machinations of the military officers, each of whom upon gaining power promised to rule only a few weeks or months and then to organize free elections for a civilian government. But power corrupted, and they ended up playing musical chairs among themselves as they jockeyed for positions of ever greater authority. Rumors of coups were rife, and martial music was heard frequently on the radio as various generals and colonels proclaimed their interest in "saving the fatherland."

In late 1964, a long-awaited civilian government emerged under the respected former schoolteacher Tran Van Huong. This offered some hope, since the cause of the previous turmoil had appeared to be largely the inner wranglings of the army officer corps. Our friends and associates, who were of course civilians, were pleased at this escape from rule by the military. But it was during Huong's time in office that the true reality of Vietnamese power politics became known to those of us who had been perhaps too naïve on the subject before. That reality was the undeniable fact of military predominance in politics. The military, after all, had the organization and the discipline (relatively speaking, at least) and, above all, the arms and support of the Americans. There was, in fact, a similar power struggle between military and civilian elements on the American side, and as the war heated up in late 1964 and thereafter, the military seemed to win out among both Vietnamese and Americans.

Tran Van Huong did not last long in office. On the surface, his downfall was attributed to Buddhist demonstrations against him and what they called his "anti-Buddhist policies." These began in Hue and included strong criticisms of American policy, culminating in the January, 1965, burning of the U.S. Information Service library there. Less than three years later, however, when the possibility of Buddhist support for Huong's presidential candidacy was aired, some Vietnamese were suggesting that Huong himself could not be blamed for the policies leading to his downfall. It was rather General Khanh, that ubiquitous *eminence grise* and then commander-in-chief of the armed forces, who was behind it all. Upon hearing of a plan calling for elections, Khanh had become afraid of what this would mean to his position. His opposition became so belligerent, in fact, that even the Americans finally lost patience, and Ambassador Maxwell Taylor bluntly told Khanh he should leave the country. In what was intended to be a clever move, Khanh had recorded the Ambassador's words on tape, and he played them back (the conversation had been in French) at a subsequent junta meeting. The other generals were supposed to react angrily toward the Americans, and Khanh thundered that he did not want a colonialist envoy. The overly ambitious Khanh lost out, however, and was finally sent abroad as a "roving ambassador." Melodramatic to the end, he boarded his plane with a little plastic sack of Vietnamese soil and a vow to the effect that "I shall return." He now resides comfortably in Paris, where Vietnamese Embassy officials claim not even to know his street address.

In February, 1965, the respected Dr. Phan Huy Quat came to the fore in another attempt at civilian rule. Although Quat seemed to have many of the necessary personal qualifications for the post of prime minister, he never really had a chance. Most of his four months in office were marked by frustrated attempts at forming a cabinet satisfactory to all the various factions in Saigon. Besides, he was largely unknown to the Vietnamese people. (In fact, this was true of every leader after Diem, with the possible exception of General Minh.) In one model village, by way of example, we noted flags flying everywhere and were told a VIP delegation had just departed. "Who was it?" we asked. "Some colonel," a villager answered. When we questioned the local district chief, however, we discovered that the visitor had been Prime Minister Quat himself! Internal fights and differences with his chief-of-state, Phan Khac Suu, finally led Quat to call on the military "to save the country." On June 12, 1965, the trim, mustachioed Air Vice-Marshal Nguyen Cao Ky came into office.

Ky was ecstatically greeted by the Americans. He was one of the "Young Turks," the new generation of military leaders who were energetic, progressive, and clearly nationalistic. More important, Ky spoke good English, better than any leader before him (with the possible exception of Khanh). Thus the Americans felt they could deal with him. But the main reason the Americans greeted Ky with such enthusiasm was the reason the climber Mallory gave when asked why he wanted to climb Mt. Everest: "Because it is there." For the Americans it had been the same with Khanh and with all the other leaders who had risen to power: whoever was strong enough to take over was presumed strong enough, with immediate American support, to provide stability. And what Viet Nam needed above all—as indeed our own experiences with the bureaucracy had indicated—was stability. With American involvement now including the bombing of the North, and with the bitter experience of ten successive Saigon governments in twenty months, the United States could not afford any more fooling around on the part of ambitious

Saigon soldiers and politicians. The situation had become far too
serious for that. Unity and stability were needed in order to prose-
cute the war against the Viet Cong. Even the question of whether
or not Ky himself was the right man for the job was no longer
relevant. Who else, Embassy officials asked rhetorically, was there?
At the beginning, in fact, Ky did not seem such a bad choice. He
had the strength of the air force behind him, he had the backing of
many student groups with whom he enjoyed the affinity of youth,
and he was generally considered to be honest, patriotic, intelligent,
and fearless. While his chief-of-state, Nguyen Van Thieu, remained
largely unknown and in the background, Ky eventually became
known among his countrymen, though largely because of his lon-
gevity in office and his flamboyance.

It was this latter trait that made Ky a poor choice in the long run.
He was too young and too boyish in a society where age and seriousness of purpose are respected. Somehow, the Mandate of Heaven
did not fit him. Darting about in black cap, purple scarf, and yellow
gloves, Ky was the exact antithesis of what, according to tradition,
a Vietnamese leader should be. His current wife, a stunning former
Air Vietnam stewardess, did not contribute to his nationalist image
by traveling to Japan for plastic surgery on her nose and eyes,
intended to make her look less Vietnamese and more Western.
Acquaintances of Ky's, who had served with him in the French
army in North Viet Nam before Geneva, confidentially expressed
their personal dislike of him. He was nothing but an impetuous
playboy, they said. He didn't have what it takes.

While Americans emphasized Ky's good characteristics, which
certainly existed, the Vietnamese tended to follow their native intui-
tion when it came to national leadership. Any prime minister who,
for example, on a state visit to Taiwan, performed daredevil stunts
at the controls of a jet trainer, might titillate his hosts but hardly the
public back home in Viet Nam. On another occasion, Ky made an
even more clownish impression. It was on July 20, 1965, officially
known in South Viet Nam as the "Day of National Shame," signify-
ing as it did the anniversary of the signing of the Geneva Accords
by which the country was divided in two. All through the morning,
truckload after truckload of local inhabitants were brought from

the surrounding vicinity to the banks of the Ben Hai River. The Ben Hai, flowing through the middle of the Demilitarized Zone on its way to the sea, marks the border between North and South Viet Nam. Sometime in mid-morning, after thousands had been assembled, the sound of planes could be heard overhead. One, a Vietnamese Air Force Skyraider, flew so close to the border itself that, in full view of the crowds on the south bank, North Vietnamese guns across the river started shooting away. Taking the hint, the Skyraider finally doubled back. The only purpose of the aerial show, it turned out, was to announce the arrival, by car, of Prime Minister Ky. Not content with this display, Ky proceeded to act like a comedian on the speaker's platform. He made funny faces and silly gestures. The onlookers could hardly be impressed by the quality of their prime minister. Those standing around us kept repeating in amused disbelief, "Oh, look how Mr. Ky is fooling around!"

Ky's personal faults were more than matched by the difficulties of the situation. Governing South Viet Nam, with all its divisions and the war besides, was perhaps the hardest job in the world. Any step in one direction would be criticized from another. The fact that he got along well with the American Embassy (Lodge called him "my second son") led nationalist Vietnamese to call him an American puppet. Later, when he publicly berated the Americans, the Vietnamese would sense the truth but still question his emotional stability. Ky once called himself "a tragic man," and in lucid moments he confessed his uncertainties about himself. In May, 1968, when he was vice-president and losing power steadily to the new president, Nguyen Van Thieu, he raised the leadership problem in an extemporaneous Saigon speech:

The whole world respects Ho Chi Minh and [North Vietnamese] Defense Minister Vo Nguyen Giap. Why? Who are they? Are they not Vietnamese too? Why can't we find a man in the South and make him be respected by the whole world? Is it because our leaders are nothing but old fashioned slaves? Perhaps I am partly responsible for this. Perhaps I haven't performed my duty with all my might and that's why our nation is still the way it is. If it is any mistake of mine, I am ready to be judged by the people and by history.

Ky will not be the only one judged by history.

During the period 1963–1966, American officials always had the idea of elections in the back of their mind. They felt, quite reasonably, that if the Vietnamese people could choose their own government, then the cause of stability would be advanced through that government's legitimacy. The Vietnamese looked at it somewhat differently. They—that is the intellectuals—were all in favor of both elections and stability, but for them government legitimacy itself was the key goal. For the American Mission, it seemed, stability was the necessary goal, for the Americans had to sell their administration's Viet Nam policy to Congress and to the American people. For this purpose, stability under a truly popular government was not required, because the American people had no way of judging what was or was not popular. But the Vietnamese could tell the difference, and they had little use for an unpopular but superficially stable government like Ky's. Theoretically, of course, only a popular government would in time become a really stable government, but the U.S. Mission was short of time—and, it must be said, of understanding for Vietnamese feelings.

As a result of the antigovernment Struggle Movement in 1966, which came desperately near to overthrowing the Ky regime (see Chapter 6), the Saigon government was forced to hold elections for a constituent assembly. The first job of such a group would be to draft a constitution, since there had been none in effect since Diem's fall, the country having been ruled for the most part by military decree. The mixed American attitude toward such elections was expressed by Ambassador Lodge, back for his second tour at the Embassy. Before the Struggle Movement, Lodge had gone on record as being against elections for the near future. Like Ky, he felt they would be too difficult to organize under wartime conditions. When the strength of the Struggle Movement's pressure became felt, however, Lodge suddenly decided that elections were a good thing and that he had been for them all along. Although the NLF were excluded from participation (which under the circumstances was hardly surprising), and in spite of a militant Buddhist boycott, the elections of 1966 went amazingly well. Subsequent balloting for hamlet and village office was also relatively successful, as was the final framing of a new national constitution—an act marred only by President Johnson's reportedly hailing it as the best gift he could ever receive, one comparable to his first look at his baby grandchild. Most Vietnamese were not pleased at the idea of Lyndon Johnson being the grandfather of their country.

It was the crucial presidential and legislative elections of 1967, however, that caused so many Vietnamese, and ourselves, so much dismay. The central problem, and one not unique to Vietnam, was the power of the incumbents to sway the vote in their favor. It was for that reason that the militant Buddhist hierarchy had gone so far in its Struggle demands as to insist on the resignation of Ky and Thieu before the campaign period. They did not succeed, however, and as a result, electioneering began well ahead of the one-month period permitted to the civilian candidates. Three months before election day, for example, signs that read "The government of Nguyen Cao Ky is the government of the poor people" appeared all over the country. In a sense, this was only a minor affront, since no one believed the slogan anyway. Most Vietnamese would point out that it was true that the Ky government was the government of the poor, but only in the sense that its corrupt leaders sucked the people completely dry.

One of the IVS volunteers saved himself some money by striking a responsive chord in taxi drivers who did not take the Ky signs seriously. Like many Vietnamese, taxi drivers assumed that we were rich like most Americans in Viet Nam, and they would try to charge us the "rich American" price. This price was usually any-where from 30 to 100 per cent more than the Vietnamese price. The clever volunteer, when confronted with the cost of a taxi ride, explained to the driver (in Vietnamese) that he was working for the Vietnamese government which, as all the signs indicated (he said with a smile), was the government of the poor people. "Therefore," he said, "I am poor and should only pay the Vietnamese price." The driver would burst out laughing. "Oh, you know much about our country," he would say. Accepting only the normal price, he would drive off, still chuckling.

Others of us used the same joke as a way of pointing out that we were not ordinary, wealthy Americans. Invariably the taxi drivers would laugh uproariously. "Those signs tell a lie," they would say.

"The government does nothing for the poor people. They just make money for themselves." One complained about the new water system built by the government with massive U.S. aid: "The problem with your water system," he said, "is that the pipes all go to the cement houses. I live in a thatch house and have to buy my water from the rich people."

Nevertheless, the fact that the Ky government had been in power for over two years gave its leaders the advantage of being better known than any of the ten civilian politicians represented on the presidential ballot. In one village of Montagnards (see Chapter 4) we noted that flimsy wooden guide rails had been built around the schoolhouse in order to usher the lines of voters into the polls two weeks later. Intrigued, we asked the schoolteacher, an old friend, for whom he was planning to vote.

"For Ky, of course," he replied.

"But Ky is only running for vice-president," we pointed out, the military junta having recently decided on its Thieu-Ky ticket.

"Oh, isn't there any way I can get him to be president?" our friend, now disappointed, inquired.

"No, he's just running for vice-president," we told him. "Why do you like him so much, anyway?" we asked.

"Oh, he's a very good man," the teacher answered with confidence and enthusiasm. "He talks good on the radio!"

"But have you seen any results of the things he's promised on the radio?" we countered, knowing the teacher would not resent our queries.

"Well, how should I know about that?" he asked.

Perplexed as to whether he knew any of the other candidates, we then asked why he didn't consider voting for Tran Van Huong, at that point the favored civilian candidate.

"Oh yes, Dr. Luong, I know about him," our friend replied. But we had to correct him. Dr. Luong was a physician in the provincial capital whom he was confusing with candidate Huong. We explained that Huong was a former schoolteacher and prime minister.

When our friend heard that he had been a schoolteacher like himself, he showed momentary interest, but then finally said, "No,

I'm going to vote for Ky. I've never seen the other man's picture anywhere."

In terms of equal opportunity for all the candidates, Ky's ticket was so far ahead of all the others in "equality" that it was surprising when he and Thieu garnered less than 35 per cent of the ballots cast. In addition to exploiting the advantages of incumbency, Thieu and Ky were able to neutralize their most powerful opposition by keeping them in exile or by refusing them permission to run. General "Big" Minh, for example, whose popularity posed a threat to the government in power, was kept in exile in Bangkok during this time. Another exiled and popular general, Nguyen Chanh Thi, was questioned by Ky's national police chief, General Nguyen Ngoc Loan, on a special trip to Washington, D.C. When Thi refused to declare his support for Ky and to join Ky's ticket as vice-president, he was kept in exile. Au Truong Thanh, the other leading contender, and a liberal, was refused candidate status because of his alleged "pro-Communist neutralism." Truong Dinh Dzu, a somewhat disreputable lawyer who came in second in the balloting because he openly made himself the "peace candidate," wisely announced his "white dove" platform and indictments of Thieu and Ky only after his candidacy had been approved. After the election, he spent much of his time in jail before being sentenced by a military tribunal (and without appeal) to five years of hard labor for his political speeches during the campaign. Finally, there was a general belief in Vietnamese circles, partly fostered by Ky, that if Thieu and Ky did not win, they would pull a *coup d'état* against whoever did succeed. All these factors, plus the knowledge that the Americans were supporting the military ticket, made their winning inevitable. No Vietnamese ever doubted it for a minute. Again, it was surprising they did not win more than 35 per cent of the total vote.

Perhaps the most ludicrous aspect of the entire process, however, was the American position. One American friend, with years of experience in Viet Nam, pointed out to the highest Embassy officials that most Vietnamese did not support Thieu and Ky. He suggested that the U.S. government urge truly free elections. Within days this friend went back to the United States and has not been allowed to return to Viet Nam since. In Washington, Assistant Secretary of State William Bundy had stated privately that "these elections are our last hope in Viet Nam." With such desperation in high administration circles, it was hardly surprising that when Henry Cabot Lodge arrived in Saigon as head of a team of twenty-two election observers sent by President Johnson, he expressed confidence that everything about the elections would prove to be above-board. Our Vietnamese colleagues, however, expressed considerable dismay over the activities of some of the observers they met or saw. They told us that several had dropped in for only a few moments at two or three polling places, then were rushed off for sumptuous meals given in their honor, usually by the local province chief. What the observers could not see, they added, were voters who were paid off by zealous government officials, military men who had received two voting cards (one through their families and another through their military unit), polling places with an insufficient number of ballots, and some ballots with the names of certain candidates missing. Some of these irregularities were of course unintentional, but others were deliberate. Finally, and particularly in the legislative elections, there were simply too many names from which to choose—a source of great frustration to voters who usually hadn't heard of any of them. One old woman, for example, angrily threw her bundle of ballots on the floor, not knowing how she could possibly be expected to make a sensible decision.

While President Johnson's observers returned to the United States with generally glowing accounts of what they had seen in their four days, Vietnamese colleagues, who knew the whole background, felt differently. "In many ways, the elections have only made our situation worse," lamented one. "They have seemingly legitimized the *status quo* of war and foreign intervention which we hate." "You held the elections to convince the American public that Viet Nam has a democracy," said another. A third cynically announced, "We are planning to send twenty-two Vietnamese observers who don't speak English to the United States in November, 1968, for four days, to see if your elections are fair."

In March 1968, the incredible Ky himself, now vice-president, gave his comments on the elections in an interview with an Italian journalist:

> In most of the cases, the men who have been elected in South Vietnam are not the men that people want; they do not represent the people. The people voted for them because someone told them to vote. Our last elections were a loss of time and money, a mockery. They were only useful to elect a regime which is wrong and corrupted and weak and would fall immediately with a revolution.
>
> It is hard for me to say so because I share the responsibility of those elections, I have been voted in them and I am the Vice President of such a regime. But at least I recognize the evil where the evil is, and I say that laws must be changed, because what we now have are laws that defend the rich. We need new laws to defend the poor.*

Meanwhile, and before President Thieu began to consolidate his own power, a Vietnamese friend described the new form of government. Power, he said, was divided among four competing forces: (1) the U.S. Embassy; (2) the two houses of the Saigon Legislature; (3) the three "cabinets" of Thieu, Ky, and Loc (the latter was soon replaced as prime minister by Tran Van Huong); (4) the four tactical zones and their commanding generals. It was hardly surprising, therefore, that the elections did little to win popular confidence for the government. Thus, while Embassy officials hailed the "new government," Vietnamese saw it as the same old regime. The only thing that had been proved was that an election could, technically, be carried off even under wartime conditions.

Since Johnson's election-observers could not understand Vietnamese, and since they knew little about Viet Nam, they could not possibly have learned the truth about the elections—or about their aftermath. But that has always been the problem: Americans have rarely known the truth about Viet Nam. When the same leaders as before were "inaugurated" in Saigon on October 31, 1967, Vice-President Humphrey was dispatched as the ranking American representative for the ceremony. Remarked one Vietnamese in Hue, "His attendance reminds us of the old days when the Chinese emperor,

* Quoted in Washington *Post*, April 7, 1968.

our ultimate sovereign, would send a delegate to supervise our vassal emperor's coronation."

Later, when the Embassy claimed that the Thieu government was making progress toward needed reforms throughout 1968, Vietnamese noted that the regime conducted overly thorough "witch hunts" after the Tet offensive, summarily closed down newspapers, arrested and sentenced even anti-Communist opponents, and generally dragged its feet on many liberalization moves that the people were demanding. Though some Vietnamese had seen promise in the Legislature, particularly in the somewhat representative Lower House, even this hope disappeared when in the course of 1968 it accomplished little. Some said that more time was required, but the problem was that Viet Nam never had much time. Others said that what Viet Nam needed was a genuine revolution.

And so, over the years, the political system has gone along, never very popular with its constituents, never very responsive to their wishes, yet surviving somehow in spite of various changes at the top, influences from outside, and even insurrection from within. The whole succession of leaders from Diem to Thieu seem to Vietnamese to have had much in common with one another. None of them could ease the burdens of life, bring about a harmony of spirit, or fulfill the Mandate of Heaven.

[4]

PLIGHT OF THE MINORITY

The Highland Tribespeople

Driving the few miles from Ban Me Thuot to Buon Kmrong Prong was an arduous experience in the rainy season, for the last part of the road was like a mud bog. Few people went there at any time of year, but during the rainy season it seemed especially isolated. Ban Me Thuot itself, particularly in the late summer of 1963, was not a bustling metropolis, even though it was the chief market and administrative center for Darlac province. Its market place was a melting pot of the Highlands, where Montagnards of several different tribes jostled with the Vietnamese and Chinese living in the town. Throughout the day, raucous sounds emanated from the streets and from public loudspeakers. The tribespeople were always distinguishable here by their darker skin and colorful dress. Sometimes they came into town on three-wheeled Lambrettas, but more often they walked along the sides of the roads, carrying in wood, squash, and cucumbers, and carrying out the wonders of the market: gongs, black cotton cloth, and salt. We often stopped to give rides to as many as could be accommodated in our jeep.

Coming from Saigon, some 250 air miles to the south, Ban Me Thuot was in the middle of nowhere; coming from Ban Me Thuot, the strategic hamlet of Buon Kmrong Prong was the frontier. To some of the military and government officials, this frontier looked like "Indian country"—and indeed was called, in the lingo of the times, "VC country." Ever-present danger overshadowed any possible constructive improvements for the inhabitants. To young volunteers, however, it was the "new frontier," where disease and illiteracy would have to be eradicated and where concentration of the previously seminomadic people in strategic hamlets could facilitate modernization.

Everything about Buon Kmrong Prong gave an impression of neatness and order. The bamboo stakes between the rows of barbed-wire fencing formed pleasant patterns, and one forgot momentarily the dangers that had led the villagers to drive them patiently into the soil. Inside the spacious perimeter of the hamlet fence, the bamboo and thatch longhouses of the Rhade tribesmen were neatly arranged in rows. Built on stilts, they could be entered only by placing one's feet sideways in the notches of a propped-up log. Animals were thus prevented from intruding.

We had come to Buon Kmrong Prong to help dig a well. To us, developing a source of relatively clean drinking water was one of the most urgent needs in the Highland villages where dysentery has always been a terrible scourge. It was, however, a need not always evident to the local people, who regarded river water as quite adequate. For us to claim that there were evil microbes in the water was to substitute one form of invisible spirit for another; a much more convincing argument to the Montagnards was that digging a well would save the half-mile walk to and from the river.

One day after the well had been completed we were invited to join the mourners at the funeral of one of the hamlet's notables, a member of the Tribal Law Court in Ban Me Thuot. "He was in the hospital for three months," one of his closest friends explained. "His stomach was all puffed out. Then the doctors sent him home again, saying he wasn't sick any more. Not sick, but now he's dead. Yes, it is true—not even these modern doctors know everything."

As we waited for the funeral to begin, Y Klar came up. He had worked with Americans for a few months and knew some English. He also knew that we were interested in learning about the customs of his tribe. "Rhade customs are very different from Vietnamese customs," he said. "Rhades have very happy funerals, Vietnamese very sad." We told him that American funerals were very sad, like Vietnamese. As the festivities got under way, however, we began to wonder whether the Rhades did not have a better approach. The spirit being liberated, according to the theology, why not show joy rather than grief?

With about two hundred Montagnards gathered outside the long-house where the coffin was lying, the ceremonies started in full force. At first they were mournful enough. There was music—the heavy bonging of gongs, the thumping of a huge drum, the warbling sound of a wind instrument—intertwined with the chanting of the mourners in the longhouse and the horrendous trumpeting of the hamlet elephants. At midday the coffin was moved to the grave site just outside the village fence, and as the music continued, a shaman, dressed in red, smeared buffalo blood on one end of the coffin and performed a ritual chant. The dead man's best friend then gave a eulogy, after which an urn containing the deceased's crossbow, blanket, bracelets, and other articles was placed in the grave. Meanwhile, the group of women had been wailing and dabbing their eyes with handkerchiefs. As the coffin itself was lowered, the heavens burst forth as if to add their tears to those of the women. The men hurriedly filled the grave with dirt.

After the shower the mourners began to ease their sadness with food and drink. We began to see why Y Klar had prepared us for a happy funeral. The meat of three water buffalo that had been sacrificed that morning was served, and dozens of jars of rice wine that had been carefully guarded from premature consumption were brought forth. The participants soon reached a stage of advanced giddiness and grew quite cheery, interrupting their laughter only long enough to empty bladders or doze off. Such parties, we knew, could go on for days. Sadness, as Y Klar said, was not the predominant mood of Montagnard funerals.

But if sadness was secondary at funerals it was not so for life in general. For the Montagnards even more than for the Vietnamese, the stresses of modernization were upsetting, adding emotional burdens to those brought about by the rigors of war.

There are thought to be nearly a million Montagnards in South Viet Nam. Divided into about thirty main tribes and language groupings, they were collectively called Montagnards by the French, the name meaning "Mountaineers." Since the French days, life has changed for them probably more than for any other group in the country. They were accustomed to roaming the forests, but the war has necessitated their agglomeration within the bounds of fortified hamlets. They had lived by a slash-and-burn economy, planting their rice in one place until the yield became too low, then moving on to clear off new hillsides and valleys for planting. Now, with movement restricted, the population more concentrated, and land less available, they have had to learn an entirely new economy and way of life. Once accustomed to an independent, even isolated, social and cultural existence, they now have had to learn to live side by side with strangers to their lands—the ethnic Vietnamese.

The Montagnards were there first, believed to have migrated into the Vietnamese Highlands some two thousand years ago. American anthropologists have devoted relatively little attention to these people, though they have been divided into two very general language groupings. One, the Mon-Khmer, includes such tribes as the Koho around the present town of Dalat; they are thought to have come originally from what are now Burma and Cambodia. The other, the Malayo-Polynesian, includes such tribes as the Rhade around Ban Me Thuot; they are believed to have migrated up the Malay Peninsula from Indonesia. To the sensitive, history was full of precedents: "You see," said one well-educated Koho friend who had read a history of his own people, "we have always suffered discrimination. Thousands of years ago we were expelled from our original homelands and we settled here. Now the Vietnamese are colonizing our lands here. They are trying to exterminate us. Where will we go next?"

While there is no certain historical indication why the early Montagnards left their original lands centuries ago, it is true that the Vietnamese have made inroads into the Highlands. This has happened particularly since 1954, when hundreds of thousands of Vietnamese left North Viet Nam and many were settled on the vast, sparsely inhabited plateau of the South. Later, President Diem's land-development program settled another large group on land the Montagnards felt was rightfully theirs. Even then, however, there was little contact between the two ethnic groups until the new outbreak of war forced the Montagnards into the lower ground nearer the Vietnamese centers. Where the French had shown a special affection for the good and simple mountain people, offering them plantation jobs and limited education and status in their army, the Vietnamese, for a variety of psychological reasons, looked down on them, sometimes referring to them as "dirty and primitive savages." Of course there were exceptions in the form of some young liberals with a developed social conscience. But more typical was the Dalat high-school student who asked, "Why do you like them so much? The Montagnards are so dirty." We American volunteers tried to bridge the gap between the two groups. When a provincial education chief said, "You know, in many ways I have come to admire the Montagnards more than my fellow Vietnamese," then we felt we had accomplished something significant for future harmony in Viet Nam.

Y Bli's story is a typical one for a Montagnard in South Viet Nam. His village was at Buon Dak Sak, located south and west of Ban Me Thuot. When he was small, he lived the traditional slash-and-burn life of his people. Every three years, his small village would shift fields, cutting down the forest and planting upland rice, a special variety requiring considerably less water than the delta paddy rice. In addition to rice, they grew corn, gourds, squash, pumpkins, peppers, and eggplant. Tobacco was planted in the location of the previous year's buffalo pen, where the earth had been fertilized by manure. As a boy, Y Bli set traps in the mountain streams to catch the tiny fish. He and the other children also caught crickets, a delicacy either cooked or raw. They developed an interesting technique: in the evenings and after the first spring rains had fallen, holes would open up in the ground. Y Bli and his little friends took cattails, or a similar plant, and inserted them into jars containing the biting red ants so common in the Highlands. Then they stuck the cattails with the ants clinging to them into the holes in the ground. The rest was automatic: the ants bit the crickets and drove them out of the holes where the boys were ready to grab them. After brushing the ants off the crickets and into an ant jar, they placed the crickets into a separate cricket jar. Y Bli could collect nearly a pint of crickets in an hour. The occasional sacrifices of their domestic animals and the shooting of a wild deer or boar in the forest added to the Montagnards' limited diet.

As for industry, village activities were limited to three: one was that of the local blacksmith, whose unique hand-bellows fanned the flames of the tiny campfire foundry in which he fashioned crude metal farming tools. A second was that of the women who wove blankets, also used as skirts, on their wooden handlooms. The third was the somewhat less specialized one of making crossbows for hunting as well as various bead necklaces and ornamental handicrafts.

With Y Bli's tribe, marriage came upon the invitation of the girl's family and was sealed by an exchange of bracelets made of brass. The husband then went to live in the longhouse of his wife's family. Y Bli was a sturdy, good-looking boy who got married early, at the age of sixteen. Jokingly, we asked him why he married so young. He answered with a grin and a shrug: "Her mother pursued me relentlessly, so I had no choice!" Soon afterward, in early 1963, Y Bli joined the Special Forces, a branch of the army popular with the Montagnards because they were trained separately from the Vietnamese and were allowed to serve in their native Highlands. Y Bli joined because he wanted to defend his people from the Viet Cong, because he liked adventure, and because he felt this was the way to advance. In franker moments he would add that with the Special Forces he could assert his identity against the Vietnamese—both those of the Viet Cong and those of the Saigon government.

Y Bli was sent for training to Camp Buon Ea Nao in Ban Me Thuot. He liked it there, his children could go to school, and he was making money. To be sure, he missed his village at first. At night he would seem to hear the familiar sounds of the pounding of rice and the joyous shouting of the children romping in the golden rice fields or splashing about in the river. But he was young, the outside world was an adventure, and it did not take him long to break the links with his traditional world. He had gold caps put on his teeth, which had been filed down earlier according to the practice of his tribe. In the market place he had contact with Vietnamese, but was hurt to note that his people, inexperienced in the ways of commerce, were being taken advantage of by the shrewd town merchants.

Y Bli began to see, understand, and become bitter about the discrimination against his people. He asked the questions posed by underprivileged minorities everywhere: How can we lift ourselves out of this rut when many in the majority, who control the economy, profit from our backwardness? How can we educate ourselves without people trained to be teachers and when our young men and women find it difficult to get into the schools? How can we use our own resources when we don't have the capital to get started and when we must accept lower wages if we are to get jobs at all? Where does one start? Is it practical to try to break down the barriers by educating our own people? Should we remain, in the eyes of the majority, the jovial but ignorant children of the forest? Or should we smash the chains of discrimination by revolution? Y Bli found himself obsessed by these questions. He tried to work out solutions by himself, and he discussed them and argued about them with his fellow Montagnard soldiers.

Early in 1964, Y Bli was transferred to another camp at Buon Sarpa. Here, with Cambodia and the guerrilla infiltration routes not far away, he participated in border surveillance patrols. But the commanding officers at Buon Sarpa were Vietnamese, and before long the new arrival felt the ethnic tensions weighing still more heavily on him. There were good reasons why they should. For example, Montagnard soldiers were not always paid the full amount they had coming to them. Besides that, the Vietnamese officers sometimes sent Montagnards out on operations without going along to share in the danger. When the officers did go along, they had Montagnard coolies carry their packs. There were smaller grievances as well. Vietnamese officers often failed to return the salutes of the Montagnard soldiers, and the Montagnards felt that the enterprising Vietnamese barbers who had set up business at Buon Sarpa were overcharging for haircuts. Y Bli began to wonder what he was fighting for. "We fought for the French and got nothing," he said. "Now we fight for the Vietnamese and *they* give us nothing."

Finally, on September 19, 1964, the Montagnard leaders at Buon Sarpa—like others elsewhere in the Highlands—revolted. At one o'clock in the morning they shot eleven Vietnamese officers. They raised the Montagnard flag over Buon Sarpa and tied the Vietnamese commander to the flagpole. The Americans in the camp looked helplessly on. Certainly they were opposed to the violence, but they had always tended to sympathize with the underdog Montagnards. (Eventually, the Americans were evacuated by helicopter.) The revolt lasted eight days, and in all the Highlands more than eighty Vietnamese were killed. Y Bham, a famous man to the young tribesmen, visited Buon Sarpa during this time. He had spent five years in jail in Hue for his role in an earlier rebellion and was the leader of the Montagnard nationalist movement, FULRO (Front Uni pour la Libération des Races Opprimées—United Front for the Liberation of the Oppressed Races). After the 1964 revolt, Y Bham, with some of the Buon Sarpa leaders and a few hundred followers, remained in the near vicinity of the Cambodian border (some thought actually in Cambodia).

At Buon Sarpa the revolt ended when a Vietnamese armed force, larger than was customarily used against the Viet Cong, arrived from Ban Me Thuot. The Montagnards surrendered. General Nguyen Khanh, then prime minister, came for a ceremony at which the Vietnamese flag replaced the Montagnard colors. The two adversaries exchanged pistols and made new promises to each other.

For Y Bli, who knew little of the larger politics, the whole series of events formed a memorable experience. After the revolt, he returned to Ban Me Thuot, then was transferred further north and east to An Khe, where in the spring of 1965 he participated in a military operation to open the Viet Cong-held Route 19. Nearly two hundred allied soldiers were killed in this operation, and Y Bli, while uninjured, became more and more discouraged at seeing his friends fall one after the other. He resolved to quit the Special Forces and, without permission, headed once again for Ban Me Thuot. The last time we met, Y Bli was very depressed. "I cannot return to my village," he said, "because life there is strange to me now. Besides, if I did return, the VC would retaliate against me. Or perhaps the FULRO would try to recruit me. Yet I cannot return to the Special Forces, for I left them before. Even though I like the military life, it is no good to fight for the Vietnamese who take advantage of us. They will not give me a job here, either. There is nothing to do."

Y Bli is not lazy. He does not want to live off his relatives. Like many of his peers, he is confused. He is disoriented not only by the consequences of war, but by the fact of being a member of a minority group in a seemingly alien master society.

"I am a soldier," he said. "I cannot go back to my village. I have forgotten the ways of planting rice. My dream is for the independence of my people. The old village is for my parents and grandparents. There is something different for me." Yet Y Bli cannot articulate what that something is. The complexities are too great, and he cannot cope with the demands made upon himself and his people by the inevitable coming of modernization.

For the Montagnards, moving into strategic hamlets has often been upsetting. Unable to roam at will in the forests because of the dangers of war, they have had to learn intensive, rather than extensive, cultivation. Now, if the soil nutrients are used up, they cannot simply clear new land and move to a new location. They must stay where they are and cope. They must learn to diversify their crops, to utilize the manure from their animals as fertilizer, and to use commercial fertilizers and insecticides. This much they must learn just to maintain their previous level; if they are to escape the ancient curses of disease and to improve their living standards, they must learn more. Planting new vegetables and raising improved breeds of pigs and chickens can furnish them with a more balanced diet, thereby cutting down on disease. Because living conditions have become more crowded, they must develop sanitary water and toilet facilities. And part and parcel of all this is the need for education, to develop the ability of the people to adapt to new conditions. All this has to come sooner or later to the Montagnards, just as it has been coming to the Vietnamese. But the pressures of the war are hastening the process and allowing little time for the necessary social and cultural adaptation.

The war, a Vietnamese province chief decided in early 1964, dictated the construction of a large Montagnard resettlement area at Gia Bac. Its purpose was to group together several villages which could not defend themselves and make them into an entity of sufficient size to defend not only its people but also the main road on which it lay. Gia Bac was built in a dramatic location atop a ridge.

From it, one could see the South China Sea to the east and the Annamite mountain chain to the west. Gia Bac was to be a model settlement, enthusiastically supported both by the Vietnamese government and the American aid mission. A health clinic was built, along with a two-classroom school and a hamlet office. Wells were dug, and new clothes were distributed to the people. An all-out effort was made. An auspicious inauguration ceremony was planned, though organized as it was by Vietnamese, it bore scant relevance to the Montagnard traditions.

Warned in advance of the dignitaries' arrival by the whirring of helicopter rotors, the tribespeople were lined up neatly on either side of the dirt road along which reviewing stands had been set up for the inauguration ceremonies. Decked out in relief clothing, the people looked bewildered as the officials from the sky staggered through the clouds of dust billowed up by the chopper blades. Some of the lesser province officials had come by jeep, making a strenuous two-hour trip. All the provincial service chiefs had been ordered to attend this ceremony. Whereas the Americans were generally pleased to have a change from their desks and the confines of the town, these officials frequently took off the rest of the day or came to work late the next morning in order to compensate for the dangers and the unwelcome excitement. Once in Gia Bac they gathered in little groups and chatted or joked among themselves. The Montagnards stood as they were told, waiting to see what would happen. They understood little of the proceedings anyway, since the majority could not speak or understand the Vietnamese language. Two buffalo also waited, with ropes tied tightly around their heads and attached to ceremonial poles.

Such occasions, no matter how remote in the jungle wilderness, were invariably equipped by the Vietnamese Information Service with portable public-address systems. A long string of Vietnamese notables made speeches, after first testing the sound equipment by blowing and tapping on the microphone. One Montagnard man spoke briefly and was followed by a Catholic priest, the only Vietnamese there who could speak Koho, the appropriate Montagnard language for Gia Bac. If the villagers were still listening, they would have understood these two small parts of the speech-making. To be sure, the buffalo sacrifice was a Montagnard custom, but the accompanying ritual of the Koho prancing around in a circle while blowing their six-piped mouth organs had the flavor of an unfamiliar and forced Vietnamese choreography. Because of the presence of the dignitaries and the late morning hour, the sacrifice, traditionally carried out at dawn in more elaborate form, was abbreviated. The legs of the huge animals were bound together with ropes which were then pulled, causing the buffalo to fall. Then their throats were slit, slowly enough so that the heaving of the suffering beasts and the stench of the fresh blood filled the air for more than a brief moment. Finally, the highest of the somewhat squeamish dignitaries were dabbed on the foot with the blood. Gia Bac was now "official."

After the ceremony, the public-address system was turned over to a blaring Vietnamese popular music band brought in from a Saigon nightclub. To its accompaniment, the guests were treated to a huge banquet. The people of Gia Bac, meanwhile, were free to go their own way. A group of small children headed for the community water hole a few hundred yards distant, farther than any of the visitors would be likely to venture. They had been on good behavior and looked spanking clean in their new clothes when the school was opened earlier. Now they were far more natural and uninhibited, scampering naked in and out of the water and splashing each other gleefully.

The future of Gia Bac would not be gleeful, however. The inauguration day was virtually the last on which security conditions permitted civilians to use the road. A few months later, with Viet Cong roving all about, the people left the settlement—some to refugee camps in the district towns, some to join the Viet Cong. This stage of their lives was without ceremony or fanfare. Gia Bac lies now abandoned, no longer a subject of pride to Vietnamese officials. It may never have been such to its own inhabitants.

Our own failure to understand both general conditions and the Montagnards was reflected in the fate of Minh Rong, another hamlet not far from Gia Bac. There had been a nice school at Minh Rong before, one of a very few constructed for the Montagnards by the French. In recent years, however, it had fallen into disuse because the people were afraid to send their children outside the strategic hamlet fence and into an area, however nearby, where the Viet Cong might attack. Every time we drove through the tea plantations and bounced along the dirt trail past the school, we felt a sense of waste. No Viet Cong had been reported in the area for a long time, yet the school was being used as a shelter for cows. Its roof was falling in, and its cement floor was being torn up by hooves.

Why couldn't a teacher be hired and the school fixed up and used again for the children of Minh Rong? we asked provincial and district authorities.

"Impossible," we were told. "The people there are afraid of the VC."

One day, however, we went with the Montagnard assistant district chief and the provincial school inspector and talked with the leaders of Minh Rong hamlet. Conversation revealed that they weren't so much concerned about the VC as they were about a genie that haunted the school grounds and would be grossly offended if the school were used again. If they were to have a school, the leaders told us, it would have to be a new school in a new place. For if they tried to use the old one, the genie would bring evil fortune upon them. Indeed, they did not sound very interested in having a school. The Vietnamese school inspector, though basically a good and jovial person, seemed equally uninterested. A new school would only mean more paper work for him. An ensconced civil servant who occasionally admitted to a kind of revulsion for the "dirty Montagnards," he had no sense of the need for social revolution in the rural areas. He snickered at the tales of genies, turning his attention instead to a twirly homemade toy with which some of the ragged little Montagnard boys were playing in the dirt. Meanwhile, with the Montagnard district official, we made another try.

"While you're waiting for a possible new school," we asked the hamlet leaders, "could the old one be repaired and used temporarily?"

"Well, probably yes," they replied after some thought.

"For how long?"

"A few months."

"If the genie isn't offended by a few months, why would he be offended by a permanent school there?"

"He just would be. The children from all over would be trampling about and disturbing him. The genie would then bring sickness on the village people."

"But only the children from your village would use the school," we said hopefully, adding that we were already sponsoring another school for the next village. "Surely the genie would not be angry toward your children in Minh Rong?"

"Well," the leaders finally agreed, "perhaps not."

"Do you think it would be all right, then, to have the school reopen?" we asked.

"Yes, all right."

By now, the school inspector was whining about wanting to go back home. He didn't like being so far out of town, it was getting late in the afternoon, and besides, it looked like rain. He had not been with us earlier in Djiramour, a hamlet in the next district, and therefore he did not know the power of the genies. In Djiramour, the villagers had been forced by the local government to move all their houses for the second time, from the slopes of a hillside to the top of the same hill. The reason given was to permit better defense of the hamlet. One would have thought those people very angry at having to move again so soon after the initial settlement. Why had the government not thought to place them on top of the hill in the first place? One day we had asked them how they felt about all this, expecting a torrent of angry words. Instead, to our surprise, the village chief had replied, "The genie wanted us to move up here. He has not made anyone sick since we moved. This is a better spot. We are glad."

In Minh Rong, however, it would remain to be seen whether the genie would, in the end, approve or not. Meanwhile, we did our job. Since no one in Minh Rong knew how to repair with cement and no one knew how to read and write, both workers and a teacher had to be brought in from outside. Ideally, the teacher was chosen from among the hamlet population, since the natural spirit of community cooperation tended to make teacher and pupils more responsive to one another. But this was not possible in Minh Rong. The district office finally designated K'Brop, a young boy from a nearby blanket-weaving hamlet, as the teacher. While K'Brop was being trained for two months, Vietnamese workers were sent in to repair the old school, to convert it from an institute for cows to an institute for basic learning. Ideally again, the Montagnards would learn to mix concrete by themselves and to help build their own school on a self-help basis. We had taught them elsewhere and found them industrious and quick to learn. But Vietnamese contractors could not afford the time and effort required to teach them. "How could they possibly learn anything?" shrieked one particularly arrogant Vietnamese district chief. "They are so ignorant! They are a prehistoric people!" When it was suggested to him that the first step toward overcoming their "ignorance" would be to build them schools, he laughed. "They don't care about such things," he said. "They want to be left alone." In the case of Minh Rong, it was considered more expedient to send Vietnamese workers to repair the school.

The school was repaired and K'Brop began teaching. But perhaps the genie had been annoyed, after all, for the school was never a success. Less than two months after it opened, the lock on the classroom door was broken and a number of books and CARE school kits were stolen. Soon after that, the Viet Cong, who had been absent from the area for some time, began terrorizing the countryside again. As a result, K'Brop did not dare to stay in Minh Rong, and it was not long before many of the hamlet people also left, seeking refuge in the provincial capital. Now the school at Minh Rong is once again unused, standing as a lonely sentinel in the midst of the tea plantations.

There were many reasons for the school's ineffectiveness. One was that the villagers did not really want it in the first place. We had been overeager in our insistence. Only fourteen students enrolled, and as many as half were absent for long periods of time. While theoretically a small class should be more conducive to learning, in Viet Nam the feeling seems to be that a small turnout reflects an unworthwhile activity. Another problem had to do with K'Brop. To begin with, he was not a cheery person and his lack of spirit influenced the classroom atmosphere. Not having advanced very far into primary school himself, he had understood little of the material presented at the short training course. And because the training program itself had been planned in Saigon, much of its content was irrelevant to Montagnard conditions. The point of the overly theoretical lessons, taught in Vietnamese, often escaped the new Montagnard teachers, who had only a rudimentary knowledge of the Vietnamese language. When questions were called for at the end of one fast-spoken lecture on teaching methods, a bewildered student asked, "Could we have more soap? We're all out of it." Until late 1964, Montagnard teachers, on returning to their classrooms, were obliged to conduct their classes entirely in Vietnamese. In practice, of course, they could not do this even if they spoke it well themselves, because their students wouldn't understand them. Still, despite all the difficulties, a beginning had been made, and even though some teachers did not perform as well as they might have under more favorable conditions, concepts of modern education were being introduced in villages that had never had schools before.

While the slipshod K'Brop was being trained as a teacher for Minh Rong, K'Xung, an alert Mnong, was being trained in Dalat. He had made the trip to Dalat, along with five of his colleagues, from the Da Mrong valley. A rutted trail, impassable even by jeep, wound over the mountains from Da Mrong to Dalat for a distance of some forty miles, and it was along this route that K'Xung had walked. The trip took a full two days on foot, and the brave young teachers spent the night in the forest. "Danger of Viet Cong? So what?" K'Xung said upon arrival.

K'Xung's qualifications for teaching were considerably better than those of K'Brop, even though his hanging earlobes, which are no longer common among the younger Montagnards, made him look more traditional. K'Xung had studied at a Catholic missionary school in Dalat, had completed primary school, and could communicate in basic French. He was conscientious and dedicated, as proven by his arduous trek through the forest, and he was extremely kind, as we were to learn later.

K'Xung's home was in Dien Krac, the most remote hamlet in the

Da Mrong area. To the people of Dien Krac the Americans must have seemed a strange, if generous, breed. After the teachers' training course, when K'Xung and his colleagues were loaded down with school supplies too heavy to carry for two days through the forests, a way had to be found to transport them home from Dalat. At the last minute, an understanding U.S. Army major offered a helicopter that had been consigned to him for "psychological warfare" the next afternoon. But there were two conditions to our using it. One was the weather, which turned out to be adequate. The other related to the "psywar" function of the mission, which the young teachers could fulfill by broadcasting propaganda to their fellow villagers while circling overhead before landing. Seeming scarcely surprised, K'Xung and the others agreed to this condition. They were, after all, ardently against the Viet Cong, and besides, retaliation by the guerrillas was unlikely since Da Mrong, for all its isolation, had been relatively free from the tensions of the war. Preparing for take-off from the little airfield in town, we must have made an unusual sight: from the airborne instrument of war dangled a huge bank of loudspeakers; they would have to be loud indeed to be heard over the din of the helicopter itself. Inside the helicopter, instead of weapons, ammunition, or leaflets, went blackboards and globes, schoolbooks, pencils and crayons, balls and visual aids, and myriad other tools for the classroom. The helicopter pilots had never visited Dien Krac before, so we would have to steer them through mountain passes and around cloud banks until the village came into view.

Only fifteen minutes later, instead of the two days it would have taken on foot, we crossed the last mountain barrier, and as the helicopter circled over Dien Krac swarms of villagers poured out from their thatch houses, craning their necks skyward. They were attracted not only by the now familiar whirring of the rotor blades, but by the announcements emitted through the hanging loudspeakers: "Hello! Hello! This is K'Xung, your teacher. I am returning home after a long two months in the city. The government has trained me to become a better teacher for our hamlet school and for our people. Our people will progress through education. All children prepare to study to read and to write. Now school will begin.

Hello! Hello! This is K'Xung. . . ." The villagers watched the heli-copter as it hovered, preparing to land, and then they streamed outside the strategic hamlet gate to engulf K'Xung as he stepped from the craft with packages of all shapes and sizes. His task was just beginning.

To us, as outsiders, there was a sense of drama in all this—drama we had tried to evoke in the course of a short talk at the closing ceremony of the training sessions in Dalat. "This is not," we sug-gested, "a ceremony just to mark the closing of this course. Rather it is to celebrate the beginning of a new phase, a new step forward. For now you will be returning to your distant hamlets to teach your own village children. The most important task is just starting. As for us, your American friends, we have tried to help you somewhat in this training course. We hope in the coming weeks and months to be able to visit you in your classrooms in the hamlets. Meanwhile, we wish you much success, for yours is a great and noble undertak-ing." Understandably, it did not seem so great and noble to K'Xung, about to labor under the daily burdens of a teacher's life. But there he was, and when the helicopter took off and puttered back over the jagged mountain barrier to Dalat, Dien Krac was again isolated from the outside world.

Actually, the question of who was isolated from whom was a very subjective one. From the town, the hamlet was indeed isolated. On the other hand, no one was more provincial—particularly con-cerning the Montagnard villages—than the city dwellers. Because of the gap involved, school inspectors seldom visited such hamlets as Minh Rong and Dien Krac. By tradition, in fact, education was considered a phenomenon limited to the towns. The Vietnamese director of a district boarding school for Montagnards, though a fine and sensitive young man, had never seen a Montagnard hamlet until, at our initiative, he led some of his students on a singing tour of their home villages. This gesture was greatly appreciated by the children's parents, since it gave them an opportunity to see what their children had been doing while away at school. But even more important, the experience proved to be a major revelation to the school director, giving him his first view of his pupils' cultural back-grounds.

It is surely this lack of contact that has led to lack of understanding between the two ethnic groups. The great Independence Day parades held in Saigon on November 1 often feature a "Highlands delegation." Intended to titillate the urban Saigonese, this delegation is primitively and exotically dressed. Its members ride shaggy ponies along the broad boulevard of the parade route. Garbed in such a way even in their own villages, not to mention in the national capital, they would appear extremely out of place. But those Vietnamese who do not know the real Montagnard way of life cannot realize that they are being duped. Instead, they point and laugh.

Because the Montagnards are often thought to be primitive, anything better than what they already have is considered too good. One province chief was asked why the hamlet schools intended for Montagnards were of a different and inferior construction from those meant for Vietnamese. Why didn't the Montagnard schools have glass windows too? Why were the walls built only waist-high, leaving the rest open with only latticework up to the roof? Wouldn't it be very cold for the children in the early mornings? Wasn't aid money provided for equal-quality construction of all schools throughout the province, for Vietnamese and Montagnards alike?

"The Montagnards are more accustomed to the cold," the province chief replied.

We, as American volunteers uninfluenced by the traditional Vietnamese prejudices, felt compelled to treat the Montagnards better. But this too could cause problems, since it tended to emphasize the poor treatment they received at the hands of the Vietnamese. When we procured army-surplus leather briefcases for all the new teachers at the end of their training course, one young Montagnard offered us profuse thanks. "Before you came here the Vietnamese never gave us anything," he said. "They treated us very badly." From our point of view, the solution was not to treat the Montagnards well in order to make up for past injustices, but rather to bridge the gap in understanding between them and the Vietnamese with a view to future reconciliation. It was, after all, their country, and the two groups would have to learn to live in it together. General Vinh Loc, a former Vietnamese commander for the Highlands region, was quite critical, however, of American encouragement to the Montagnards. Along with his subsequent replacement, General Lu Lan, he was the subject of a joke told in Vietnamese military circles: "Under General Loc the Montagnards were allowed to keep their loincloths. With Lu Lan, they will lose even those."

Certainly there has been improvement in the last few years. For one thing, the word "savage" has given way to the word "Montagnard" in everyday usage. When Lieutenant Colonel De was province chief in Dalat, he frequently sang duets with the Montagnard teachers: "Kinh Thuong Mot Nha"—Vietnamese and Montagnards share one home. Colonel De insisted at one point that all his civil servants begin to study the Koho language, and he proceeded to master it himself. He appeared genuinely to like and admire the Montagnards, and they liked him too. Late in 1964, after he failed to declare in time for General Khanh during an attempted *coup d'état* in Saigon, Colonel De was transferred to a coastal province. And although he was elected in 1967 as Dalat's representative to the Lower House in Saigon, he was no longer in a position to give much help to the Montagnard people.

Meanwhile, in a hamlet not too far from Dalat, Colonel De's replacement decided to prove to the Montagnard inhabitants that the government still cared for them. He ordered ten or twelve Vietnamese service chiefs to spend the night there. But the gesture was timed to coincide with an expected visit by Pham Khac Suu, then the Vietnamese chief of state, in order to impress him with the provincial administration's concern for the tribespeople. The Vietnamese were thus highly annoyed when the chief of state failed to appear, and they were left waiting forlornly and feeling quite out of place in the strange hamlet surroundings. They formed a clique of their own, effectively ignoring the Montagnards. Finally, to accommodate themselves overnight they made some of the Montagnards leave their homes, the eviction belying any gestures of friendship.

There were other exceptional Vietnamese, however, besides Colonel De. One group of action-minded students spent a full month in a muddy Montagnard refugee settlement, helping the uprooted tribespeople to build new homes. Some Vietnamese were associated with the foreign missionaries in converting the animist

Montagnards to Christianity. In spite of the missionaries' sometimes self-righteous competition with one another for the allegiance of various villages, their contributions to the physical well-being of the people were often considerable. Although some Montagnards were unimpressed by all "Yuan," as they called the Vietnamese, and thought of them as being lazy, weak, and arrogant, many could indeed distinguish between the good and the bad Vietnamese.

Miss Tu, the provincial school inspectress in Dalat, was widely considered to be a good Vietnamese. She had a friendly smile for everyone and, in spite of being a woman, was one of the few civil servants who seemed to enjoy visiting the people in their hamlets. Her colleagues in the education office, all good people in themselves, seemed to permit her this strange predisposition in favor of the Montagnards, though never fully understanding it or sharing it. They would pay lip service to the desirability of helping all the rural people, but when it came to bouncing around on wilderness trips to see them, they were either too busy, too fearful of their lives, or didn't feel very well that day. Miss Tu, putting the men in her office to shame, was always willing to set out at the crack of dawn and often stayed out until dusk. She never complained. She was particularly friendly to the Montagnards, and it was a rude awakening for them when, like Colonel De and so many effective civil servants, she was abruptly transferred in 1967 to a job in Dalat City, leaving the problems of the countryside to two old men who rarely left their desks and never visited hamlet schools. "The situation is very bad now," Miss Tu wrote to us recently. "The teachers become lazy, because nobody comes to see them. I met K'Xung and some other teachers, our mutual friends, who came to see me when they went to the education office to get their salaries. Now, nobody comes to give them money like we did before, so they must go by foot to get it themselves every three or four months."

She knew K'Xung well. She had helped him, and he would help her. On one visit we took CARE school kits, soap, student chalkboards, wall decorations, maps, a ball, and hair clippers to his village of Dien Krac. The helicopter, as usual, dropped us off outside the village entrance. (The first time, it had landed inside the village, but the rotor blades threatened to blow the thatch roofs off the houses.

Thereafter, we always discouraged the pilots from landing too close.) A throng of children came to greet us and helped carry the supplies to the schoolhouse. The helicopter then flew off for other supply missions, the pilots promising to return for us at two-thirty that afternoon. While making visits by helicopter certainly afforded great ease of transportation, there was always an element of uncertainty. Sometimes we barely had time to complete our business before it returned, and always we had to keep an ear cocked for the sound of the rotors so as to be at the landing spot exactly when it descended. Although army officers occasionally used it to make weekend pleasure trips, we were advised to respect the time of the helicopter, since it allegedly cost at least $200 an hour to run the flying wonder.

This time we would not have to rush our visit. We watched while K'Xung locked the things we had brought in the school cabinet for safekeeping. The soap was especially precious because all we could obtain was expensive shampoo, donated by an American firm. Cheap bar soap would have been better, but it had not been budgeted locally and so we had no means for buying it. The Montagnards stood in awe, however, of our affluent and foamy green suds. Then we helped K'Xung hang some of the decorations on the wall, along with maps of Viet Nam which we had procured free of charge through a kindly officer at the National Geographic Service. Miss Tu used the maps to assist K'Xung in giving the pupils a spontaneous geography lesson. Names they may or may not have heard before, like Saigon or Dalat or Ban Me Thuot, were related to points on the map on the wall. K'Xung's globe, made at the training course but in most classrooms destined through lack of use to remain a mere ornament, helped to explain the origin of the different-looking Americans. The fifty pupils, dressed virtually in rags, did not appear visibly impressed.

Not wishing to cause an added burden, we had brought along our own sandwiches for lunch. K'Xung offered us rice wine to wash them down with, though Miss Tu declined, Vietnamese women normally confining themselves to tea and soft drinks. K'Xung, however, spoke highly of the rice-wine custom as we sipped the cheering liquid through a tube enmired in the depths of the tall heirloom

jar. "Oh, we drink it often," he said, "especially when we have
guests." Indeed, it is a sociable pastime, within the family as well as
during festivals and funerals. The oldest woman in the household
usually takes her place before the jar and sips first, the society being
matrilineal. She then cedes to the guest and finally to the other
members of the family in turn. One man is designated to keep up
the water level in the jar. With a metal cup, he takes fresh water
brought directly from the river or well and adds it to the rice mash
which has been fermenting in the bottom of the jar for up to one
month. This pastime is frowned on by the Protestant missionaries,
but it is not interfered with by the Catholics. As K'Xung put it with
a grin, "It's quite all right for us Catholics to drink rice wine. It is
only the *Protestants* who protest!"

At two-thirty, the helicopter was not yet in sight. We waited.
K'Xung, meanwhile, gave the children the ball to play with, and
they found this much more exciting than the geography lesson. As
they kicked it about the open area in the center of the hamlet, we
scanned the skies. But when the monsoon clouds floated over the
mountains, followed by the daily torrential rains, we began to believe that we would end up spending the night, for helicopters did
not fly in bad weather. By the time the rain had finished clattering
onto the metal roof of the school and pouring into a barrel set up at
one end, the afternoon was drawing to a close. We concluded for
sure that we would be spending the night. While Miss Tu sat alone
on the veranda and got used to the idea (before that day, even she
had never been inside a Montagnard longhouse), a soldier across the
way played the *kamboat*, a six-piped mouth organ. Though most
foreigners (including the ethnic Vietnamese) found the music monotonous and simple, the instrument turned out to be a difficult one
to play.

Although Dien Krac itself was little affected by the war, it was
highly unusual for an American, or a Vietnamese from the city, to
dare spend a night in the village. Furthermore, Miss Tu was concerned that her family would worry about her safety, which they
certainly did. Never having been there themselves, of course, they
naturally conjured up the most grotesque images of a frontier post
peopled by savages. At five-thirty we asked if the military two-way

radio could be used to call Dalat in an effort to determine whether we'd been forgotten. Every hamlet has a two-way radio for use in case of Viet Cong attack, yet we were told that the only times it could be heard at the other end was at 6:00 P.M. and at 6:00 A.M., the monitoring times at Da Mrong post. Half an hour later, the soldiers tried to radio in, but since all the other hamlets were calling at the same time, Dien Krac had to await its turn. By the time the operator finally got through, the Da Mrong monitor had been turned off, not to be heard again until six the next morning! One could not help wondering about the system's efficacy in case of attack, though possibly the sound of gunshots would have carried the three miles along the valley floor even without the radio.

With embarrassed apologies for the primitiveness of the dinner available, K'Xung offered us a more than adequate amount of red rice, along with some river fish and tea. Then, as darkness fell on the hamlet, he and the village chief found blankets, suggesting some of them for use underneath us in order to make the woven bamboo sleeping platform softer. K'Xung's whole extended family slept raised above the dirt floor on the same long bamboo platform in the single long room of the Mnong-style longhouse. The only other furniture, aside from a crude table and some chairs, was a smaller platform which hung from the center roof pole and served as a granary. The valuable heirloom vases that were used for the rice wine were lined up along one wall.

In addition to blankets, K'Xung produced two mosquito nets, perhaps the only two in the hamlet. But they were scarcely needed, we discovered, because the indoor cooking fires were allowed to smolder throughout the night; the suffocating smoke they produced tended to discourage all insects. Finally, the soothing sounds of the village lulled us to sleep, as occasional low murmurs and muffled coughings from the other huts mixed with the loud calls of the denizens of the forest around us.

The next morning, the radio operator reported having made contact with Da Mrong at six, but added that Da Mrong had claimed it did not know how to contact Dalat. Its line reached only to Lac Duong, the district headquarters. After a cursory washing, and over more rice and fish offered by K'Xung, we decided the only way to clarify our situation was to walk to Da Mrong. For this it was fortunate that Miss Tu, before undertaking the helicopter trip the previous day, had changed her high-heeled shoes and *ao dai** for sneakers and slacks. K'Xung, leaving his not-too-saddened class to the pleasures of the new ball, accompanied us. By then the sky was blue and the sun bright, and the valley was a luscious sight with its towering green peaks on either side. We could hear children shouting from afar in the golden rice fields. These were children who could not go to school, for it was their job to scare away the birds that threatened to eat the precious ripening grains.

In Da Mrong, word had just been received that the helicopter would come. It was being repaired from a breakdown the day before. Although hot and perspiring from the relentless sun, we decided in the meantime to walk on to see Ha Jah, a teacher at the nearby hamlet of Yengle who seemed to appreciate our periodic encouragement. Being an easygoing fellow, Ha Jah had difficulty keeping discipline in his class of eighty-five pupils. Every setback— even so minor a one as the soccer ball's wearing out—was discouraging to him. This time, as it happened, Ha Jah's pupils were off burying a small classmate who had died from sickness the day before. Still Ha Jah persevered at his job. Finally, when the sun was already high, the unmistakable sound of rotor blades could be heard, and the helicopter descended first at Dien Krac, to learn we'd gone to Da Mrong, then at Da Mrong, to hear we'd proceeded to Yengle. Responding to our waving of handkerchiefs in front of Yengle's stockade fence, the helicopter touched down. We bade farewell to both Ha Jah and K'Xung and climbed aboard.

Inside the chopper were four Americans, annoyed that we had not stayed to await them at Dien Krac but had caused them to take several expensive minutes to trace us to Yengle. "What's the big idea?" one of them asked. "We got up early this morning. We have to get back to our base. This picking you up was only a favor. We just about decided to leave you right where you were." Miss Tu smiled wanly.

It was always encouraging to visit Dien Krac and the other schools in the Da Mrong valley, for in spite of their remoteness and

* The *ao dai* is the traditional Vietnamese women's dress.

the difficulties of transportation, they were among the best-run schools and they attracted the largest numbers of children to class. It seemed that aside from the differing attitudes toward education on the part of various parents within a given community, different communities also displayed varying collective appreciations for a school in their midst. The Da Mrong villages were highly appreciative, thus the crowded classrooms and conscientious teachers. The attitude in Minh Rong, by contrast, was not favorable and enrollment was low.

In working with Montagnard villagers, as well as with Vietnamese, it was important to be able to recognize the moods and attitudes of the community and of the leaders within the community. It was easy to make mistakes. On an initial investigating visit to one isolated hamlet with the Montagnard deputy province chief, we received the impression that a school was not desired by the people there. The inhabitants we met showed no interest. We consequently proposed that a planned classroom should be placed elsewhere. Several months later, the people of that hamlet opened their own school in a new wooden building with crude, though adequate, furniture. They had selected their own teacher from among the local population, and he had begun lessons for more than thirty children. Such efforts at self-help were all the more impressive for their rarity. More often, luring Montagnard children to school was very difficult, as it had been at Minh Rong. This was hardly surprising, for having only recently moved out of the forests into the fortified settlements, parents frequently did not know the meaning of education and had no clear idea of what a school really was. It was difficult to persuade them that a better life lay in store for them if they would send their children to school, rather than keeping them at home to help in the household and to guard the buffalo or chase away the birds that threatened the rice. Often a family would designate one child, the smartest of the brood, to attend school by way of token representation. In some schools, only boys attended. "Oh, is school for girls too?" asked one teacher.

The romanticists among us questioned the need for urging these contented children of nature to attend school and thus to succumb to modern life and its inherent woes. The overriding reason given was that education was critical to the war effort. Schools, according to this line, represented the winning of hearts and minds, and the conquest of ignorance implied that educated people would never choose communism. Of course, the counterinsurgency motivation was not the only one, though it was the one that gave impetus to school construction and teacher training programs. It was also seen that general economic development, which was after all the need of the times, could only be based on a literate population and the ability to link cause with effect—fertilizer with larger crops, sanitation with better health, and ability to read and reason with participatory democracy. Of special significance to the Montagnards was the need to catch up with their Vietnamese compatriots, so that they would not be cheated in the market place or discriminated against because of inferior opportunity to advance. Among Montagnard nationalists, this last reason had a special appeal and helps to explain why their leaders were often very willing to cooperate in modernization programs for their people.

Much has been done for the Montagnards. In a sense, it was the pressures of the war that both led to their problems and opened up solutions to them. It was the pressures of the war that brought them into frequent contact with the Vietnamese who looked down upon them. But this same contact over the years has begun to bring them together in a limited bond of understanding. Six years ago Vietnamese would have denied any similarity between the way they looked upon the Montagnards and the plight of the black people in America. Now, at least, the problems of the Montagnards are recognized. Increasing numbers have been absorbed into the government, and a few have even learned the techniques of bureaucratic corruption. In some areas Montagnard high-school enrollments tripled between 1965 and 1967, thanks in part to American scholarships. Montagnard pupils are given handicaps on the competitive government examinations for diplomas. A majority of children have for the first time been able to attend primary schools either in or near their villages, although many of these have been ravaged by war soon after opening. Each Highland province now has an agricultural training center where new seeds and animals are furnished and new methods of farming and home economics are taught. In national government, a previously insignificant Commissariat for Montagnard Affairs has been elevated to the ministry level, and a proportionate number of Montagnard representatives serve in the Saigon Legislature, their place assured by the Constitution. More Montagnard military units have been placed under the command of Montagnard officers.

Yet many continue to dream hopefully of a separate Montagnard nation. These nationalists feel uncomfortable in any association with the Vietnamese government, and a handful (predominantly from the educated elite) continue to hold out in the mountainous border regions against any form of Vietnamese hegemony. They look skeptically upon government attempts to mollify them. When in 1967 a Montagnard lieutenant colonel was appointed province chief in Pleiku, a move intended to please the Montagnards, they reacted by taking offense at the government's choice of a man lacking in administrative experience: "This is ridiculous! This man is ignorant; he does not know how to read or write! To call him chief of province is to demonstrate to what an extent the Vietnamese make fun of us. The government appoints this so-called lieutenant colonel just to better oppress us and to laugh in the nose of all the Montagnards." That same year, one of the most educated and reasonable Montagnards reacted to the news of a mysterious poisoning of his people: "This recent news concerning the relations between Vietnamese and Montagnards disturbs me. I have just heard the very bad and shocking news that 140 Montagnards have died, poisoned by alcohol and dried fish—30 in Djiring and 110 in Ban Me Thuot. I believe that we are going to disappear little by little. I am afraid of that. I don't know why they did it. I'm afraid this will create another tension between the two races. I know very well that to live in peace it is better to be friends than enemies; but this time events have exceeded their proper bounds. You see, the weak are always in the wrong. Thus, it seems, might makes right." The causes of the poisoning were never proved, but the Montagnards did not care; they blamed the Vietnamese.

The problems of reconciling embittered ethnic groups have never been easy. In North Viet Nam, it is believed, separation was relatively complete, since the Montagnards there were granted nearly autonomous status on their own lands. Those Vietnamese adminis-

trators who did work there were apparently required to learn the
Highland tongues and to treat the tribespeople as equals, or even as
"comrades." Montagnards in the North were appointed to high positions, especially in the military. To be sure, some of the North
Vietnamese tribal societies are considered more advanced and sophisticated than those of the South, thus facilitating equality and
cooperation. On the other hand, rumors during the period of
American bombings and the outpouring of Vietnamese into Montagnard areas have suggested that relations in the North may have
become more tense anyway.

For the Montagnards of the South, life will never again be the
same. The old generation that longed to return to the life of slash-
and-burn is dying. Among the young generation, some have been
integrated into the Vietnamese world and others will be. But the
majority, represented by men like Y Bli, are caught in the middle,
unable to return to the old ways, yet frightened before the specter
of the new. Their eyes have been opened to promise for the future,
but their darker skins, their imperfect accent in speaking Vietnamese, and the weight of discrimination have left them with feelings
of inferiority. Finding for themselves satisfying roles in the larger
society will take time and understanding. Like all peoples struggling
for identity, they are tormented and confused.

Americans have greatly influenced the slow emancipation of the
Montagnards. Without them, it might not have come about. But it
was never really fair for Americans, of all people, to criticize Vietnamese for their bigotry toward the tribespeople. The racial problems of the United States have not escaped notice in Viet Nam, and
one sensitive Montagnard turned down the offer of a study trip to
America. "I am afraid I would not be regarded well by the American people," he said. What Americans in Viet Nam could and did
do, however, was to set an example of concern for these people so
that some of the racist, or just plain nonthinking, Vietnamese would
see the Montagnards as fellow citizens. Miss Tu is pleased with the
progress she has seen in her country: "It was right when you compared the situation of American Negroes with the situation of the
Montagnards. But now, I remark that the situation of the Montag-

nards is better. They occupy some important places in society. Most of them are very emancipated. But there is still one problem," she adds. "They keep their inferiority complexes." For the Montagnards, the struggle will continue long after the war.

[5]

HUMAN FRAILTIES

Red Tape, Corruption, and Lethargy

Some five miles up the coast from the seaside resort of Nha Trang is the village of Cat Loi. In 1964, Cat Loi was to receive a school from the government. The villagers were enthusiastic about the prospect of a new school, and it was the first time the government had ever sponsored one for them. When Gene, the IVS volunteer working in the province, visited there, the people proudly showed him a freshly painted hamlet office which they had just built for themselves. Then they told him of their plans for helping to construct the school. They were prepared to do this on a self-help basis and had further proved their enthusiasm by selecting one of the hamlet's budding young intellectuals to attend a provincial teacher training course.

The villagers' high hopes for the school were not matched by government action, however. There were repeated delays until its construction was finally begun. In spite of the people's desires, and contrary to their expectations, it turned out not to be a self-help project at all. The government had hired a contractor to build all the schools in the district and had given him a certain amount of roofing, cement, and money to complete the job.

On one visit after work had finally started, Gene found the villagers deeply disturbed. The contractor's workers were laying out the foundation and making cement blocks for the building, but the villagers complained that they were using too little cement in the mixture. They feared that the structure would not be strong. A week later the walls were up and already crumbling. "The contractor uses only part of the cement which you Americans have given for the school," the people complained. "He sells the rest. He gives the money to the government officials who gave him the contract. Because they are crooked our hamlet will have a poor school."

Gene dutifully reported this reaction to the education officials in the provincial city of Nha Trang, but they replied that they couldn't do anything about it because the contractor was a friend of the province chief and the district chief. The American AID representative said that he had already taken the matter up with the province chief and could not bother him with it again for a while. Gene then went to talk with the contractor and was immediately invited to dinner at one of Nha Trang's finest restaurants to discuss the issue. At the dinner, the contractor promised to do a better job and gave assurances that the bad work was due simply to an oversight on the part of his foreman. After the contractor paid the restaurant bill, they agreed to meet at the district chief's house the next week to discuss the situation further. Meanwhile work had stopped on the school, and rain began to wear away at the thin cement walls. The villagers continued to complain and said that since the Americans were paying for the school they should have the power to do something about it.

The visit with the contractor at the district chief's house was short and theatrical. It consisted of a pointed reprimand given by the district chief to the contractor in order to demonstrate the good intentions of the district chief and to protect everyone's ego. After the scolding, the contractor left the room and the district chief followed him out to have a few private words with him. Then the district chief returned and said that "everything has been taken care of."

In Cat Loi, work resumed a month later. Many of the walls had to be rebuilt because children playing in the area had pushed them over. The villagers said again and again what a bad job the government always did. When the school was finally finished, Gene asked the villagers whether he could walk on the floor. "Be careful," they warned. "The cement is only half an inch thick." Feeling they might be exaggerating, Gene stomped on the floor. The cement crumbled under his weight. When he bumped against the wall, cement fell from it to the floor. The villagers asked how such a building could ever stand up to daily use by the pupils. They pointed again to the much sturdier hamlet office that they had built themselves. Before school opened, the villagers had to raise money on their own and repair the walls and floor in the new school so that classes could be held at all.

When Vietnamese list their criticisms of the Saigon government, corruption is universally mentioned as the leading factor undermining confidence in the regime. Government officials and contractors frequently work together in construction jobs where they skimp on materials and the quality of their work and then divide the amount saved off the American grant. Yet there are other methods of corruption too. Destitute refugees often complain of having to pay about $5.00 for identification papers, without which they would be arrested as Viet Cong. The sister of a close Vietnamese friend was told by a Vietnamese employee in the U.S. Embassy personnel office that she would have to pay $50.00 for the processing of her papers so that she could get a job more quickly. Another girl told of her sister's recent departure for Thailand with an American soldier; in itemizing the amount she had to pay for her exit visa, the bribe given to the bureaucrats involved was but a matter-of-fact part of the whole cost.

On very rare occasions, and mostly as symbolic gestures to placate critics—especially the Americans—corrupt administrators are removed from their posts. In late 1967, for example, there was a thorough shake-up in Binh Dinh province. The U.S. Embassy was ecstatic—until one of the very worst offenders, the refugee-service chief, turned up in an equally high position in another province farther north. Administrators with enough influence to get good jobs in the first place and then to last in these remunerative positions also seem to have enough influence to save their necks even if they are finally caught. Some flagrant cases may be brought to court, but our Vietnamese associates have been quick to point out that these usually involve only relatively minor officials. To take on the worst offenders, they add, would be politically impossible, since it would affect the highest ruling echelons—if not the ruling men, then at least their wives, who sometimes act as a "cover."

One district-chief friend suggested that a certain level of corruption can exist even while the government is responsive to the people at large. "Of course I steal from the government," he said without apology, "but I try to do my job well, to work hard when I work, and then to play hard when I have finished the work. As for my corruption, I try to do it intelligently, and I tell all my subordinates to do the same. I tell them they can take a little here and there, but not too much. That's as good as anyone can expect." He was, in fact, a very competent and efficient district chief.

In 1968, and in spite of visible government efforts to root out corruption, Prime Minister Tran Van Huong admitted that it could never be entirely eliminated. For some, it seems necessary for survival under difficult wartime circumstances. With such a large percentage of the country's male population in the armed forces or the civilian government, relatives at various levels have found ways in which they can help and enrich each other, even though these ways may not be considered ethical in the West. Corruption in the best interests of supporting one's own family, in fact, is not only excusable, but even morally right in the family-oriented Vietnamese society. We found an example of this attitude in a letter from General Nguyen Huu Co, one of the biggest profiteers in all South Viet Nam. Having held the various positions of corps commander, minister of defense, and deputy prime minister, he is known to have fired at least one province chief because the latter refused to give Co's wife a large piece of property in his province. Finally Co himself was ousted from the country and sought exile in Hong Kong. Writing from there to a former colleague in 1967, he explained his position:

My family of 12 children is now fine. My oldest child, nineteen years old, passed the first exam and is still studying at Lycée Yersin, Dalat. The other children are also in school and I don't have to worry much about my family. Luckily, while General Khanh [the former prime minister] hated me, I took my cue and constructed a house in Nha Trang on government land which the Americans rent for three million [piasters] per year. After annual taxes and maintenance, I still have half that for myself, enough to raise my 12 children. If it weren't for that,

I don't know what 1 would do for a living. In our career as generals, and once we are turned to pasture, it is very difficult to change profession.

The removal of corrupt officials does not necessarily bring about an amelioration of the original conditions. The refugee-service chief who was ousted from Binh Dinh province, for example, was replaced by a competent man, but American AID officers pointed out that the honest replacement was so afraid of making a mistake himself that he hardly dared act at all. Provincial programs were thus stymied because no one would take responsibility, fearing a new accusation of corruption if something were done wrong. Another exceedingly honest civil servant felt responsible for three pit-privies that pupils had dug and constructed at their boarding school. Since government funds and materials had been used, the education administrator refused permission for the privies' use until the province chief himself approved it. Broaching the matter to the province chief proved delicate and embarrassing, and the lesser official refused to act on his own. Finally, the pupils' urgent need of the facilities pressed us to resolve the issue by interceding with the province chief ourselves.

Another education official was relegated to the out-of-the-way Highlands province of Lam Dong after being accused of corruption in his previous job on the coast. In this case, however, the administrator showed more than reluctance to commit himself because of fears of new corruption charges. He also manifested a supreme disdain and indifference toward the job itself and the everyday problems he should have been solving. His attitude resulted in a particularly mediocre training course for hamlet teachers, and very nearly resulted in out-of-town participants' having no place to sleep or eat because he did not feel like making the necessary arrangements. Worst of all, the province chief, equally disturbed over the man's hostility toward his job, could not oust him because of the latter's "highly placed friends in the Saigon ministry."

If Vietnamese are disgusted with the corruption and nepotism exhibited by many of their government officials, they are often quick to add that Americans too are guilty. Saigon's *Cong Chung* newspaper charged in March, 1968, that "American aid is entirely responsible for the current corruption in Viet Nam," adding that this was one of the reasons why "Americans have earned more enmity than sympathy from the Vietnamese people." Others, like the Saigon *Daily News* columnist Van Minh, were less harsh on the American role, placing the onus instead on "the irresistible impact of the American way of life" on Vietnamese society and noting that it is difficult for Vietnamese to resist the many opportunities for corruption caused by the Americans' tempting display of riches:

Vietnamese civil servants, who have been the hardest hit by the current inflation, are not expected to watch this mad scramble for the U.S. dollar with equanimity and detachment. Being human, they are most likely to resort to corruption or moonlighting, not only to cope with their financial difficulties, but also, and sometimes mostly, to be financially in the swim with other people. For one's inability to make as much money as one's equals, according to psychologists, is a forceful cause for an inferiority complex.

Americans participate even more directly in illegal practices. The most common is exchanging money on the black market, for which some Vietnamese criticize not only U.S. government personnel and private contractors, but also the very journalists who publicly accuse the Vietnamese of corruption. There are more enterprising Americans, too, and Van Minh described their roles as follows:

Saigon and other cities have been flooded with stolen PX goods. It is logically assumed that the goods have been stolen by Vietnamese. But I wonder if any Vietnamese, however cunning and resourceful they may be, could afford to steal so many goods as to regularly feed the innumerable open black markets without the connivance of Americans themselves. How could Vietnamese alone, say, steal tons upon tons of steel bars from the American military installations along the Bien Hoa highway which are guarded only by Americans? How could Vietnamese alone get huge cases across so many checkpoints manned by none other than Americans? It is a well-known fact that some American guards at U.S. warehouses often come to a curious deal with Vietnamese crooks. In exchange for a certain amount of money or for some cute girls, those guards agree to let the crooks have absolute freedom to steal anything. . . .

"Of course, I never expect the Americans to be morally better than the Vietnamese or any other people," Van Minh concluded. "We, Americans and Vietnamese alike, are human beings and share the same capital of human frailties."

Government responsiveness on the local level is seriously affected not only by corruption, but also by more directly political considerations. Competent administrators, it seems, are continually transferred because their competence is seen as a threat to those around them or because they have supported the wrong side in this or that *coup d'état* or because they lack the right friend at the right place in the hierarchy. One very kind and sophisticated gentleman who had been chief of primary education in Ban Me Thuot in 1963 was transferred to Hue in 1965. According to his version of the story, he had been in his new post only three or four days when antigovernment riots broke out in the city. The education chief went out to some of the schools and tried to keep them functioning in spite of the disturbances. His move was interpreted, however, as a "counterrevolutionary gesture," and the wrath of the demonstrators then turned upon him. "Kill him, kill him," they apparently shouted. In the end, they only beat him, after which he managed to escape south to Phan Thiet. When things quieted down again in Hue, he asked to return there. The request was granted, but since he was still considered a controversial figure, he was placed in an office without any job. The last time we saw him (he has since been transferred again), he was spending the day sitting at a vacant desk with nothing to do except talk to the new, but only temporary, education chief, who was himself fervently hoping to be sent elsewhere. There were too many political problems for them to work effectively in Hue, they both said. Meanwhile, the only progress made in education was the stamping and signing of the most routine paperwork.

The bureaucracy, through little fault of its own, is ill-suited and untrained for the task of carrying out the various new development programs, which are intended primarily to show the government's responsiveness vis-à-vis the NLF. The task, of course, is a supremely demanding one—in these difficult and competitive times it would require no less than a revolutionary approach to problems, particularly in the rural areas. It would mean that government cadres, like their counterparts in the NLF, would have to become much closer to the people. Like NLF cadres, they would have to assist old widows in harvesting their crops or in carrying water, to give poor peasants needed rice, and generally to show an interest in the people's problems. But very few government bureaucrats can do these things. They were trained in the French civil service techniques of shuffling sheaves of papers, and they are very uncomfortable among and condescending toward the rural people. As family-oriented individuals, these officials cannot readily comprehend the idea of philanthropy on a larger social scale. As security has become a more sensitive issue, of course, the problem has grown even more serious, for government civil servants with family responsibilities feel that they cannot afford the risks the job demands. Since their isolation in the provincial or district towns keeps most of them from having any up-to-date idea of security conditions in the countryside, however, fear of the Viet Cong often serves more as a pretext than as a legitimate constraint.

One of our primary roles as volunteers, as it turned out, was to act as catalysts in urging Vietnamese administrators to do their jobs. Agricultural extension agents would whine that they didn't have enough gasoline to take their jeeps far out of town, though they often seemed to have enough for the service chief to drive around town on his personal errands. School inspectors would ask in all honesty, "What's the sense in going out there? There's nothing to do." But the fact was that their visits, if sincere and constructive, could do much to buoy the morale of rural workers who felt, usually with justification, that no one outside cared about them or whether they worked or not. The statistics that urban administrators spent hours and reams of paper compiling were absolutely meaningless because no one had ever been to the area concerned to see for himself what was really going on.

The management of the self-help program was an example of this lack of communication between rural and urban areas. According to the program's theory, the people of each hamlet would decide what their community needed most. They would then submit a request through their village headquarters and then through district and on up to province levels for any necessary construction materials, food commodities, or a certain minimum of cash, at first limited to about $200 per project. At the same time, the people were responsible for providing the labor themselves, thus the principle of self-help. On paper, this was an excellent program: it offered government assistance without making the people overly dependent on such aid, and it urged democratic community action on the part of the hamlet people in determining their own local priorities.

In practice, however, villagers found it difficult to distinguish between the various government offices and to know which one to approach. They got discouraged when they were sent from one narrowly defined service to another. Furthermore, the transmission of documentation through all the layers of bureaucracy could delay implementation by a full year or longer, so that we often found ourselves being begged by the villagers to give the assistance directly. But we could not in good faith do this, because another aspect of the program was to develop the government's responsiveness by having it handle everything. In the end, not only did projects often fail to materialize, but the government machinery showed even more evidence of its inability to respond. Equally bad, in some districts local administrators decided for themselves what the hamlet people wanted. It was certainly easier for them than going out to the hamlet to explain the program and then wait while the hamlet people made up their minds. In one such district, we suspected something was amiss when every village in the entire district requested the purchase of water buffalo. When we went out ourselves and talked with the people, it turned out they knew nothing of any such request or of any such program, and most of them asked for something like a well or a school instead. The district officials, when confronted with this discovery, merely noted that "buffaloes would have been better for them."

In more recent years, as American aid flooded in, harried Vietnamese administrators were often at a loss where to put it all. Fertilizers and improved pig and chicken breeds usually were lavished on nearby villages where transportation was easiest. Schools were assigned to hamlets at random, usually in response to the district chief's suggestion, even though investigation of these selections in one province revealed that 75 per cent of the locations either had a school already or else showed scant interest in having one. Meanwhile, other localities in the same province were crying out for such assistance, having gone so far as to recruit their own teachers and to open schools in the most humble available shacks.

In another province, the hamlets had been blanketed with so-called information halls. These were listed as self-help projects in many cases, though in reality they fulfilled the function of the government's generally irrelevant information service. Their doors were always locked, since the building was for information-service use only, and their cadres almost never appeared in the distant hamlets. Meanwhile, the education service had plans to construct elaborate new schools in the same localities—until we suggested using the information buildings as schools and thus saving money. The problem here was not only that the government services had little contact with the villages, but that these services had little contact with each other. It became part of our job to coordinate the projects of the information and education service chiefs in this case. Finally, the information halls, with the addition of furniture, were opened and "doubled" as schools.

For us, particularly in the early years, the hazards and roadblocks of government corruption and bureaucracy were far more aggravating than Viet Cong terrorism. For the rural Vietnamese we were trying to help, on the other hand, there was nothing new in government unresponsiveness. Naturally, they complained about it—often bitterly—but when promises were made to rural people they knew from experience not to take them very seriously. Even in years of relative peace, such as 1958, government workers at the agricultural experiment station in Ban Me Thuot were going for months without their salaries—even though they were entitled to only fifty cents a day. In 1963 and 1964, rural health-workers and schoolteachers went without salaries for up to a full year. It was surprising that any of them bothered to keep working, though some of course did not. For us it was sometimes both easier and more humanitarian to lend small amounts of our own money to particularly hard-hit worker friends in our provinces. When we sometimes made a point of keeping a promise, the people were surprised; it had never happened before.

Bitterly frustrated, those of us working in the provinces would search for scapegoats, and it was usually the bureaucrats in the Saigon ministries whom we blamed. Certainly we knew that all bureaucracies are cumbersome, slow, and full of red tape, and that of the American Mission in Saigon was no exception. Yet the one the French bequeathed to the Vietnamese was especially slow. When corruption and the reluctance of petty administrators to make decisions were added to this, it was perhaps no wonder that nothing happened. We were even more frustrated, in fact, when we occasionally met some of our scapegoats in Saigon and found that they were nice people. Politely and patiently, they would look up from their piles of papers and dossiers to assist us. Yet it seldom did any good to appeal to them. Either they knew nothing of the problem, or else they indicated that the province or district had not sent in the necessary papers. Sometimes they suggested that the crucial file must have been delayed somewhere else along the line, perhaps in one of the piles on one of the desks of one of the other friendly and patient bureaucrats. Their job was not a particularly pleasant one, though many of them had given large bribes for the privilege of working in Saigon. When told that rural workers had not been paid for months, their response was invariably, "I'm sorry, but we don't have the necessary papers here." It often seemed as though every slight transaction required ten carbon copies, each of which had to be stamped at least once and often twice or three times, and then laboriously signed and countersigned in some unreadable signatures.

If the bureaucrats did not seem as concerned about the problems in the field as we thought they should have been, they always said it was not their fault. After all, they too had problems, many of which, in the final analysis, concerned the larger political context. And so it was that we were led into a vicious circle where nobody was at fault more than anyone else. The whole nasty situation, it seemed, was to blame. And that was the problem of Viet Nam.

[6]

DEFENDING THE INTERESTS OF THE BELIEVERS

Catholics, Buddhists, and the Struggle Movement

"Ap buc, ap buc," we repeated, thumbing through the dictionary to see what the monk's words meant in English. It was August, 1963, and he had been using the word with increasing frequency during the Vietnamese-English language lessons we had been exchanging. "Ah, here it is—'oppression.'" The monk looked at us benignly. "Yes," he said softly, "oppression." We smiled in the satisfaction of having learned a new word.

It seemed an appropriate word, for upon entering the pagoda grounds that afternoon we had been startled to note that there were soldiers everywhere. At first we had been afraid to enter, thinking we would be stopped by the guards. But though they looked at us with some suspicion, we rode in freely on our bicycles. The monk, after all, expected us, as he did every afternoon, and we did not want to let him down. We had first come to know him upon hearing of his desire to learn English. Then, as principal of the Buddhist high school next to the pagoda, he had also asked us on occasion to teach pronunciation to his students. In return, he helped us with our Vietnamese. He was only twenty-four years old, but he seemed older and wiser.

Greeting us at the door to his quiet cell, he invited us in. Some of the other monks with shaved heads and dressed in the same gray robes brought tea and oranges. Our special friend surprised us then by taking out a bottle marked Gilbey's Gin and pouring some of the contents into his tea. When we gently teased him, he explained that the bottle contained nothing more than purified water; his tea was a bit too strong. Then we began our lessons. Although we usually drilled each other from textbooks or recited into the school's tape recorder, that day we decided to hold conversation practice.

"There are so many soldiers surrounding the pagoda," we noted.

"Yes," he said. "Today all the pagodas in Viet Nam have been surrounded by the military. It is a very bad situation."

"Are you at liberty to leave the grounds?" we asked.

"I dare not," he replied.

"How long do you think the martial law will continue?" we asked, after a pause to look up the Vietnamese term for "martial law."

"I do not know," the monk said. He wanted to say more, but his English, and at that point our Vietnamese, was too limited. So he shook his head and said only, "I am very sorry. I am very sorry."

That evening, when we left our house to go to the photo shop across the street, there were still a few people walking about. Outside our window three people squatted around a small fire on the sidewalk, saying prayers and lighting incense. We thought that perhaps the martial law, particularly in this small provincial town, would not be taken so seriously after all. But by nine o'clock everything was deadly silent except for an occasional military truck passing by. It was a stark contrast to most nights, when the streets were active until late, particularly with hawkers of *pho*, a popular and delicious noodle soup, and of half-hatched duck eggs, a great delicacy for those who don't mind the taste of tiny feathers and partially formed beaks that go with it. Each hawker had a different call, and some tapped rhythmically with a wooden stick on a sonorous piece of bamboo in order to attract attention. But not that night.

Many people listened to their radios, particularly to the respected BBC broadcasts from London, which were generally considered the most objective. In Saigon, the radio said, troops had invaded the main Xa Loi Pagoda, which only days before was seething with activity. Government authorities were claiming that arms had been hoarded in the pagodas and that many "pro-Communist, rebel Buddhists" had to be imprisoned or killed in order to preserve the national unity.

We continued to visit our friend every afternoon at four. Two days later, in another "conversation class," the school principal's weekly radio program served as the point of departure. The latest script, and our lesson, was entitled "Liberty and the Buddhist Religion." After laboriously looking up the words we did not know, we emerged with a fervent plea for freedom of religion and thought and a denunciation of everything that went against it. "We are given no freedom," the monk explained. "The government leaders are all Catholics and they do not give freedom to the Buddhists."

"But aren't you afraid of being arrested for saying such things in public?" we asked.

"Perhaps I will be arrested," he said. "But I would be very happy to die in defense of freedom." We sat and looked at each other for a few seconds. He was smiling sweetly.

Tension had been building up throughout the country to the point where even we felt somewhat nervous about reading aloud from the monk's writings. We had occasional visions of hidden microphones picking up our words as we repeated his antigovernment remarks in an effort to master their pronunciation. As we left his monastic cell, the gongs were ringing, drums were pounding, and the faithful were chanting their prayers in the pagoda. We walked our bicycles through the mud of the compound, wondering what the armed soldier at the entrance thought about all this and about those praying inside. We wondered whether he himself might be a Buddhist.

A few days later, we were again together in the monk's cell. He was just taking up a knife to cut an orange for our refreshment when a messenger ran into the room and handed him a letter. It demanded his immediate presence at the office of the local province chief. That night, when we turned on the radio to hear the monk's regular Saturday broadcast, we heard nothing that sounded like a religious talk. There was only the usual variety of Vietnamese popular songs. Returning for class the next day, we learned that the province chief had summoned the young monk merely to inform him that his radio program was being canceled. "We have no freedom," our friend said again. "I am very sorry."

As if to underline his words, the pagoda and school grounds had become by then a virtual campsite for soldiers. Some had set up tents, while others slept in a crude barracks built across the street. There were more than a hundred soldiers in all. But our friend showed no rancor. He did not blame the province chief or the soldiers themselves. The orders for all this, he said, came from President Ngo Dinh Diem. As we left, he handed us a pamphlet in both Vietnamese and English, entitled *Principles of Buddhism.* "All life is suffering," it said.

The Buddha taught that men must follow the Eightfold Path of self-development which leads to the end of suffering. The Eightfold Path consists in Right Views or preliminary understanding, Right Aims or Motive, Right Speech, Right Acts, Right Livelihood, Right Effort, Right Concentration or mind-development, and finally, Right Samadhi, leading to full Enlightenment. As Buddhism is a way of living, not merely a theory of life, the treading of this Path is essential to self-deliverance.

The pamphlet ended with an admonition: "Cease to do evil, learn to do good, cleanse your own heart: this is the Teaching of the Buddha."

On entering the pagoda grounds some four days later, we were stopped for the first time by one of the soldiers on guard. He wanted to know where we were going, but we had barely answered when another soldier across the street shouted to his colleague to let us go. We rushed inside, but our friend was nowhere in sight. Another monk ushered us into his cell, served us tea, and asked us to wait. After a few minutes had passed, we asked whether it might not be best to return the next day. We thought our monk might be busy elsewhere. But we were kindly advised to wait. Fifteen minutes later, our friend arrived—accompanied by half a dozen military police. It was, in effect, a small pagoda raid.

Although they were not brutal, the police had a job to do and they did it: they confiscated the prized tape recorder and four tapes, taking them to the province chief's office. The machine had of course been used for the "subversive" radio program, but the majority of the tapes contained only our own English lessons. The monk was a pathetic figure as the police walked off with the expensive machine which the school had purchased with its own funds. "Now my students will not have English tapes from which to learn," he muttered. But we could do nothing except sit there silently. We wanted to go and wait outside, but the door from the narrow cell was blocked by the police. After they left about half an hour later, the monk told us that they had also been there the night before and had confiscated his typewriter and mimeograph machine. Neither of us, to be sure, felt much like studying language at that point.

Yet even in adversity there were small things for which to be thankful. Another monk, the one who had told us to wait, came in a few moments later and dramatically lifted the small pillow from our friend's bed. With a mischievous grin he removed a transistor radio from its hiding place—one item saved from the eyes of the marauding military police. We all sat back and laughed together. Then, feeling the need to release our pent-up tensions, we walked over to the schoolyard and joined a group of students playing volleyball. The young principal seemed to forget his woes as he played joyfully, unimpeded by his long gray robes. When we left, however, he turned serious again. "Can you write articles on what you have seen for foreign newspapers?" he asked. We had to explain that we could not. As IVS members, we were supposed to stay out of politics.

Still, we had come to feel great admiration and affection for this young monk who faced such adversity and had said with a calm smile that he would be quite willing to die for his cause. Even though we knew the secret police were well informed of our actions and associations, we continued to visit the pagoda every day. But the worshipers did not dare to come anymore. The pagoda was quiet and the usually happy monks seemed sad and dispirited. Yet they seemed to appreciate our coming, providing them as it did with a daily ray of sunshine from the outside. Oddly, perhaps, we never knew any of their names. We were taught to address them as "thay" —teacher—and that was name enough for us.

On what was to be our last visit—it was September by then and we were moving to another town—things seemed to be going better for them. The day before, our friend had announced in the course of the conversation class that the province chief wanted to see him at five o'clock in order to tell him to teach a civics course at the school. "Civics," naturally, meant government propaganda—a course on President Diem and his theories of ruling. But the monk did not want to go to the province office again, so, in our presence, he signed a letter to the chief saying that he was too busy with school affairs. In his place he sent two other monks, noting to us that if he were forced to teach such a civics course he would cease all work and go on strike. At five fifteen, however, an official car and a messenger were at the door. The province chief was demanding his presence. Still, relations seemed to have been smoothed over in the end. The monk had not only succeeded in avoiding the necessity of teaching a Diemist civics course, but he had also been assured that his tape recorder, typewriter, and mimeograph machine would be returned. Pleasantly surprised at his victory, we asked him how he had managed it. "I just talked with the province chief calmly and reasonably," he said, smiling.

That evening, black rain clouds gathered on the horizon. The murmurs of twilight mixed with the gong and drum sounds emanating from the pagoda. "Reality is indescribable," admonished our pamphlet on the principles of Buddhism. Although we had promised to visit whenever we could return to his town, we were never to see the monk again. A month later, we received a letter from another Vietnamese friend:

I have one mourning news for you. The monk headmaster of the Buddhist secondary school was died about a week ago in a very fatal automobile accident. I was informed that you had sent to him a letter. But he didn't alive to read it. May God Bless you.

Even now, more than five years later, our friend's picture sits on the altar of his pagoda, alongside that of the famous Thich (Venerable) Quang Duc, who had burned himself to death for his faith. For the monks believe that our friend too had been a victim of the government. Although the details are still enshrouded in mystery, people in the town later told us that his automobile "accident" was intentional —he had been hit head-on by a two-and-one-half-ton Saigon government military truck. It was only later that we noted some uncompleted handwritten notes on the back of the pamphlet he had given us. Translated from Vietnamese, they read as follows: "I am a person who has failed on the road of life. When I was young, I always searched for a way of living appropriate to high ideals. But alas, I have been mistaken and I erred in misery."

The role of religion in Vietnamese life and politics is very complex. On the local level, religious leaders have been particularly important in community affairs. Government-appointed village officers, in fact, often have little influence, owing their positions largely to the fact that they are considered politically loyal and that they can read and write well enough to handle the paperwork involved in their jobs. Village priests or monks, however, enjoy considerable influence. We soon learned that any projects we undertook in the hamlets would need to have the approval and support of these religious leaders in order to succeed. Without their support, projects might be subverted or they might fail.

We found that Catholic priests were the most patriarchal in their attitudes toward "their" villagers. While Catholic hamlets usually gave the impression of being the best organized, and while their strength usually served as a source of support to the government, in other cases overzealous priests could cause a certain amount of trouble. In Thanh Binh hamlet, for example, the government had constructed a school with three classrooms, since there was no other public school in the vicinity. Teachers were trained in the province capital and sent back to open classes. But they did not teach, and right beside the empty government school three new classrooms were being constructed in exactly the same style. The priest, toward whom the villagers themselves expressed a combination of respect and some fear, refused to give permission for children to attend any school other than his own. When we last passed through Thanh Binh, almost four years later, his private school (for which the children had to pay tuition) was still full while the government one was being boycotted and falling into disrepair. The local province chief, in addition, admitted he was helpless in the matter, since he was afraid that any action on his part would be interpreted as being anti-Catholic.

In another hamlet nearby, it was the same story. The hamlet chief stated the council's decision to request a school as a self-help project. Then the priest walked up. When he heard of the plans, he did not even turn to the hamlet chief but rather to us directly. "No, we don't need a school here," he said. "We already have one up the road." He was referring to his parochial school. We asked the hamlet chief again. Intimidated, he agreed with the priest, and the whole project was dropped, though not without some discussion among the men standing around. A few weeks later another council meeting was held and somehow, it seemed, they decided to go ahead with the school idea in spite of the priest's negative position. It was unusual to circumvent him in this way, and there was some speculation that province authorities had applied pressure. But the priest won anyway. In the end he managed to control the new school as well as his older parochial school.

For official American aid representatives, Vietnamese Catholic priests and nuns were at times the bane of their existence. Again, it was because they were so well organized. In one Highlands province heavily populated by Northern Catholic refugees, the "little black ladies," as the AID man called the nuns, seemed to appear every day with a new request for cement or bulgur wheat or something else. In return, they would offer him various vegetables or potatoes from their gardens, or even guinea pigs for him to eat. They were not begging, really, because the people in those villages devoted a considerable amount of work to improving their own lives and facilities. Schools, orphanages, and libraries sprouted up everywhere. Some of the cement, to be sure, they wanted in order to construct magnificent cathedrals, and it was always questionable in U.S. circles whether American aid should be used for such ends, or even to support private religious groups at all. But while the constant requests for materials became bothersome at times, they reflected an admirable will on the part of the nuns. Even the construction of cathedrals might have been justified in terms of the psychological advantages it offered the people—advantages which may, in the end, have contributed more to their well-being than endless material goods.

After a time, the Buddhists, too, began to request assistance from the Americans, particularly as they gained new confidence in the aftermath of the Diem period. Still, and especially to Americans, the Buddhists seemed less organized and less interested in helping their own people than the Catholics. The refugee camps they sponsored often appeared physically inferior to Catholic camps. (Government camps were the worst of all, both physically and psychologically.) Our own volunteers, who often associated spiritually with the Buddhists over the sometimes "grasping" Catholics, wished that they could find ways to help Buddhist orphanages or Buddhist villages. But as a rule the Buddhists tended to be less interested in our help. The explanation for this lay in the differences between the two religions themselves. Thich Nhat Hanh, a leading Buddhist monk and social worker, put it this way:

The West . . . , when it looks at Buddhism, tends to make a comparison between its subtle and ingrained relationship to the people and the highly organized, structured organization of such religions as Catholicism. The Christian missionaries are far better in terms of organization than the local Buddhist institutions. The extensive Western resources behind them make it possible for them to establish impressive schools, hospitals, and other forms of social organization. . . . A superficial comparison of these highly organized activities with the local Buddhist structure is likely to convince the observer that Buddhism has no future. But when one goes more deeply, one discovers that the strength of Buddhism does not lie in organization, but in the deep roots of the psychological and moral values held by people.*

Buddhism, in fact, is to some extent a part of all Vietnamese. Its long history in Viet Nam, dating back to the second century A.D., has made it a strong element in the cultural ethos of the country. In the eleventh century, under the Ly dynasty, Buddhist monks exerted considerable influence on the national government, and their faith was virtually the state religion for a time. After the Ly and under the Tran, a gradual "confucianizing" occurred and Buddhism was influenced by the folk beliefs and animistic ideas already present in the society. Then, around the end of the seventeenth century, as Buddhism rose again in importance and as the strength of Confucianism faltered, the various thought patterns of the people tended to mix. What resulted was the present, peculiarly Vietnamese synthesis of religions mentioned in Chapter 2.

When the French took over Viet Nam, installing and quite natu-

* *Vietnam: Lotus in a Sea of Fire* (New York: Hill & Wang, 1967).

rally favoring Catholicism, Buddhism first came to be associated with nationalism. This was in a sense inevitable, since Catholicism was associated with the foreigners and Buddhism was an indigenous force. The pagoda was a religious and social center to which only Vietnamese would come, whereas the Christian churches were built by foreigners and worshiped in by those who followed and worked for the foreigners. Little changed, in fact, when the French left and Ngo Dinh Diem took power. Diem was a Catholic (he nearly became a priest), and as president he ruled the country with what many called a combination of Catholic morality and Confucian mandarin paternalism. The Buddhists later charged that under his rule they had been repressed. But they were not really repressed so much as they were discriminated against or by-passed as favors tended to go to Catholics. Most land grants, for example, went to Catholics to build schools and hospitals, as did the most favorable agricultural credit loans, most lumbering privileges, and certain export-import monopolies. The influence of the priests was great, and conversions became numerous among opportunists. As Communist insurgency accelerated, and Diem became more and more frightened, he relied increasingly on those he could trust—fellow Catholics. Vietnamese Catholics later admitted the preferences they were shown under Diem, preferences which were denied only by U.S. Ambassador Frederick Nolting, who said in the summer of 1963 that he had never seen "any evidence" of anti-Buddhist discrimination in Viet Nam.

On the morning of May 8, 1963, there was a Buddha's birthday celebration in Hue. It was a peaceful celebration and the atmosphere was festive, though speakers did protest a government decree prohibiting the flying of the Buddhist religious flag. This seemed to them a special sign of intolerance since days earlier the streets of Hue had been decked with Catholic flags for the anniversary of Ngo Dinh Thuc's (Diem's brother's) investiture as archbishop of Central Viet Nam. On the evening of May 8, an IVS English teacher at the boys' high school was on his way home from a coffee shop in the Citadel. Accompanied by one of his students, he crossed the main bridge across the Perfume River and immediately noticed a group of some five hundred people gathered around the Hue radio station. They were demonstrating, it turned out, because the government radio had refused to play any Buddhist music or otherwise acknowledge the holiday—a peculiar stand since at least 80 per cent of the people in Viet Nam consider themselves Buddhist.

As time passed, the teacher later reported, the crowd grew to almost two thousand. A few students managed to get to the top of the radio station where they proudly displayed their flags, much to the pleasure of the onlookers. Still, everyone was quite orderly. The announcement was made that if the head monk was not permitted inside the station to plead their case, then everyone would remain until he was heard. Shortly after that, it was said that the mayor of the city had arrived and would be followed by military forces to "protect the Buddhists." "From whom will they protect the Buddhists?" the IVSer asked his friend. "Everyone here *is* Buddhist!"

Deciding it would be wiser to leave, the teacher and his friend made their way slowly through the crowd to their bicycles. But the military had already arrived with foot troops, armored trucks, tanks, and fire trucks. The latter suddenly opened up on the crowd with their water hoses. "At this point," the IVS teacher told us, "I was right at the corner trying frantically to get my bicycle and get out, but with no success as I couldn't get through the people. Just then I heard a terrific explosion and the sounds of rapid fire from a rifle. Thinking some fool VC had gotten into the crowd and thrown a bomb into the radio station causing some trigger-happy soldier to open up with his rifle, I got scared. People were running in every direction. Suddenly I heard another terrific explosion and actually felt the heat of it against my cheek—the tanks had begun to fire. The soldiers seemed to be shooting right into the crowd. I dropped my bike and took off. People and bikes were strewn all over the street. I knew that I had panicked and that I should stop and be more careful, but those fool guns were right at my back and I was out to save my own life. Explosions and machine-gun fire followed the crowd right down the street. It never ceased. I finally got far enough away to take stock of the situation, but found myself totally confused. The only thing that I could think of was, 'Why aren't I dead?'

"Then the rage hit me," he continued. "The Vietnamese government had fired on its own people who were peacefully demonstrating. I have now joined the ranks of the average Vietnamese who don't know what to think. We're fighting a war against the Communists and our own government attacks us. For the government to fire on the crowd, to create a panic in which eight people—mostly women and children—were killed and others hurt, has further alienated the people. This is a bitter experience which no one who was there will soon forget. The government and its fight against communism has lost an important battle."

This incident was only the first of many that would bring some of the Buddhist groups into the political limelight for years to come. Tensions became almost unbearably high, particularly in Hue. The same volunteer teacher was asked by a seemingly desperate Vietnamese student whether he could have asylum in his house. He said he was being chased by the Diem police. The volunteer did not know quite what to say, fearing political involvement and trouble, but he could not, in the end, resist the urge to help. He invited the boy to come, only to have him then decline, saying he had only wanted to "test" the American.

The following summer saw the immolations that were to shock the entire world. It was very difficult for foreigners to understand the meaning of these actions. Their purpose was not to shock so much as to call attention to the need for changing the government's repressive policies. Among Vietnamese Buddhists, suicide is committed for a noble cause, not to escape from one's own problems but rather to make difficulties for those whose behavior has impelled the act. Through this form of sacrifice, according to Buddhist doctrine, one gains merit, and therefore it is an honor to be allowed to perform this final gesture as a human being. A Buddhist friend later recounted the story of one monk's burning which he had witnessed in Hue. It sounded ghastly, perhaps, to us as Westerners, but to him it was nothing less than awesome.

"He tried three different times to burn himself," our friend said. "The first time was at the spot marking the May 8th shooting by government troops. But he could not do it there; the police made him move on. Then he crossed the bridge and tried again at an intersection downtown, but once again he was pushed on by the police. He felt very sad; he felt that he had not been chosen by Buddha for this great sacrifice. But on the third attempt he succeeded. That was on the grounds of Tu Dam Pagoda—probably you know the spot, for there is a big urn there to mark it now—at three o'clock in the morning. His helpers poured the gasoline all over him, and then he himself lit the match. Immediately he was enveloped by flames. His straight-postured body drooped forward several times, but each time a strong sense of will-power brought him back up. His mind was holding sway over his body. But finally his hands, held together in prayer, slowly spread apart, and then, suddenly, he collapsed, dead. All the bystanders, watching there in the pagoda yard, cried. It was so impressive."

In Saigon's Xa Loi Pagoda, which, until the August raids, was the center of 1963 Buddhist activities against the government, the heart of Thich Quang Duc was on display on the main altar. It was in a glass vase and appeared quite black, but the monks said that it was "the only part that would not burn." To Vietnamese, this seemed to lend heavenly approbation to their cause. Meanwhile, banners hung all around, begging for freedom from tyranny and for decency toward Buddhists. At the same time, loudspeakers broadcast prayers, religious music, and chants for the milling crowds. The atmosphere was electric—until the raids, and then everything was deadly still.

We volunteers were not directly affected by all these events, but again, we could not help being influenced and saddened by them. They were a major cause of resentment against the Diem government, for the President was unwilling to make any concessions to the Buddhists' legitimate demands or even, it seemed, to give them the benefit of the doubt and admit they were not all Communists. The *Times of Vietnam*, the daily mouthpiece of the Nhus, printed article after article quoting one venerable after another who had praised the government for its stance. There was no reason why these monks should not praise the government, however, for either they were forced to do so or else they were really secret police-agents, taxi drivers, or other miscellaneous persons who had been disguised as monks. One Vietnamese friend was surprised to find a pedicab driver she knew dressed in monk's robes at the local pagoda. The real monks were in jail, but appearances had to be kept up.

In late October, a United Nations observer team came at President Diem's invitation to see how happy the monks really were. In the main pagoda in Dalat, however, there was only one real monk remaining. The rest were taxi drivers. Such distortions for the benefit of the U.N. observers went beyond the pagodas. All the waiters in one hotel where the observers were to eat lunch were dismissed and replaced by government agents who wanted to overhear their comments. Some Vietnamese wondered why the service was so poor. The U.N. team members were not all fooled, however. A secretary with the group said that while the "planted monks" were talking with the visitors, real monks were whispering in her ear, "Don't believe them."

The Buddhists, along with the students, were instrumental in bringing about Diem's fall. The army, to be sure, struck the final blow, but it probably would not have done so had popular feeling not been as strong as it was. After the coup there was concern that the tables would simply be turned and that Buddhists would now discriminate against Catholics, but this did not happen. On the other hand, with the new climate of freedom, expensive Buddhist pagodas and meeting halls did seem to sprout at a faster rate, some monks rode in fine cars, and May, 1964, saw the largest celebration of Buddha's birthday within living memory—at least, friends said, since the French had first come to Viet Nam. It lasted an entire week, cost $40,000 (high for Viet Nam), and culminated in a mammoth parade with floats and more than 100,000 marchers spread out as far as the eye could see down the fashionable boulevards of Saigon. Also, friends who had been equivocal about their religion before, like the one who had closed his letter "May God bless you," now proudly admitted their identity by signing off, "I pray that Our Lord Buddha will extend to you happiness and prosperity." Vietnamese in general admitted that they could be more friendly to Americans, since the Diem government policy had been rather hostile, partly because of American sympathy for the Buddhists.

By early 1965, however, religious differences had again become quite sharp, in some places approaching the intensity of 1963. Where many Vietnamese, particularly Catholics, had dismissed the religious question as a divisive factor in Vietnamese life and politics prior to

1963, they now saw it as another woeful stumbling block to national unity. Americans probably made more of the issue than Vietnamese, but government cabinets were chosen as much for religious balance in that period as they were for regional and other considerations. Again, it was at the provincial level that we had the most experience with these phenomena.

In Hue the lines seemed especially sharply drawn. Catholic student leaders claimed that in the early part of the year, during the Buddhist demonstrations against the Tran Van Huong government, they had been pursued by Buddhist student leaders with evil intentions. "They tried to have us kidnapped," said one, "and they are always pouring recriminations upon us Catholics." Capitalizing on the apparent preference of American officialdom for Catholics because of their outspoken anticommunism, he reminded us that it was the Buddhists who had angrily burned the American library. Anyone who was anti-American, he said, must be pro-Communist. Yet to some extent the change in fortunes was borne by these Catholics as being part of the rules of the game. The same leader who complained of Buddhist designs upon him once accompanied us on a visit to a newly opened dormitory for fine-arts students in Hue. As we were being shown around, he turned to us with a tolerant smile and said, "I don't know why I'm taking this tour. This was my uncle's house until the government seized it and threw him in prison." His uncle had been a Catholic and a member of the hated Diemist Can Lao party.

By mid-1965 these wounds, which probably had more to do with political associations than with religion itself, were healing. The new phase that was developing, while led by one faction of the Buddhist hierarchy—Thich Tri Quang's militants—did to some extent cross religious lines. (It did not draw active support from all Buddhist quarters, since the Buddhists were divided into several groups.) This was the Struggle Movement, the civil war within the war that would finally explode in 1966. We were getting hints of what would come from friends and associates before that, however, and we felt that a responsive government in Saigon could have avoided it. Again, however, the government was not responsive and neither were the Americans.

"Why, after all we've done for them, are those Vietnamese so anti-American?" Americans back home would ask in hurt astonishment. Others read about the demonstrations and decided that the only answer was to "bring the boys back home." "If the Vietnamese don't want us," the argument went, "to hell with them." Neither reaction was a fair one, and indeed it took patience to understand just what the Struggle Movement was all about. *Dan Toc* (The People) magazine asked itself this question in a summer 1965 article, "Why Do We Struggle?" "When we deal with the purpose of defending the national sovereignty and the self-determination of our people," it began, "we do not mean to be anti-American as the innocent and superficial people usually think. It's not our problem to object against the U.S.A., our best allied country, since we accept in principle the presence of the Americans as a necessity in our special present situation. We only want to call the attention of the Vietnamese and American governments to carry out concrete solutions to make the relationship between the two countries become better and better."

Some of the problems for which the Struggle Movement people were asking solutions seemed vague or minor to many Americans. They were essentially political, economic, and social problems, not religious ones. The Buddhists were involved only because they had taken up the nationalist banner. "You must bear in mind that Buddhism in Viet Nam is not the same as when it was first born," said Thich Tri Quang. "Our most sacred duty is to preserve our faith and to advise our followers. . . . If our country is lost, then our people would lose their identity and Buddhism could no longer survive. In other words, the Buddhists must vigilantly protect their country's interests, because that is in the interests of their own faith."

Those who would become active in the Struggle cited the issues: they wanted the two governments concerned, Vietnamese and American, to make known the exact number of foreign soldiers in the country, the military bases where they were stationed, and their rights and the period of time they were to stay in Viet Nam. In addition to concern over such arrangements between the Saigon government and U.S. authorities, they were disturbed that the use of American currency was interfering with the sovereignty of their own currency. The behavior of American troops and the disposition of their garbage were equally severe problems. One bright young professor at the University of Hue raised the issue almost every time he met Consulate officials. Although tradition-oriented Hue itself was kept largely off-limits to U.S. military personnel—an extraordinarily wise move—Da Nang at first was not. And since the two key cities were only three hours apart by road, people from Hue traveled frequently to Da Nang, where they got a first-hand look at cultural disintegration. On either side of the main highway, and in between vast refugee settlements stuck on the sand, the marines were depositing their garbage. The nationalistic young Hue professor was appalled not only at the sight of beer cans and cigarette cartons everywhere, but even more by the idea of Vietnamese children scrounging for any still usable items amidst it all. "Can't you dump your garbage somewhere else?" he asked. "Somewhere so it isn't so visible and degrading to our self-respect?" The American consular officials finally did take up the matter with the marines. The next time the professor asked about it, he was told that according to the marines a Vietnamese trucking company was responsible for carting off the garbage and there was nothing the Americans could do about the problem.

As for the carousing of the troops, there was little the American authorities could do to prevent this either. Officials would report that American troop behavior was much better than it had been in past wars where the Americans were occupying powers, and certainly the tensions the troops were under made it thoroughly understandable that they should need to let off steam. The Vietnamese were not unreasonable; they understood all this very well. Yet they could not help resenting it, particularly the way their girl friends were treated and the way prices soared because of the spendthrift Americans. The intelligent and dignified wife of one friend got especially tired of having her fanny pinched every time she went downtown for errands. A staunch anti-Communist Catholic, she said, "I sympathize with those young boys and they are good for coming here to help us. But now I am really disgusted by them. I can't stand them. Why must they be so rude?" Ambassador Lodge knew about the problem and issued a special memorandum about it:

In expressing our friendship for the Vietnamese people, I ask the help of each American in Vietnam. We have left our homes thousands of miles away to serve here among a brave people as their friends from the free world. Yet, as always, the process of living closely together demands more than ordinary attention to common courtesies and to signs of respect. We are not only partners of the Vietnamese people, but also we are guests.

The American smile and a friendly greeting are part of our best heritage and assets. Let us be more generous in using them every day —with the Vietnamese with whom we work, with the Vietnamese who see us passing by in the streets, with the Vietnamese who have become part of our social lives.

Let the Vietnamese get to know us as we really are. In their hour of national need, this can be very important.

Most important to the Vietnamese, however—and their demand for it could be called neither minor nor vague—was the need for a broad-based and popular government to replace the unresponsive military junta under Thieu and Ky. Vietnamese reasoning on this matter not only concerned the short-run desires for justice and peaceful social revolution, but it also related to the problem of an eventual negotiated settlement of the war. Its logic was explained to us by a Buddhist friend, a student leader who, according to the Catholics, was behind the burning of the American library a few months earlier. (He himself impishly explained away his role in the incident by saying, "I was sick the day that happened.") Whether he was behind that particular incident or not, it is important to understand his outlook and that of his colleagues. We talked with him late one October afternoon at a small and rustic coffee house inside Hue's Citadel.

He began by asking us what we thought about the progress of the war.

"Well," we said, "it seems to be going better now than before. There seem to be a number of victories over the Viet Cong." This was after the first few months of direct American troop participation.

"That's true," our friend agreed. "But have you ever noticed that all the big victories seem to be scored by the Americans? Our own Vietnamese troops don't appear to be doing much. That is not a good sign." We wondered what he was leading up to, and soon found out as he continued: "Our troops don't have a good motivation for fighting. They don't like the government they see directing them—the corrupt generals and all. And they don't understand why the Americans are fighting here. They are a little suspicious. They do not have anything clear-cut to fight for."

"What do you suggest?" we asked lamely. It was the moment he had been waiting for.

"We must declare the goal of our fighting, and the goal of our fighting is an ultimate peace. Peace is the most urgent desire of all our people, and the soldiers, after all, come from the people at large. If our troops know that they are fighting for peace, they will fight hard in order to get the war over with. But there is one problem: up to now, anyone who talks about peace is considered to be a Communist or at least pro-Communist. This is very wrong. Why should the Communists have a monopoly on the desire for peace?"

To us, his observations made a great deal of sense. Popular folksingers like Pham Duy were officially frowned upon by government leaders because they sang passionately of the yearning for peace.

"What we need in Viet Nam now," our friend told us, "is a third force. To understand this, just look at what we have: on the one side is the Viet Cong and China behind them; on the other side is the regime in Saigon, supported by the Americans. They are deadlocked. Neither one can win. They fight against each other. But in the middle are the Vietnamese people. They are the ones who suffer. We must organize these people who are caught in between and who cry out for peace. It is they, the People of Viet Nam, who can save their country from this evil war."

"But how would this Third Force operate?" we asked. It sounded rather amorphous to us, though fine in principle.

"The Third Force will cooperate with the government in order to bring about a settlement between the Viet Cong and the United States. It will serve as a kind of intermediary between the two."

"Then it will have to take a somewhat anti-American position at the same time as it takes an anti-Viet Cong one," we pointed out.

"Yes," he said, "by definition. But when the Third Force begins to operate, you must understand its reasons: it is for the sake of the preservation of our country against both the Communists and arbitrary military dictatorship. We are not really anti-American. We like the Americans and we appreciate all your help, but we must have a better solution than this series of unresponsive governments in Saigon."

So far we could not disagree. His platform made sense, and his criticism of the Saigon regime corroborated what we had seen ourselves and heard from others. Since American policy was involved, we asked him if he had discussed all this with the Consulate officials.

"No," he said, sounding reluctant, in fact, to do so.

"But you should," we urged. "If they knew about your views, perhaps they would improve the American policy accordingly."

He smiled disbelievingly and said, "Why don't *you* tell them?"

As he drove us home on the back of his motor scooter, he turned and smiled again. "You see, I'm not anti-American. If I were, I wouldn't ride around with you in public like this."

Feeling that we had been given a deep and unusual insight into the Buddhist view (though our friend did not refer to Buddhists, but rather to "the People"), we passed on the gist of his remarks to officials at the Consulate in Hue, as he had urged us to. The young officers there had rather limited contacts with the local population—partly because their staff turnover was so frequent and partly because ultranationalists tended to avoid American officials—and they were delighted to have such information. With great enthusiasm they sent a report on our conversation to the Embassy in Saigon. Whether anyone in Saigon ever read the report, however, or whether anything that happened in Hue was ever taken with any seriousness by the Embassy, would remain a matter for grave questioning in the months to come. Certainly the Embassy was not prepared when matters came to a head.

On the evening of March 10, 1966, our IVS agriculturalist in Hue returned to the house excited by news he had just heard. At the USAID office, where he had stopped to pick up mail, a radio message had been received from civilian regional headquarters in Da Nang. "General Thi has just been ousted from his command," it said. "The Embassy supports his ouster, but if anyone asks you about it, say you don't know." General Nguyen Chanh Thi was the highly popular corps commander for the Hue–Da Nang region. He was from a village near Hue, spoke the local dialect, had a charming personality, and enjoyed excellent relations with the various political and religious groups in the region and particularly with the Buddhists and intellectuals of Hue University. In fact, General Thi was the only high military commander or government official in whom these people seemed to place any confidence at all. He was staunchly anti-Communist, having been imprisoned as a young corporal by the Viet Minh in 1945, at which time he experienced great suffering and brutality. Yet he felt deeply the need for a social revolution and responsive government for his people. When few other high officials dared to act, General Thi supported progressive social-action programs, such as those undertaken by various youth groups in his region. It was for all these reasons that he was fired by the other generals—among them the one he humorously called "our young prime minister," Marshal Ky. Although the ouster was disguised as a resignation for health reasons (sinus), the reality was that Thi was too popular and the generals felt him as a threat to their own power. Yet Thi had already refused at least two opportunities to become prime minister. "I am a military man," he would say. "My place is in the army, not in politics. Politics is for civilians and a civilian should be prime minister."

Presumably no one realized the furor that Thi's ouster would cause. Prime Minister Ky had just returned from the Honolulu Conference with President Johnson and was full of confidence. The American Mission itself presumably thought the confidence was justified. The fact that the Mission publicly denied any complicity in the Thi affair was a most unwise blemish on its credibility, especially since the evidence is so clear on this point. On March 11, one day after Thi was "urged to resign," General William Westmoreland wrote him a letter, expressing the belief that Thi was "interested in securing medical attention in the United States." It had therefore occurred to him, the letter went on, that Thi "might welcome an invitation," on behalf of the U.S. Department of Defense, to use American medical facilities. Westmoreland concluded by noting that he could make all the necessary arrangements immediately, and he conveyed to Thi "every good wish." Eventually, Thi did go to Washington and to Walter Reed Army Hospital. But, as he explained later, he did not go for treatment; he went merely to visit and cheer up wounded American soldiers from Viet Nam.

Meanwhile, the Buddhists under Thich Tri Quang called for demonstrations. Even military troops, police, and government civil servants—including the deputy province chief—joined the marches. Schools and markets were closed (we had to stock up ahead on food), meetings were held, and government fell apart. It was the opportunity the Buddhists had been waiting for to press their demands, demands that had been ignored up to then. Incredibly, and for reasons that only he could understand, Ky sent the ousted Thi back to Da Nang with instructions to "calm the population." It was then, at a downtown rally, that General Thi explained his new position to his people. "I have decided to retire," he said, "because of my sinus condition. It especially affects my nose—so that everything seems to smell very bad." Things would smell a lot worse, however.

The demonstrations completely immobilized IVS activity in the northern regions, though volunteers in the delta continued work without even realizing that anything was amiss. (The delta region was frequently unaffected by religious or political movements that began in Central Viet Nam.) In Hue, long lines of demonstrators marched by within half a block of our house. At the beginning, friends sometimes waved to us from their ranks, though some later said they had been pressured into joining the Movement. The women were the most vigorous demonstrators. Wearing purple blouses and conical hats, they swung their arms back and forth and shouted in unison, "Down with Thieu and Co! Down with Thieu and Co!" It was interesting to note that during the first few demonstrations Ky was never mentioned. This was exactly as our Buddhist student leader friend had forewarned us. Co was chosen instead because of his known corruption, and Thieu was the Catholic and Can Lao chief-of-state. Ky was not initially included in the number of "nefarious gangsters" because the Buddhist hierarchy did not want to strike at the whole government structure at once. "It is better to divide them so that they cannot get back at us so easily," we were told by one of the clever planners.

Although many of our more moderate friends and associates in Hue became concerned as the Struggle Movement took a more violent direction, more of them than ever before agreed this time with the general principles of the Struggle: namely, an end to arbitrary and unresponsive government (of the kind that so crudely dismissed the popular General Thi) and a call for democratic, popularly elected, civilian government. Anything that stood in the way of these goals, they were also against, and it was in this respect that they became anti-American and carried anti-U.S. banners: "Viet Nam for the Vietnamese," "Down with U.S. intervention in Vietnamese internal affairs," "Down with U.S. hindering the formation of a democratic, popularly elected government." The Americans, everybody knew, were wedded to the Ky regime, believing that even this time Ky could "carry it off." If anyone had doubted this for a moment, or if some had hoped for a more enlightened policy for change, these feelings were crushed when the U.S. Mission in Saigon agreed to transport Ky's troops to Da Nang to quell the rebellion. Ky's impulsive announcement that the whole movement was Communist-inspired and that its participants were Communists was a source of further outrage to the people. "Do you think we are Communists?" asked one very outspoken friend, in an attempt to bait us. When we said no, he was satisfied, adding that if the government continued to treat the people in such a way, then he was afraid it would only play into the hands of the Communists.

No one could ever be certain just how much Communist infiltration there was among the Struggle group. A French-Canadian priest likened the atmosphere in Hue to what he had experienced in Peking in 1949—just before it fell to the Chinese Communists. General Thi himself, still at liberty in Hue and Da Nang, warned the leader, Thich Tri Quang, that his movement was being infiltrated by Communist elements. Tri Quang, it seems, was not pleased by the implied criticism and did not respond. Although most of our friends reserved their strongest attacks for the Saigon government, many did become fearful of a Communist coup that could capitalize on the violence and turmoil. Yet, the younger Buddhist leaders insisted that they knew exactly what they were doing and were certain that they were in full control of the situation. The monks, for their part, had a Buddhist solution to the Communist problem. Thich Don Hau, then the chief religious monk in that whole area (he was always considered very nonpolitical), would recite parables of love and peace when one raised the subject of communism. Looking over from the terrace of Linh Mu Pagoda toward the gardens and the seven-storied tower, he once said that the only way for man to be saved was not through doctrines like communism or capitalism, but through man's own individual goodness and through practicing love. "Yes, Venerable," we had said, "but how is man to achieve this individual goodness?" "Buddhism teaches 80,000 different ways," he assured us with supreme confidence, but without elaborating.

Americans could never understand the faith of the Buddhists, which seemed to apply to politics as much as to religion. Even some Vietnamese could not understand it, and one friend, a deep thinker himself, reported that he had been entirely mystified by a conversation he'd had with Thich Tri Quang. If one asked the Buddhist leaders who would fulfill their qualifications for a national leader and who could thus replace Thieu and Ky if the latter two were deposed, the answer was invariably, "Oh, there are many good leaders. That is no problem." It was never explained whether such a person should be a Buddhist or why he had not come to the fore already in a country searching for capable leadership. It was possible they were only expressing a truly religious faith that someone would emerge, without having any clear idea themselves who he would be. It was even more possible that when they assured their questioners that the Communists would not win out in the shuffle, they meant that Buddhism would prevail over communism only in the spiritual sense—that the country might indeed fall to the NLF, but that Buddhist ideals would hold sway in the minds of the people over whatever new ideas the Front tried to impose. Buddhist leaders sometimes said that if the Communists tried to profit from their movement, then they would have to fight the Communists. But again, it was never clear whether the Buddhists would wage a war of guns, or whether it would be indeed a war of mind over matter. No American could ever understand this. But what Americans did decide was that they would not take any risks, no matter what assurances the Buddhists would give them. And thus it was that the last hope for political compromise and a third force passed by the boards, and the Saigon government and the Americans opted for a military solution to the Struggle and to the war itself.

For us, the last days in Hue were full of tension. We would listen to the local radio station, which was held by the Struggle forces, and even hear the names of our former students who were now leaders of the movement for their schools. We could have very little contact with Vietnamese, because it would have compromised them to associate with us during those times. Some of our closest associates were already being insulted for their friendship with Americans. Probably this hurt us, as sympathizers, even more than it hurt them. It was curious that while some Vietnamese could not be seen with us because we were American, top American government officials in Da Nang's regional headquarters were at the same time accusing us of supporting the Struggle Movement. In any case, we were on extra good behavior, aware that the slightest mistake might provoke an incident.

Rumors, meanwhile, were spreading like wildfire throughout the city. It was said that Ky would send tanks, particularly when the new corps commander, Thi's replacement, also came out in favor of the Movement. (He had little choice, really, since the Movement was so powerful in the region.) General Chieu, a top Ky aide, also came to Hue to negotiate with the rebels. He might well have been stoned by angry mobs had Thi not saved him. After that, Chieu was "invited" by students to stay for lunch with them, then to go for a pedicab ride in order to show his solidarity with "the People" (who did not travel by Mercedes), and finally to stay overnight in Hue, again with "the People"—all of which was a face-saving way of making him a hostage. By early April, as all this had been building to a crescendo, all airplane flights were restricted and then canceled, principally so that agitators could not move around so easily.

After a while, some Vietnamese who were stunned at the increasing virulence of the antigovernment campaign, though still agreeing with its principles, tried to moderate it somewhat. But the Struggle had gathered a momentum of its own and they did not succeed. For the Americans, too, it was a hectic period, and the increasing bitterness on both sides was reflected by the American vice-consul, whose nerves were not holding up well at all for a diplomat. "Why, that goddam Buu Ton!" he said, Ton being one of the student leaders. "He came storming in here the other day and demanded that we take down the barbed wire around MACV [Military Assistance Command Vietnam] so they could have a demonstration there. He demanded that of the most powerful nation in the world!" But the vice-consul was caught in a trap. In order to avoid further anti-American feelings, he would have to give in to the demand. And he did, blustering all the while. A few weeks later, the U.S. Consulate, along with the Information Service Cultural Center, was burned by angry mobs—for the second time in less than eighteen months.

On the evening of April 5, we were expecting our Vietnamese neighbors to join us for dinner at the IVS house. Just as they arrived, two men from MACV appeared and announced with characteristic military precision that we, along with virtually all non-Vietnamese civilians, would be evacuated from Hue the following morning at 0830 hours; each person was permitted sixty-six pounds of baggage. That was all. We did not even know to where we would be evacuated, whether to Saigon or, if things were upset there too, to Bangkok or Hong Kong or what. The dinner, after that, was pretty dreary, and we had to stay up much of the night packing. It was true that we had no work in Hue, since everything was closed down because of the turmoil, but we were still not very happy about picking up and leaving just like that.

Next morning, as instructed, we reported to the Citadel airstrip at 8:30, passing, en route, a procession of citizens on their way to the day's demonstration, which was expected to be the biggest yet. Most of Hue's foreign civilians were there: a German psychiatrist from the medical school, the Filipino wife of a Vietnamese dean who later became rector of the university, a kind old musician, also German, from the Conservatory of Music (he had just recovered from a case of cholera), an American missionary family with a sick baby, and so on. We boarded the special planes, army Caribous, buckled our seat belts, and waited for take-off. We waited and waited. Nothing happened. Finally we got up and started walking around. Somebody said they didn't know yet where to send us, and a little later there was some question about whether we would be evacuated at all. People from the Consulate drove in and out, a two-star American general flew in on a private plane, more rumors spread, and everyone got very tired and hot and irritable.

Some army C-rations materialized from somewhere for lunch, and then sandwiches and soft drinks arrived. Reporters wandered about, also curious as to what would happen. The German psychiatrist speculated that the Ambassador was in the middle of his siesta in Saigon and that President Johnson was asleep for the night in Washington, so no decisions could be made. As we waited and watched, army enlisted men pulled a light spotter plane out of a Citadel moat; it had crashed there the night before. The weather kept getting hotter, and we reminded each other that in the summertime Hue was the hottest place in that entire tropical country. Finally, around five, as shadows were beginning to lengthen on the little airstrip, a temporary senior consul, dispatched from Saigon just to handle the crisis, came to make an announcement. As we had suspected by then, we were being used as political pawns in a game with the Vietnamese generals. If they could not guarantee our safety in Hue, they were told by U.S. officials, the United States would evacuate us, an act that would presumably be embarrassing to them. A few American military men had already been evacuated temporarily, also as an admonition to the Vietnamese to mend their ways. Although it seemed the generals had made some concessions, they were still turning their guns on each other. Thus they were endangering us, so the argument went, to a Viet Cong takeover that would profit from the power vacuum. And so, the consul concluded, it was regrettable that we had had to wait all day long, it was admirable how we had stood up to it all, and now we would be evacuated to—Phu Bai, the marine base nine miles away! Although further evacuations followed the next day, it was an anticlimactic destination, to say the least.

In the weeks that followed, there were immolations once again. A novice nun proclaimed to President Johnson that by her act of self-immolation "I will serve as a flame to enlighten your policy." When Mr. Johnson undiplomatically replied that such acts were useless, Thich Tri Quang lashed out at him: "This declaration proves two things," he said. "Mr. Johnson understands nothing that is happening in Viet Nam; Mr. Johnson is impertinent." Tri Quang himself, however, soon lost some of his support. Having succeeded in the Struggle Movement's aim of forcing elections, he continued to fight for the immediate resignation of the government in power. Not surprisingly, he did not trust the government in its election promise. As an American observer saw it, however, "The Vietnamese government by now doesn't know what else it can do. It handed everything to the Buddhists except its own head on a platter. Then it turned to them and said, 'What more do you want us to do?' and the Buddhists said, 'Drop dead.'" Tri Quang's last move of defiance was to instruct all faithful Buddhists to place their family altars in the streets of Hue to prevent Ky's troops from moving into the city. But by this time, the people were becoming disillusioned, objecting to the sacrilege of subjecting their Buddhas and sacred altars to the ravages of weather and possible crushing by army trucks. They were tired of violence and intrigue and the idea of their soldiers fighting one another. Hue, in a state of numb shock, was retaken peacefully by Ky's riot police in June of 1966.

After everything that had taken place, however, it seemed that neither the Saigon government nor the Americans had learned any lessons. Elections, to be sure, were held. But the lack of communication and understanding that had led to the Struggle Movement in the first place continued and later caused even greater problems. When reconciliation was called for, continued repressions were the answer. In the aftermath of the movement, hundreds were arrested, some of them remaining in jail without trial for over a year. There was a washed-out feeling in Hue throughout 1967. It was not surprising that many disillusioned people, those who were released or who had managed to hide from the police in the first place, could not follow the government anymore. Several of our friends from this group joined the Liberation Front soon afterward. They were not Communists. Certainly many of them believed in the third-front principle. But the government, in its blindness, forced them into the arms of the opposition. Two months after the Movement was crushed, a friend described the situation in a letter to us:

I am saddened to see that the government is looking for ways in which to take revenge against the people of Central Viet Nam, especially those in Hue: they imprison, they persecute, and they restrict the necessary provisions of life through a kind of economic blockade. These methods truly serve just to provoke further the anger of the people toward the authorities and I think that the situation is not yet calm. There will surely be another explosion and perhaps even more dangerous events than those just past.

The Americans were equally shortsighted, refusing as they did all aid to Hue. They also kept the U.S. Consulate and the Information Service library in the black and gutted condition in which the angry Hue crowd had left them, intending these physical reminders of the Struggle Movement to serve as permanent monuments to shame all of Hue. The Vietnamese understood this and resented it immensely. Bitterness toward American policy increased. Meanwhile, some Vietnamese, including high officials, claimed that the two burning incidents were perpetrated by the American CIA in the first place. Thich Tri Quang, they said, had specifically told student leaders not to perpetrate any such violence. One old acquaintance, a top Struggle Movement leader whom we were able to visit once in prison in 1967, was particularly insistent on this theme. (A law student, he complained that his confinement to prison, in addition to being unjust for lack of a trial, interfered with his examinations!) "I don't feel quite so bad about the whole affair," he said of the burnings, "because your government was also involved." He explained that three of his colleagues, who were released "surprisingly early" from prison (meaning they probably had official "pull"), had admitted to receiving CIA directives (and money) to burn the Consulate. "But why?" we asked. "In order to give the government an excuse to strongly suppress the Movement once and for all," he said. Whether this particular story was true or not, there was no doubt that both Americans and the Saigon government were anxious to repress those who had started the rebellion against them.

The final irony of this policy became known when Hue was the scene of the most savage treatment in the Tet attacks of early 1968. Substantial parts of the city were held for nearly a month by the Liberation Front, which capitalized upon the people's natural hostility to their repressive government. "During the days when the VC first came in," wrote a friend, "the people were stupefied, but they were not afraid of the VC because the latter were very wise in using every form of propaganda; therefore many people sympathized with them. The VC invited the people to meetings and to join in the various jobs of defending the city. Labor and working-class circles, to whom the government had never paid any attention, now were catered to by the VC and were used by them in many jobs. Thus, these people sympathized with the VC."

Students who had joined the Front after the Struggle returned during the time it controlled Hue in order to serve as guides and to visit their old friends. Repressed by the Saigon regime, they now had weapons and enjoyed considerable authority. One of them told a friend that he had waited four months for the authorities to pardon him after the Struggle Movement. But the government authorities didn't do anything of the sort, and he was living in extreme misery. Caught in the middle, he was afraid both the government and the Front would try to arrest him, and so he finally chose sides. The side he chose was the Front.

It is true that many people in Hue were deeply shocked during this time by the Viet Cong atrocities and mass murders, some of them involving live burials. Their first sentiments favoring the NLF changed to horror as they saw what was happening. "When the people saw the broken-up situation of their families and of the city," wrote our same friend afterward, "and especially when they saw brothers and sisters, friends, and relatives taken off or killed, then no one sympathized with the VC anymore, especially in student circles. I'm sure that none of the people of Hue like the Viet Cong now."

What he added, however, was more ominous: "But the local government authorities don't think this way," he said; "they are looking for ways to arrest all the people who were active for the VC, including all those whom the VC forced. I think the authorities need to have a clear reconciliation policy. Otherwise they will *push* many, many students in Hue into the arms of the VC"—as in the case of the friend cited earlier, he added. It was always the same. Another close friend, a young girl, was arrested by the Hue police (on false charges) and tortured so brutally that she had to spend several weeks in the hospital. Still another friend, a student, wrote of his desire for the University of Hue to open again after the offensive so that he and his colleagues could continue their studies. (They were already being trained in self defense, but the problem, he added, was for defense of whom—corrupt generals?) Here it was the Americans who were directly at fault. "The sad and regrettable part," he wrote, "is that the majority of American notables are applying pressure to close the university. I think this is an extremely mistaken position if the Americans still want to punish the anti-American spirit and attitudes in Hue two years ago." He added that when he had requested local American authorities for air transportation for Da Nang students to come to Hue and join the relief effort, the U.S. Army major had asked whether the students concerned were Buddhist or not. "If so," our friend noted with amazement, "he would not let us go by airplane! I had to explain for him at length that not all Buddhist students like the VC. I was most sad that the attitude of the majority of Americans is intolerant and misunderstanding like that."

The witch-hunting spirit in Hue after the Tet offensive was hard on IVS volunteers too. One of our refugee men was asked by an American intelligence agent if he knew any students who were anti-American. The IVSer, who had been teaching in Hue throughout the school year prior to the offensive, was in a tight spot. Most of the Vietnamese he knew were to some extent anti-American. Not wishing to indict all of them as Viet Cong, however, and knowing that the American official would see every anti-American as being just that, he casually replied that he knew of just one or two. Immediately the official wanted to know their names. When the IVSer rightly refused to betray any innocent friends, the tough senior American in the province denounced him roundly, called him a Communist himself, and came very close to banishing him from the province. It was not surprising that a high Buddhist monk once said,

"The Vietnamese Buddhists resent America only for misunderstanding the whole Viet Nam problem."

Hue was subjected to still worse. A Vietnamese friend cried out about the corruption that siphoned off rice from the thousands who were living in crammed conditions in temporary refugee centers. "You can't imagine it," he said. "Their conditions are dirty, smelly, in lack of food, and in especially tense spirits in the face of the sound of the bombing and shooting of all kinds that was bursting forth right before their eyes. Many of the dead had to be buried on the spot, barely covered with earth. Yet, of the rice transported from Da Nang to Hue in convoy last week, 1,000 bags were lost! During this time, the forces doing the transporting were the military and military police." He appealed to us for help from America. "I hope very much that you will find a way to inform those with power in America to be sure to raise their voices about the corruption in the relief (rice, medicine, foodstuffs) and rebuilding efforts (money, cement, metal sheeting, etc.). I hope there will be some committees to investigate immediately in order to help the refugee people in Viet Nam, especially the people of Hue in this period. That is the reason why I must write you this letter for two hours this morning."

The Struggle Movement is not over in Viet Nam, though it has been seriously weakened. Led by Thich Tri Quang, it has not been only a Buddhist movement. Liberal Catholic elements also participated, while certain of those who would call themselves Buddhists did not. The fact that the Movement was centered in Hue and Central Viet Nam (the big fighting was in Da Nang) shows that regionalism also played a part. The failure of Saigon and the Americans to understand the special characteristics of the Central Vietnamese was much to blame for all that happened.

What, then, is the Struggle Movement? In its previous manifestations, it was just what our friend in Hue had described to us under the concept of the "Third Force"—"the People." Because neither the Liberation Front nor the Saigon government seemed a satisfactory alternative to the majority of Vietnamese, it was up to someone else to lead them to a middle way. In times of social chaos, religion served as the vehicle. Here was one institution in which the people still had confidence; they could follow the pagoda's moral leadership. Some of course felt that Tri Quang's forays into the political world were for the sake of personal ambition, and Americans, though they had given him asylum from Nhu's police in 1963, could not understand him at all. "If you want to talk about charisma, Tri Quang has got it," said one official. "With his thick lips, shaven head, and intense searing gaze, he gives the impression of an ascetic from another world. God, he is an artful bastard." But Tri Quang claimed he was not engaged in politics. "I restrict myself to defending the interests of the believers," he said. There were many among the Vietnamese who felt that the Struggle was the only way to improve conditions in their country.

The Struggle, though now quiescent, is not over. How long will it last? One young student leader, before going into hiding, told us: "Until my beard reaches down to my waist," he said. "That will be a long time." The monks phrased it differently: "Cease to do evil, learn to do good, cleanse your own heart: this is the Teaching of the Buddha."

[7]

THE NAME OF THE GAME

Pacification and Its Effects

Duong's home was simple, like that of most rural families. In the middle of its one room was a handmade table flanked by two wooden benches. A large wooden bed filled the back side of the room and was the center of most of the family activity. Here Duong's father sat as he watched the youngest child while Duong, his wife, and three older children were working in the fields. When there was no company, meals were also eaten here, for Vietnamese find squatting on a wooden bed far more comfortable than sitting on wooden benches. Not only is the wooden bed the most versatile piece of furniture in the house, but it is also responsible for the excellent posture of the Vietnamese.

It was 1959 and we were visiting Duong to look at some plots of improved sweet potatoes grown from cuttings that we had given him. He had begun to harvest and other farmers in his village were interested in trying the new varieties.

On first entering the house, however, and out of respect for age, we talked with Duong's father. We had always wanted to ask about his family's trip to the South. "When did you come to this place?" we asked him.

"Our whole village came in the tenth month of 1954," he replied. "First we had a meeting in our village and discussed whether to come or not. A few wanted to remain because they did not want to leave the graves of their ancestors. Of course none of us wanted to do that, but we were afraid of the Viet Minh. We talked long into the night and decided to move to the South where we knew we would be free to follow our religion."

The old man paused, and it was Duong who took up the story again. "You see, we are Catholics," he explained. "The Viet Minh claimed that Catholicism was the religion of the French and of those who sympathized with the French. Even though they sent a man to our village to tell us that we could live in peace with the Viet Minh, we did not believe them. We had heard too much about their tricks."

"Did those who wanted to stay in the old village come also?" we asked.

"Oh yes, we all came. It was the entire village's decision. But some of our relatives in neighboring villages stayed. Sometimes we hear from them when their priest writes to Father Nam. They must send their letter to a man in Hong Kong who sends the letter to us here. It takes many months to hear from them."

"Do they like life in the North?" we asked.

"They tell us that they do. But we do not believe all they write. How can they criticize the Communists? Perhaps their letters will be opened. But the church is still standing. And all are free to attend church."

As Duong talked, the old man was fumbling through a pile of papers. "They sent us this picture of the church," he said, passing us a photograph. The edges of the picture were frayed and the front and back were grimy with thumbprints. But it was their old church in the North, still standing and obviously still in use.

"Tell us about your trip to the South," we urged the old man.

"It was very difficult," he said after a deep sigh, "—especially the day we left. We sold or traded all of our possessions except the few things we would take. I traded our beautiful blue vase and two pigs for gold earrings for my daughter-in-law. But you see that she does not wear them now. The Viet Minh took them. We sold or traded everything—my plow, the chickens, our furniture, everything. We only kept enough rice to last until we got to the city of Hai Phong and our two buffalo and the cart to carry things. After two days of travel, we were stopped. The captain asked where we were going and we told him that we were taking advantage of the agreement that allowed us to go to the South. At first he was very kind. He told us that life in the North would be very good now because the

French had been driven out. He said that Ho Chi Minh was the new president and that all religious beliefs would be respected. But we told him that we must go South."

"What happened then?" we asked.

"Then he told us that we could not take the buffalo, or the cart, or the dishes. These, he said, were the property of the state. We were very angry and sad. But we could do nothing. He left us only the pictures of our ancestors. He said that these pictures would remind us of our home in the North. After this, the trip was very hard. Only Father Nam remained in good spirits, even though he had the greatest burden of all. In the evenings he would gather us around the fire and pray. My son and grandson would go out and steal fruit and ears of corn so that we could have enough to eat. We told Father Nam that the food was given by kind villagers, but he must have known. It was a time of great shame for all. After many days of journey, we finally reached Hai Phong. There was much confusion in the city. At first we could not get to the boat area because the Viet Minh soldiers told us that no more boats were going South. But we did not listen. Finally they let us through. We found a spot for our belongings and waited for the boat to take us South."

"Tell us about the boat ride," we urged.

"The boat was crowded with people. Almost all of them were rural folk like us who had never been on a boat before. At first we liked to watch the waves and the children looked for fish. But on the second day, the waves rocked the boat and we were all sick."

"What kind of a boat was it?" we asked.

"It was an American boat," the old man answered. "Your sailors were very kind. But at first the children were all frightened. The American sailors were so big and we had heard such awful stories. Before long, however, the sailors were teaching the children how to tie knots in the ropes and showing them pictures of their own children. They became very good friends."

"Did you have any problems on the boat besides the waves which made you sick?" we inquired.

"Oh yes, we had one other problem." This time it was Duong's wife who answered. "After the waves stopped rocking the boat, we were very hungry. But the Americans cannot cook rice! Sometimes it was hardly cooked at all; sometimes it was too well cooked; but it was never right. We had to form a cooking committee to cook our own rice. Then things got better. The sailors sometimes watched us, but mostly they stayed on the deck with the children."

"When we arrived in Saigon we were taken by truck to a Catholic church," the grandfather continued. "There we were met by the priest and some Saigon soldiers."

"How funny we found the language of the soldiers!" Duong's wife interrupted with a laugh. "Even though they were Vietnamese, their accent seemed almost as strange as the language of the American sailors on the ship." She laughed again, trying to imitate the slurred tones of the southern Vietnamese.

"But we soon found out that there was little difference in language," Duong's father said. "We had to listen carefully at first, but most of the words were the same. The Saigon soldiers were very well prepared for us. They passed out sleeping mats, cooking pots, and even some rice. All the children scurried around to find some wood and paper to build a fire by which to cook."

"Father Nam was so happy," Duong said. "Now he could have mass in a church. He asked permission of the priest at the church and then rang the church bells loudly. We all went to mass before the evening meal. We prayed that we would be able to live in peace, and most of all we prayed for the safety of our relatives and friends still in the North."

"Five days later we began our last move, reaching this place which we named Ha Lan after our village in the North. The whole village always stayed together." Duong's father emphasized this last point. "We were brought here in government trucks. It is good that the government gave us our own village. It would have been hard to live in the same village with the southerners. Here in the Highlands we have room too."

"How much land do you have here?" we asked Duong.

"The government gave us one hectare [two and a half acres] of cleared land, and I have cleared two more hectares. At first I planted rice, but it does not grow well here. Now I plant only enough rice for our family. I have planted coffee on two hectares of land and corn, beans, peanuts, and sweet potatoes in between the coffee, now that the coffee plants are small."

We were all tired of sitting, and since we had come to see the sweet potatoes, Duong led us to his farmland. Part of his land was in a valley formed by a small stream, but most of it, where the coffee was planted, was on a hillside. Before the refugees had come, the area had been owned by Rhade tribesmen who practiced slash-and-burn agriculture. Now Duong was fighting the erosion that threatened during the monsoon rains. He dug small diversion ditches along the contour of the land. Occasionally, the rain had washed out the banks of one of the ditches, and we helped him to repair it while we chatted together.

"Do you like life here in the South?" we asked him.

"We want to go back to the North. I cannot grow rice here. My father has caught malaria from the mountain air. Viet Nam should not be divided. We have often talked with Father Nam about this. He tells us that we shall go back to our village in the North when there is no longer a Communist regime there. But you can see that I do not expect any change to come quickly. Coffee takes five years before it begins to bear. Some of my other neighbors only plant crops like corn and rice, saying that we will return to the North soon. They don't want to waste their time planting permanent crops like coffee and rubber. But I think we will be here for a long time."

"Has the government been of much help to you?" we asked.

"Oh yes. The government has been very helpful from the day we first arrived in the South. During the first year, until we could harvest a crop, they provided us with rice. They gave us cement to build a school, and our teacher is still paid by the government. In fact, they gave us enough cement so that we could also build our church with it. The agriculture agent from Ban Me Thuot has been helpful too. Two years ago he showed us how to dig a fishpond. We have dug the pond near our house and constructed the outhouse over the water. This way the fish feed on the night soil and we do not have to feed them. We have fresh fish throughout the year. They are a special kind that President Diem got from the Philippines. The Viet Cong propaganda said that the fish were poisonous, but President Diem came to Ban Me Thuot and ate some of the fish before many people. One of my friends saw him do this. Now many people here raise them. My father caught some this morning because he knew that you would be here for lunch. Yes, the government has been very good to us."

"Do the other villages grow the fish from the Philippines?" we asked, anxious to find new ideas to try ourselves.

"Only a few."

"Then you must show us your pond. Perhaps we can help other villages to start raising fish."

After showing us the pond, Duong pointed to the fiber crop growing in his neighbor's field. "This is kenaf," he said. "Sometimes the government does make mistakes. They told us that we could grow this and make a lot of money. Now, however, my neighbor finds that he can sell it for only a very low price. Fortunately, I didn't grow any. But he must sell it and take a loss. What else would he do with it?" We knew the story well: Viet Nam had needed a fiber with which to make rice bags, and the government had encouraged farmers in the Highlands to grown kenaf. A grading system had been carefully set up. However, no system of enforcing the grading was established, and the farmers were forced to sell all of their kenaf at the price set for the poorest grade.

"How have your sweet potatoes done?" we asked, turning finally to the original purpose of our visit.

"I have harvested many of them already," Duong replied. "The yield is good. My neighbors have asked for the vines so that they can take the cuttings for their own plots. I will sell a few at the market place in Ban Me Thuot next week."

As we returned to our own home, we discussed the fortitude of the northern refugees who had left their homes with no idea of what they would find in the distant South. Probably the most important element in their success was the guidance and inspiration that priests such as Father Nam had given them. After the priests, however, a great deal of credit for the resettlement of these approximately 900,000 northerners was rightfully earned by the American aid program and by the new Saigon government. In 1954, South Viet Nam was exhausted and in chaos after eight long years of war.

Americans were almost completely unaware of Vietnamese customs and language. Yet the tremendous job of transporting the refugees to the South and resettling them was accomplished in an orderly and efficient manner. Two essential lessons could be gleaned from this exemplary experience. First of all, the refugee program was one that everyone wanted. The refugees themselves wanted to move to the South and the Diem government wanted them to come. Second, the refugee villages, because of their unquestioned loyalty to the Diem government, were allowed considerable autonomy in governing themselves. They did so almost always through their priests, respected local leaders who enjoyed the confidence of the people.

Unfortunately, not all American and Saigon government assistance was as effective as the aid to these early refugees. Much of what followed was never seen by the population. What was seen was often not needed, not understood, and sometimes even resented. Farmers around Ban Me Thuot, for example, complained that the new superhighway there was not only irrelevant to their needs but also hurt the hooves of their buffalo when they did try to use it. The farmers also saw little benefit from U.S. assistance when it involved supporting the police in fingerprinting the population and passing out plastic identity cards. To them, the necessary I.D. card simply provided dishonest officials with another opportunity for selling government services at a profit. Nor did the Vietnamese ever understand why schools without electricity were given record players and tape recorders, or how the "national prestige" was increased by the Saigon government's decision to build a multimillion-dollar nuclear reactor in Dalat.

Some of these aid efforts were dedicated to superficial appearances or to impressing the various national leaders, especially President Ngo Dinh Diem. When it was learned that Diem was going to Dalat, for example, trees and branches were cut and driven into the ground along the full length of the fifteen-mile highway from the airport into town. Villagers were told to put up large gateways prior to his visit with the slogan "Long Live President Ngo Dinh Diem." Even American technicians joined in, each trying to outdo the other in ingenuity. A major effort was made to make muskmelons grow because it was learned that the President liked muskmelons; in the end, these attempts failed. A radio broadcasting studio was installed in one of Diem's palace bedrooms; the control room, in a bathroom next door, was elaborately soundproofed to avoid embarrassment if the toilet were flushed while he was on the air. In the end, the studio was never used.

In these projects, one element was forgotten: the people. Dignitaries involved in the aid program visited the villages, taking picnic lunches and cameras, but seldom seeing what was really going on. Their trips were usually planned around a swim at Nha Trang's beach, a tiger hunt, or a visit to an "exotic" Montagnard hamlet. Occasionally, we were asked to go on these tours to explain what the "rice-roots level" was like. In one typical case, we had received a telegram to meet visitors at the airport at 8 A.M. We arrived at the airport just as the province chief got there. The province chief had a list of those expected and he carefully arranged the cars and jeeps. At 10:30, late as usual, the plane landed. The band that the province chief often seemed able to find on such occasions played the Vietnamese national anthem, and after everyone had shaken hands all around, we headed for the prewarned village. We arrived an hour later, by which time the business suits of the visitors had all assumed the same dusty red color of the Highlands soil. About a mile before reaching the new gate of the village, the advance guard had turned on its siren. Thus, by the time we reached the tiny thatch houses, children were out cheering and clapping their hands. The visitors waved and smiled back. The children's parents stood at attention as we drove by, looking neither left nor right. The advance jeep came to a screeching halt at the village headquarters and six soldiers jumped out. They stood at attention while the dignitaries filed into the meeting room where a lecture was presented on the progress of the village. It was the province chief who gave the lecture, though his only knowledge of the village was what he had gathered during earlier tours there with other visitors. Then we were all taken to the dispensary where a local girl who had received some training in Saigon passed out medicines to a long line of villagers. One of the guests complimented her on her clean, new uniform, and we rushed back to Ban Me Thuot, the cheers still ringing in our ears from the little children as we drove away.

Two weeks later we returned to the same place with an agricultural agent to distribute a few fruit trees. Most of the villagers were out in the fields tending their crops. The dispensary was closed. One of the little boys asked us why we didn't have a siren, and the village chief asked if we knew anything about the new tractor "the American aid man promised" on that earlier occasion. We told him that we knew nothing of the promise. If aid for his village would be limited to our fruit trees, he must have wondered, then why all the hoopla before?

Somehow the drive that had been so effective in resettling the refugees from the North lost steam in later years. Civil liberties were curbed, and more and more of the country's able leaders were imprisoned or left the country in exile. In An Giang, the province chief, accompanied by an armed escort, told refugee farmers that just because their land had been "distributed" to them did not mean that they would not have to pay the "rightful owners." The farmers were upset, feeling they had been duped when given the land. But this soon became common practice; as the government gained control in an area, the old landlords returned and collected past rents. The Saigon government, as it grew stronger, became more repressive and less responsive. The government had forgotten the people.

To meet growing insurgency among the rural population, the strategic hamlet program was initiated in 1962. The purpose of the strategic hamlets was to prevent contact between villagers and the Viet Cong. Villagers were either encouraged or ordered to move into central locations and then to dig a moat and build a stockade around their settlement. It was felt that by concentrating many people in one place, the Viet Cong could be prevented from getting food and intelligence. At the same time, social and economic services such as schools and first-aid stations were to be provided. By the end of July, 1963, Councilor Ngo Dinh Nhu estimated that approximately 75 per cent of Viet Nam's hamlets were completed in strategic hamlet form. This represented 8,737,613 people, the government news agency, Vietnam Press, added. These were highly inflated figures, however—like those in most other progress estimates on Viet Nam.

Part of the theory behind the strategic hamlet was that by moving all of the "friendlies" into concentrated areas, everyone outside these areas could be easily identified as the "enemy." In a frank admission of the earlier problems faced by Saigon troops in pursuing the Viet Cong guerrillas, Nhu had said: "Since we did not know where the enemy was, ten times we launched a military operation, nine times we missed the Viet Cong, and the tenth time we struck right on the head of the population." The strategic hamlets made the decisions easy: anyone caught outside the designated areas was considered a Viet Cong.

American officials found the strategic hamlet idea exciting. At last, it seemed, there was a "revolutionary" program. The American aid office passed out yellow strategic hamlet pins, strategic hamlet stamps, strategic hamlet matchbooks, and strategic hamlet school notebooks. All bore the strategic hamlet symbol: a flaming torch of freedom. The notebooks were to cause certain difficulties later, after Diem's fall from power. Because a short history of his rule had been included in them, and because history then had to be rewritten, an order was issued by the Ministry of Education stating that the otherwise beautiful and valuable notebooks could no longer be used or distributed. This seemed like such a waste that we often neglected to abide by the order, much to the chagrin of fearful Vietnamese officials. In any case, the optimism of American officials toward the strategic hamlets was expressed in an AID report of mid-1963: "The strategic hamlet program is a daring, imaginative effort to build a nation and in so doing, to defeat a long-continued, cancerous insurgency." The program was compared with the successful British counterinsurgency campaign in Malaya. Those who made the comparisons, however, failed to take into consideration the tremendous differences between the two situations. In Malaya, for example, the insurgents were almost all Chinese. They were thus easily distinguishable from the darker Malays, the predominant element in the rural population. In Malaya, during the ten-year period from 1950 to 1960, relatively few people had to suffer the upsets of relocation, while in Vietnam over half the population was claimed to have been put in the strategic hamlets in slightly more than a year. Alienation was thus less in Malaya than in Viet Nam.

Ngo Dinh Nhu saw the strategic hamlets as changing the whole strategy of the war. "From now on, whenever Communists want to launch an attack they must attack the fortified villages," his officials claimed. The strategic hamlets, Nhu reasoned, would put the Viet Cong into the position of "fish out of water." "Now," he argued, "our forces are able to conduct guerrilla warfare while the Communists are forced to fight a conventional war." He envisioned the strategic hamlets as the vehicle for bringing about a social revolution. "A new social hierarchy will be established," government propaganda proclaimed. "At the top of this new social order will be the anti-Communist combatants and their families."

But the people were unhappy. Many of them complained to us that they did not want to move into a strategic hamlet. "It is far from our gardens and riceland," one farmer told us, "and we have to walk a long way to work our land. How can we protect the mangoes from the birds when our children are not playing nearby? How will we keep strangers from catching the fish in our pond when we are not there? Who will watch over the graves of our ancestors? The hamlet chief, who was not selected by us, has ordered all of the people to move to this strategic hamlet so the army can protect us. But do they protect us? The Front has burned this strategic hamlet three times. Each time the Saigon army ran away. We are prisoners here. We cannot leave until eight in the morning and we must be back before six in the evening. If we are late, we are insulted and sometimes even slapped by the Civil Guardsmen. Our chickens are stolen by the soldiers. But we are forced to live in the strategic hamlet."

In a strategic hamlet near My Tho, the villagers complained about not being able to harvest their rice. "I had two hectares of rice in the old village," one old man said bitterly. "Now it is ripe and the grain falls into the paddy mud. I cannot harvest it. There are men here with guns who tell me that we must dig a ditch more than a meter deep and two meters across. In the bottom of that ditch we must put sharpened bamboo stakes and on each side of the ditch there must be a fence of barbed wire. When it is finished, I can return to harvest my rice. But my rice will be gone then. Who will feed my family?"

In another hamlet, people complained that the government-appointed hamlet chief had taken advantage of them. "We had to go into the forest and cut bamboo to make a stockade around our village. This was very hard work, but we did not complain. Now we have learned, however, that in the other hamlets the people were paid three piasters for each piece of bamboo. We got nothing. We were only told that it was our duty to cut the bamboo. Now the hamlet chief is gone, taking the money that we should have received. You Americans have a very good heart to give the money for the bamboo stakes, but the money goes to corrupt officials."

The Saigon government overextended itself, and even the best-intentioned officials could not meet the promises made for new schools, dispensaries, and various self-help projects. Often a school would be built, but there would be no teacher. A dispensary would be set up, but a nervous district chief would not allow the villagers to have any medicines because he was afraid that the Viet Cong would get them. A community fishpond was dug, only to have the fish die because some official forgot to deliver them on time. Local officials did not always know what the program was about. Frightened by the pressures from Ngo Dinh Nhu, they used forced labor to build the stockades and moats, and false statistics to give the impression that they were moving faster than they actually were. One Vietnamese official summed up the program to us in this way: "Asking the villagers to dig a hole around their village in the hot sun while their rice became overripe and fell to the ground was perfect propaganda for the Viet Cong. Instead of separating the population from the Viet Cong, we were making Viet Cong."

Militarily the hamlets never worked as well as it was hoped they would. Many of them stretched along a road for several miles, making it impossible to defend any particular spot. In the Highlands, some were built so low that they were especially vulnerable to attack from higher ground overlooking the hamlet. When they were attacked, assistance seldom came because the Saigon troops were afraid the Viet Cong might have set an ambush along the canal or highway as part of their attack on the hamlet. Often there were

Viet Cong agents within the hamlets themselves, agents who had at least the tacit support of the villagers. It was not difficult for Viet Cong to infiltrate, as we found on a midday visit to one hamlet in Kien Giang province.

While we were there, the sentry stood at the gate of the fortified hamlet, shirt unbuttoned, his hot steel helmet placed to one side. A woman approached, then stopped at the gate. The sentry pointed at a bundle which was securely wrapped in a newspaper. An argument followed. After three or four minutes the woman turned and walked deliberately into the hamlet. The soldier watched, helplessly.

We wandered over and asked, "What did she have in her bundle?"

"I don't know," the soldier answered sheepishly. "She wouldn't tell. She said I was nosy and that it was none of my business. She is a friend of my mother's cousin. What could I do?"

"Did you explain the military regulations?" we asked, thinking it might make the task easier in some later crisis.

"No. How could I? That would mean I didn't trust her. Besides, people don't like regulations around here."

"How long has the hamlet been here?"

"Only about three months. We came at the time of rice harvest. Many people are angry about this because they could not harvest their rice. They had to dig the moat in the hot sun. One day a government official came and Mr. Tan, one of the villagers, gave him a very difficult time. 'Why dig this hole in the hot sun?' Mr. Tan asked the official. The official gave a very long lecture. He told everyone that the moat must be dug so that the Viet Cong could not enter the hamlet. After he left, everyone laughed for many days." The sentry stopped and, seeing our perplexed look, added, "You see, Mr. Tan was a Viet Cong himself!"

"But why didn't someone report him?" we asked.

"Well, you see, the official was from the city." This seemed reason enough to the guard at the gate, but we kept pressing him, and he added the other problems involved: "If we had told the official that Mr. Tan was a Viet Cong, he would have been taken away. He has five children, you know. Besides, maybe if the government keeps all the promises that it has made, he will decide to join the government side. People in this hamlet think he would make a good hamlet chief." The confusing array of statements by the guard was made carefully, as if he felt it might be dangerous to commit himself too far. The situation in that strategic hamlet was obviously a very fluid one.

After Diem fell and the strategic hamlet program disintegrated, an attempt was made to salvage the best parts in a "new life hamlet" plan. As far as we could tell, however, only the name was changed. Attempts to maintain control over much of the rural population were rendered futile through a combination of factors: one was the peasants' resentment against the strategic hamlets; another was the lack of central direction due to rapid changes in government; and a third was the growing strength of the Viet Cong, particularly in these rural areas. When the military regime of Nguyen Cao Ky took over in 1965, a new thrust of energy was directed at the village level, and the name was changed again, this time to "pacification."

"Pacification" was an old term. It was first used hundreds of years ago by the Chinese who talked in terms of pacifying the rebellious villages and provinces that objected to the foreign Chinese rule. Partly for this reason and the historical memories raised, the word "pacification" was not used for very long in modern Viet Nam. It was soon changed to the currently used "rural reconstruction" in Vietnamese and to "revolutionary development" (RevDev) in English. The difference in names between the two languages was attributed by a Vietnamese involved in the program to the American desire to invoke dramatic images of progress. "We know we're not all that revolutionary," he said with a knowing smile. Yet, no name has been permanent and little has been new. Along with RevDev have come more reminders of the past. Some especially superior hamlets came to be known as "Ap Doi Moi," usually translated in English as "*new* new life hamlets." And to the American military, the name of the game has been not so much pacification or RevDev or new new life as "winning hearts and minds"—also known by its pungent acronym, WHAM.

The emphasis in all these stages has been on protecting the villagers from the Viet Cong and on destroying the Viet Cong infrastructure in the hamlets. To do this, the villagers are "won" through economic and social improvements, often measured in terms of bulgur wheat, cement, schoolbooks, and aspirins. "Every quantitative measure we have says we're winning the war," it was often declared. Yet such a materialistic approach has failed to move the peasants, and even the best-conceived plans have seemed to go awry in practice.

To say there are no differences among the various programs would of course be unfair. Certainly there are some. While the strategic hamlet concept relied mainly on the personnel resources of the villagers themselves, for example, the RevDev teams have introduced something new: the fifty-nine-man team from outside. In theory, these cadres, as they are called, are to re-establish self-defense in the village, uncover Viet Cong agents, initiate self-help projects, and in general develop village loyalty to the Saigon government. In theory, the plan may sound good: The cadres are to act as "imitation VC" for the Saigon government, fighting the enemy by using his own methods. By general function, the primary emphasis of forty-one of the fifty-nine members is in the military and intelligence fields. The largest group, consisting of thirty-three armed propaganda members, is responsible for detecting and destroying the political/military infrastructure of the Viet Cong in the villages. Six census grievance members are to survey and classify the people in the area being pacified and "keep track of the thinking and activities of the friendly and enemy infrastructure, gather information, and report about the genuine aspirations of the rural people." The functions of two psywar and intelligence specialists are more or less evident from their titles. Secondary emphasis, to the tune of fifteen members, is devoted to assisting the villagers solve their problems of administration, health, agriculture, and education. The six civil affairs members are prepared to temporarily take over the village administration and generally assist in starting village organization, including the election of administrative committees and village councils. The three medics and six new life development cadres pass out medicine, treat cuts and skin diseases, encourage self-help projects, and distribute relief goods. None of these functions are seen as narrowly defined. The armed propaganda cadres are admonished to help the villagers in such daily tasks as harvesting rice and carrying water, while the economic cadres are also trained to help protect the village in case of attack.

The cadres are trained near the coastal resort town of Vung Tau. A two-hour drive from Saigon, Vung Tau once provided the most popular weekend diversion for middle-class Saigon residents. Now, off-and-on security and the presence of thousands of American GI's have made the trip less appealing. In a rather secluded spot outside Vung Tau, Vietnamese and American instructors teach the trainees a few basic technical skills, propaganda techniques, methods of self-survival, and village defense. Above all, they try to instill an *esprit de corps* and loyalty to the Saigon government. Lieutenant Colonel Nguyen Be, director of the training center, seeks to produce cadres who will bring about a revolution not only against the Viet Cong, but also against corruption and apathy among provincial authorities. Patriotic songs are sung, slogans are learned, and such intricate skills as setting traps to ambush Viet Cong are mastered. After ten weeks at Vung Tau, the graduate trainees go out into rural Viet Nam, ready to combat the enemies of the people: Viet Cong terrorism and corrupt government officials.

The cadres leave Vung Tau with instructions to become part of the villagers' lives. Each of the fifty-nine members is to move in with a family and "dress the same as the people, speak the same as the people, work together with the people, and share the people's pleasure and sadness." The members are not to steal anything from the people, and everything that they use is to be paid for. In other words, they go into the village with the same instructions as the Viet Cong, who solemnly repeat as part of their oath of honor, "I swear that in my relationships with the people I will do three things and refrain from three things. I will respect, protect, and help the people; I will not steal from, threaten, or inconvenience the people. I will do all things to win their confidence."

It has been upon arrival in the villages that the shortcomings of the program stand out clearly. Although some teams have been successful, the program has grown too fast. The first ten-week course, beginning in early 1966, trained 4,700 cadres. The instructors have not been prepared for such numbers, many have never taught before, and there was no precedent for handling the kinds of problems that such massive training and indoctrination required. Moreover, the provinces have not understood the principles of pacification or how to use the cadres properly. The government cannot recruit large enough numbers of cadres locally, and so young men have been selected from Saigon, Da Nang, and other provincial towns. Being outsiders, they have then been subject to local suspicions. Often only 17 or 18 years old and without a rural background, the draft-exempt cadres have sometimes hidden behind the façade of authoritarianism that their rifles give them. The cartoon of the Vietnamese peasant, just freed from Viet Cong rule, protesting that "sure we're glad to be free, but do we have to be pacified?" has a bitter ring of authenticity. Finally, even the best trained and most highly motivated cadres have found the harsh realities of both rural life and government bureaucracy to be deeply discouraging. Thousands have written to Colonel Be for advice on the problems they face. But for most, the only answer is patience and dedication. Against the staggering conditions they confront, the cadres must wonder whether there is any hope at all for their mission.

On the surface, the job does not sound so difficult. The first duty of the pacification team is to map the villages. The members of each family are carefully listed, indicating age and occupation; later those with suspicious Viet Cong connections are marked for special attention. While the mapping is going on, some of the team members work on establishing rapport with the villagers. The medics set up a special sick call, those with a flair for music or dramatics organize evening programs, and the agriculturalist demonstrates such specialties as how to grow mushrooms. Gradually "interfamily groups" are formed for each five houses, and the head of one household is appointed group leader. Sometimes photos of the young people are collected which, along with the population map, help the team to spot suspicious strangers when they appear.

The task of the six census grievance members is the most delicate. Their purpose is, first, to find out the villagers' grievances so that the other team members are able to meet local needs more effectively, and then to find out the make-up of the Viet Cong infrastructure in the village. Moving too fast would cause distrust, resentment, and even fear among the villagers. The approach is to interview the villagers separately and over a prolonged period. This way the interviewer can instill a feeling of trust and assure the interviewee that no one will ever know the information that has been revealed. The first questions deal with the villagers' needs and are intended to establish a feeling of trust. "What are the needs of the community?" "Is there anyone sick in your family? We have a medic, you know." "What do you think about the local government officials?" "Do you know of examples of corruption?" "Are your children going to school?"

Gradually the interviewer gets into more sensitive questions: "Do the VC visit your hamlet often?" "How often?" "What do they say?" "Who do they visit?" "Who speaks out against the government during these meetings?" "Does anyone in the hamlet have relatives with the VC?" "Who are the VC sympathizers in this hamlet?" Many of the peasants never dare to give information. Although for some it is because they sympathize with the VC, most pretend ignorance because they do not wish to get involved. Some do give information: sometimes out of loyalty to the government side, occasionally out of spite, and often unconsciously.

Once a VC member has been identified, the government has several courses of action, depending upon the local situation and the position the VC holds in the Viet Cong structure. If he is not important, he can be confronted with the evidence against him and offered a chance to renounce his VC ties. Under certain conditions, an attempt is made to recruit him as a double agent. Sometimes a VC agent is just arrested and put in the provincial jail. If he is an important member and it is felt that the villagers need to be taught a lesson, then arrangements can be made for him to have an accident.

Such "accidents" can be arranged by any one of three groups involved in the use of terror against the Viet Cong. The most obvious of these is the national police. Unfortunately, guilt is often difficult to prove and the police have not been known for their kindness or even for their objectivity. In carrying out their job, they, too, often forget the people. The name of the game has seemed more and more to be not pacification or winning hearts and minds, but arbitrary repression and losing the people's allegiance. In mid-1968 the Saigon *Daily News* made an editorial plea for curbing the power of the police:

Torture and arbitrary arrests make a mockery of the Constitution. It is idle to pledge to uphold the Constitution without stopping the police from resorting to torture to obtain confession. The Constitution says "no citizen can be tortured, threatened or forced to confess."

An insufficiently supervised police force like our present police force becomes a terror. The gist of the matter is that a policeman is promoted for action leading to the conviction of a criminal, that the courts accept confession as evidence of guilt, and that, in consequence, it is to the interest of individual officers to torture arrested persons until they confess. This evil has been rampant. . . .

To us the arrests were very real. Vietnamese we had known or with whom we had worked, and friends with whom we had perhaps discussed such ideas as democracy, would one day disappear. In 1963 it was Hanh who was taken away by the secret police. In 1965 it was Khanh who was thrown in a horrible prison for not carrying his military deferment certificate one day while walking downtown. We told the police chief we would be glad to take his place in jail long enough for Khanh to run home and get the missing document. Finally, after he was released, Khanh told us that if anything could convince him and his fellow prisoners to join the Viet Cong, it was the appalling conditions to which the government subjected him in that prison. There was no end. In 1966 it was a friend involved in the Struggle Movement who disappeared. Later we found that he too was in prison, and we drove out to visit him. The director of the camp was friendly; he served beer and asked if we could teach him English. But we couldn't visit the prisoners; that was illegal.

One evening an IVS volunteer, hearing that one of his Vietnamese coworkers had been suddenly arrested, went to see the young man's father. The old gentleman invited him inside and then passed over a note he had written. The note said:

My son was arrested by the National Police, 237 Cong Hoa, Saigon's street, from March 31, 1967. Since my son is not released, I please you intervene for my son, thus he can free and come back home.

As you know, I am recently lose my younger son, death in the battlefield. I am very suffering. Before my bitterness situation I hope you to pay attention for my family, to interfere for my son.

The brutality of the police became still more painful to us when another friend was picked up. For years Mai had been unable to return to her native village because it was insecure. Because she could not go back to her village, she had no identification papers. She worked with Americans, however, and did not worry. One day, though, she was stopped at a checkpoint after visiting a friend in the countryside. The officials demanded her identification papers and permission to enter the city. She replied that she had no such papers, but that she worked for Americans and they could vouch for her identity.

"If you work for the Americans, then you can work for the Viet Cong," she was told.

She was beaten for several hours until she was senseless and had to be taken to a hospital. There she spent the next two and a half months. Then she was taken to jail, where she continued to be kept on the charge of having relatives with the Viet Cong and of having worked with the Viet Cong. "I am so miserable," she told us in a crudely written letter smuggled out of the hospital. "They beat me so badly. Can nobody help me?"

In 1968, a Saigon newspaper estimated there were about 100,000 people in prison, many of them existing in horrid conditions:

The Can Tho provincial jail was built by the French for 500 prisoners, is now used to keep over 2,000. Other prisoners through the country are under similar situation. Detainees have no room to sit. Legs of most prisoners have been swollen for having to stand on their feet to sleep. . . . They are also trained to live without washing like hyppies [*sic*], although the Mekong River which flows across Can Tho never dries. They are also trained not to go to the toilets, because in fact, there are only some toilets which have been out of use for how long nobody knows.

One of the most striking [things] at the Can Tho jail is that it is really a nudist camp. No prisoner has a piece of cloth for their bodies, but so far they have not been accused of indecency. Is this a compensation for their other freedoms? The prisoners do not see any beauty on their skinny bodies, and never like to look at them. They have to expose them because it is as hot inside the prison as it is in an oven.

The image of the Saigon police and of the forces of "law and order" was further blemished when a deputy of the Constituent Assembly, Tran Van Van, was assassinated in late 1966. Though the Saigon government blamed Viet Cong terrorists, most Vietnamese felt that the regime itself was responsible for his death. Van had been an outspoken critic of the Ky regime and was widely respected by Vietnamese at large. Suspicions over the incident grew when the Saigon *Guardian* printed a picture of the assassin at the time of the murder. When this picture was compared with the man Ky later executed for Van's murder, it became obvious to Vietnamese that the executed man was not the man who had committed the crime. Intrigue heightened as the Ministry of Information then suspended the *Guardian* for publishing "a photo which does not reflect the truth and which causes confusion in the public mind." Nineteen months later the editor felt free to comment on the charge: "To me," he said, "a photo is not supposed to reflect anything. It simply shows a scene. And how a photo can tell a lie is beyond my comprehension."

In addition to the national police, there have been two military groups involved in counterterrorist activities: the provincial reconnaissance units (PRU) and the civil irregular defense group (CIDG). The ranks of the PRU have included many Viet Cong returnees and ex-convicts. "Sat Cong," or "Kill Communists," is tattooed on the right side of their chests to prevent them from returning to their comrades in the jungles, and emblems are sewn on their camouflage shirts, giving them the nickname, "skull and crossbones." In the case of the CIDG, American Special Forces have recruited most of them from the ethnic minority groups. Since these minority groups were already considered "savages" by many of the Vietnamese majority, one of the sad by-products of this policy is to further this image and thus make understanding and reconciliation more difficult after the war.

Both the PRU and CIDG have received their pay from U.S. sources, in the first instance from the CIA and in the second from the Green Berets. Part of the reason for this direct American involvement is that the Saigon government cannot justify paying a higher wage than it gives its own soldiers. More important, however, has been the opportunity for more U.S. control over the groups. In the words of one Green Beret, "We had no control over Diem's secret police. By having a direct association with the CIDG we can direct their activities." When asked why the "counterterror" squads were formed in the first place, he shrugged and said, "Somebody has to do the dirty work."

To Vietnamese, the use of these methods of control has meant that the Saigon and U.S. governments are willing to use the same methods as the Viet Cong, to "fight fire with fire." The same disgust felt among the citizenry over inhumane Viet Cong tactics has been felt by Vietnamese who note the similarity between the Viet Cong and the PRU or the National Police. They nod and observe that "it is usually the poor who suffer." Or, as one old man commented upon reading the description of a particularly brutal deed, "One is never quite sure which side did it."

The use of force and military strength has not always been bad, of course. When such force is used to protect the people rather than to terrorize them, it is often appreciated. One of the best examples of this is the program to protect the rice crops. At harvest time, RevDev teams go into the fields with the farmers, guns strapped to their backs. They remain long enough to complete the harvest and to allow the farmers to sell the excess production. In fact they often force the farmers to sell any excess so that it will not later go to the Viet Cong. This assistance has been hard for the NLF to counteract. If they go into the village after harvest, they can extort some rice, but only from that amount which the farmer and his family have saved for their own meager needs. Taking this rice would clearly be detrimental to their desired image of being the people's benefactors.

The civilian side of the pacification program has also brought many improvements to the villages. Schools have been provided where none existed before, and textbooks have been given to tens of thousands of school children. Village wells have been dug, bridges repaired, and water-management schemes developed. Medical dispensaries have been built and nurses trained to pass out medicines and give thousands of immunizations. Self-help instruments, ranging from sewing machines to blacksmith kits, have been presented to needy families. Self-help projects, supported by U.S. goods, have made canals, new market places, and roads possible.

In the end, however, many of the good deeds have been over-shadowed by the bad. The former have seemed too much like a drop in the bucket or a corn plaster on an amputation. Besides the matter of police excesses, one of those deeds which has negative effects is defoliation. Defoliation is not a part of pacification, yet it affects pacification efforts, making them very difficult to carry out. While the military has seen it as "resource control," or a way of keeping food from the enemy, the farmers see the "medicine from the sky," as they often call it, as their biggest agricultural problem. The military defoliates the roadsides and canal banks to prevent Viet Cong ambushes, but it is also here that the farmers grow most of their fruits and vegetables so they can get them easily to market. The generals order jungle areas defoliated to destroy the cover for the enemy, yet wind carries the defoliant ten or fifteen miles and it destroys the farmers' bananas, papayas, and coconut trees. The military policy of destroying rice fields in NLF-controlled areas is intended to deprive Viet Cong soldiers of their source of food, but, as in any famine, it is the weak—the women, children, and old men who grow the rice—who suffer most.

Despite elaborate plans for reimbursement to farmers whose crops have been damaged by defoliants, payments are rarely made. The paperwork is too difficult and the procedures almost impossible to follow. For example, the government requires that an official visit the damaged area, but the farmers cannot get the officials to come to their farms. Many of the province chiefs report the damage, collect the payments, but never repay the farmers. One former minister of economy complained that many province chiefs actually ask for defoliation of large areas of their provinces so that they can collect the payments for themselves. Over a million acres of jungle and cropland were defoliated in one year, 1967, and many more were partially destroyed by wind drift.

There has been growing concern about the long-term adverse effects of defoliation. One danger is laterization, or hardening of the soil, which would make the soil useless for agricultural production. This occurs in the tropics when there is lack of sufficient vegetative cover to afford protection from the blazing sun. There is also a danger that the widespread destruction of plant life will starve to extinction rare species of wildlife such as the Douc Langur monkey and the Indochinese gibbon. Yet no one knows what the final effects of such massive defoliation will be. "The extent and pattern of herbicide treatment in Vietnam have no precedent," a Defense Department study concluded. "Therefore it is difficult to predict the effects . . . with any accuracy." Despite this ignorance of the long-range effects on the soil and on the fine balance between plant and animal life in Viet Nam, defoliant expenditures were nevertheless increased from ten million dollars in 1965 to seventy million in 1968.

There are, of course, military advantages to defoliation. Still, the long-run disadvantages outweigh them. Thus, while defoliation increases the visibility of pilots flying over jungle areas, it creates a new cover for the Viet Cong—in the farmers' houses. While defoliation makes it more difficult for the enemy to set up ambushes along the roads, it alienates the population and creates more Viet Cong to set up ambushes elsewhere. Failure to fully consider the feelings of the people has destroyed many of the positive effects that pacification workers in the area might have enjoyed.

One Viet Cong prisoner explained how he used defoliation for his own propaganda purposes. "We told the people that the Americans sprayed the chemicals to destroy crops and starve the people so that they could invade the country. Thus they should fight the American imperialists." When he was asked whether the people believed him, he answered, "Yes, they believed us and hated the Americans." We saw this ourselves. When a farmer's watermelons turned black, the allegiance of that farmer to the Saigon government was lost. Instead of reporting Viet Cong activities in his area, he then showed the Viet Cong his blackened watermelons and tomatoes, invited them in for tea, and sent his children up and down the road to whistle when the Saigon troops came. The Viet Cong, as a result, could then escape or push the plunger on a mine they may have set. In 1958, villagers remembered vividly the French who had said, "Killing one buffalo is as good as killing one Viet Minh." They remembered the French practice of trying to destroy the Viet Minh by destroying the food source for them. Ten years later a Vietnamese columnist would write about the American presence in the same way: "Our peasants will remember their cratered rice fields and defoliated forests, devastated by an alien air force that seems at war with the very land of Vietnam."

One high official who seemed especially aware of the negative effect of this military approach on pacification was Deputy Ambassador William Porter. We found that we could discuss with him the problems of defoliation, refugee generation, indiscriminate bombings, and general over-Americanization and expect that the matter would be taken directly to the Ambassador or to the military themselves. His concern about the indiscriminate bombings in the South led him to spend part of his Sundays listening to the radio transmissions by forward air controllers, the men in the light planes who direct the bombing strikes. "When I returned from church today," Porter is reported to have once told a military officer, "I was listening to one of your forward air controllers. He called in a strike on a village, giving a set of coordinates. A while later he said the bombers had hit the wrong village and he gave them a new set of coordinates so they could hit the right one next time."

On another occasion, the Vietnamese leaders of the Eighth District in Saigon complained that too many Americans were visiting their district as a result of the publicity received from Vice-President Humphrey's visit. Local people began to feel that the project (see Chapter 12) was "just another American program," and the leaders found that much of their time was being used in showing the Americans around. Porter immediately issued orders that in the future all visits by Americans would have to be cleared by him.

In arguing against over-Americanization and overmilitarization, however, even Porter was unsuccessful. More and more of the control over pacification slipped from his hands, and eventually he left Viet Nam. In mid-1967 the whole program was placed under the ultimate control of General Westmoreland and the military. This large role of the military in pacification has had disastrous effects. The province chiefs who are responsible for cadre assignments have thought of them as a military force rather than as economic and social cadres. Consequently, they have been used to plug up holes in the defense perimeter around province capitals and sometimes even as "shock troops." The NLF has thus seen the teams not only as a threat in winning the hearts and minds of the villagers but also as a direct military threat, and it has taken every opportunity it can to annihilate the teams.

The villagers have been caught in the middle of all this. To refuse the "protection" of a pacification team causes them to be suspected of having Viet Cong sympathies. To accept the team puts their village on the VC blacklist. Even if the pacification team can give the needed protection, it is likely to leave in six months or sooner. Stability has little improved since the days of 1964 when a U.S. government report summarized military movements in a small area of Long An province:

January 15	One battalion occupies the first four hamlets.
January 28	Troops ordered into second four hamlets over objections of MAAG and USOM [Military Assistance Advisory Group and U.S. Operations Mission (AID)]. Minimum essential tasks in first four not yet complete.
February 23	Troops withdrawn from hamlets.
February 24	New battalion assigned to hamlets.
February 26	Troops withdrawn from hamlets.
March 9	Troops returned to hamlets in anticipation of visit by Secretary McNamara.
March 12	Troops withdrawn from hamlets.
March 14	Troops return, occupy four new hamlets without prior planning or notification.
March 15	New battalion assigned to hamlets.
March 17	Troops withdrawn from hamlets.
March 18	New battalion assigned to hamlets, but does not actually occupy them.
March 24	New battalion assigned to hamlets; security of Highway #4 takes priority.
April 2	Troops withdrawn from hamlets. Replaced same day for visit by Mr. Richard Nixon.
April 7	New battalion assigned to hamlets.
April 8	Troops withdrawn from hamlets.
April 11	Troops return to hamlets. Using them as base only to protect Tan An City and Highway #4.

An example of the problems this kind of "protection" can cause for the Vietnamese is reflected in the fate of Son Tra. A pacification team and a small group of U.S. Marines forming a Combined Action

Platoon were stationed in this refugee hamlet to provide protection and carry out economic programs. On a June night in 1968, in what U.S. authorities described as "perhaps the worst atrocity of the war," Viet Cong forces entered the village and killed eighty-eight of the inhabitants. When they left, they erected a sign: "Don't cooperate with the Americans."

Pacification has been seen by the Vietnamese as an American program. It was, after all, conceived of and financed by the Americans, and to a large extent by the CIA. The national cadre training center at Vung Tau was founded by the CIA, and the American advisers there, so Vietnamese say, are CIA members. Many Vietnamese have felt uneasy about this cloak-and-dagger backing. It has branded the operations as clandestine rather than economic. To Vietnamese it has seemed there must be something beneath the surface. "What is this secret society of young men paid by a foreign government doing in our villages?" they asked in various ways. By 1968, in fact, over forty thousand cadres, better trained and more highly motivated than many army units, had gone through the Vung Tau training program. Not only is the pacification program important in military terms, but it has the responsibility for administering large amounts of money. Thus, control over the whole apparatus, whether by Americans or by certain Vietnamese, can be a source of considerable power in doling out jobs, reconstruction funds, and materials. To further complicate this element, there is the unstated policy of employing right-wing political factions. In Central Viet Nam, where the antigovernment Struggle Movement is the most powerful political group, it seems that members of the pacification teams were carefully selected so that the Catholic religious minority and the right-wing VNQDD (Viet Nam Quoc Dan Dang) and Dai Viet parties dominate membership. Many Central Vietnamese have seen this as a move to arm the political opposition and to hold it as a threat over the followers of the Buddhist Thich Tri Quang. This feeling was strengthened when some of the cadres were used by the government at the time of the 1966 Buddhist crisis in Hue.

To the peasant, the most compelling argument for the pacification program has been the promise of protection while he receives the economic improvements. But the government has not always been able to keep this promise, as the 1968 NLF Tet offensive proved. First, enormous numbers of U.S. troops were tied to defending outposts like Khe Sanh. Then with lightning swiftness and very detailed coordination, waves of NLF and North Vietnamese guerrillas began to attack the cities. With these attacks, the pacification teams, not to mention the Saigon government troops assigned to protect them, were pulled in to protect the cities. The rural areas were left to fend for themselves. It was clear that American and Saigon troops could not provide security for both the cities and the rural areas. It was also clear that in case a choice had to be made, the cities, the fortresses of the governing class, would get the troops. Later the pacification teams went back to the rural areas—but they themselves would have less confidence and their military functions would be emphasized over their civilian functions. After all, they now knew that in case of emergency they could no longer depend on the troops to protect them. The villagers were even more convinced that they should not put their trust and allegiance in these "visitors from the cities."

No matter how many times the program or the program's name has been changed, and no matter how good the theories have sounded, pacification has never seemed to work very well. The villagers, in short, have not been impressed. They have become rather cynical of the crazy new plans emanating from Saigon or Washington, each one intended to save their country. To them, it is all the same game.

We tried to understand how one village saw pacification one hot August afternoon. We were working in a new refugee camp where a pacification team had been assigned. A group of refugees huddled around their few possessions. On the north side a long pit privy was being dug. From the east the sound of a water pump could be heard—a pleasant reminder to us that the water shortage had been solved. Pacification cadres scurried about in their black peasant pajamas. Young Miss Van was leading a group of children in song. Two of the cadres were operating a health clinic nearby. Above the putt-putt of the water pump, the smack of lumber hitting the ground mingled with the curses of the GI's who had brought it. And close by, the bomb crates the soldiers brought were being torn apart by the cadres for later use. We had been working with these cadres, carefully pulling nails from the crates and putting them into a salad-oil can. We used our rest break to talk to the villagers.

"Have you selected the site for your new home?" we asked one man who had looked up as we approached.

"Yes," the man smiled, "we have."

"Where will you live?"

The man seemed confused at first, but then smiled again. "I am not sure. The man in the tent put an 'X' on a piece of paper. We will live in that place. He said it was a good place."

"What do you think of all the young cadres here to help you?"

"We like them. They are helping us to have new homes." He stopped and smiled again, though nervously this time. Perhaps he thought we were government agents.

We wandered on and stopped and squatted by an old woman. We asked her what she thought of the situation.

"We were forced to come here," she said in a tired, monotonous voice. "The enemy came to our old village four times. Twice it was the men from the jungle and twice it was you foreigners. Each time we suffered. You came last and brought us here. You ask me what I want. I want to be left alone. I want to grow rice."

Further attempts at conversation proved useless. On the way back to the bomb crates and the can half full of bent nails, we tried again. This time we spoke with a young woman who sat fanning a tiny glow of embers under a blackened rice-pot.

"What are you cooking?" we asked.

"Rice," she answered, her tone indicating that the question was a rather foolish one; after all, the contents of the pot were obvious. But we were concerned about the hamlet. What did they need? What did they want? What skills did they have? No one seemed to know, or want to talk about, these things. We decided that perhaps we should discuss something less personal. "When do you think the war will be over?" we finally asked.

"How can I answer that?" she replied sharply. "I have three children to care for. I have a husband, and I do not know whether he is alive or dead. These worries take my time. Ask the old men. They sit in one place and think much on these problems."

We left, telling the woman that we hoped her husband would be all right—a last clumsy attempt to be of some kind of assistance.

As we finished pulling nails from the pile of boards, the American Army major who was responsible for pacification in the province stopped by. "How are things going?" he asked. "Get the water pump working yet?"

"Bob did." We nodded in the direction of one of the volunteers who was talking to some cadres nearby.

"You guys sure are a help," the major commented. "We can help bring these folks in, but what you're doing is the really important thing. We'll have this place looking better than what they had before. These folks will really like it here. It's winning hearts and minds that's important. That's the name of the game. By the way, what did that woman say over there? Did she tell you how happy she is?"

[8]

CANDY AND TOYS

The Problems of Refugees

Every night, beginning in the latter part of 1965, we saw Kim Quy at the screen door of the Hollywood Bar in Da Nang. One tiny hand clutched her little brother and the other reached forward as soldiers passed in and out of the bar. She collected a variety of things: money from all over the world, chewing gum, candy, cigarettes, and sometimes a small toy. At midnight an old woman came for Kim Quy and her brother, and the three of them wandered into the darkness beyond the Strip, the bar and brothel section of the city.

Kim Quy was one of the few Vietnamese whom soldiers in Da Nang knew. Most important, they could help her.

"She sure is cute," they would say to one another as they dropped a piaster coin (one penny) into the outstretched hand.

"Yeah, I wonder where her mom is?"

But they didn't pursue the question. There wasn't time, really. Either the soldiers were pressed on by the heat and the thirst that only the tropics can bring, or else it was curfew time. Besides, Kim Quy didn't speak English.

One evening Kim Quy saw us, came over, and tugged at a loose shirt flap. "You O.K. You gimme chew gum?"

"Where are you from, Kim Quy?" we asked her.

Her eyes glowed and she shouted to the shoeshine boys nearby, "Mr. Foreigner speaks Vietnamese!"

We repeated our question. This time she spoke shyly: "Out there, a long way away."

"And now where is your home?"

This time she took us by the hand and led us through the alleyways to a thatch hut dimly lit by a candle. In the semidarkness, we made out an old man wrapped in a couple of blankets. As our eyes adjusted to the dim light, the old woman, who had come to take Kim Quy home late each night, walked in.

"Hello, Mr. Foreigner," she said. "Please sit down. I will bring tea." She left the room and returned shortly with a cup of lukewarm tea.

"Have you always lived here, old woman?" we asked her.

"Oh no. We are farmers. But there is a war in our village. The old women and old men must leave. We brought the children, too. It is not good for the children to live where there is fighting."

"What has happened to the young men and women?" we asked.

"Oh, they are fighting the war," she replied. "All the strong ones must fight. We got slips of paper that the airplanes dropped and we came here." She referred to the safe-conduct passes which are dropped in NLF-controlled zones and allow the people to come unmolested into the Saigon-controlled areas.

"How do you live?" we asked. It seemed obvious that neither she nor the old man on the bed would be able to work.

"Oh, life is difficult. The government never gives us anything. We had to put our thumbs in ink and press them on paper so we could get money. But the government didn't give it to us. Now our granddaughter makes a little from kind soldiers."

No one knows how many refugees there were then or are now in Viet Nam. The official U.S. government estimate at the end of 1967 set the figure at more than two million. That did not, however, include those who had moved into the cities and somehow made it on their own, or the hundreds of thousands who had moved in with their relatives. For example, no refugees were listed for Saigon. Yet people fleeing the countryside had so overpopulated that city that in August, 1968, the Saigon *Post* quoted a high-ranking government official as having said that the capital's population had increased fivefold over the past few years; Saigon, it was said, now had the highest population density of any city in the world, twice that of its nearest rival, Tokyo. A task force sent to Viet Nam to study refu-

gee and social-welfare problems for AID reported that the number
of uprooted people not accounted for in the 1967 official statistics
ranged from two to two and a half million. By late 1968, with the
addition of more than a million new refugees from the winter and
spring offensives, it was clear that at least five million persons had
been forced to move at least once, many of them several times. This
figure represents a quarter to a third of the entire population of
South Viet Nam.

Refugees who are fortunate enough to meet the government's
requirements for refugee status and who overcome the necessary
red tape receive, regardless of age, a daily allowance of one pound
of rice for up to six months. For the first sixty days they are also
entitled to eight piasters ($0.07) a day. Unfortunately a great deal
of red tape is involved, and the refugees often do not receive the
identification papers necessary to make them eligible for the allowances. One Vietnamese government official explained some of the
problems: "Their homes are destroyed or burned while they are
fleeing the countryside, and the papers are lost. Often people are
separated from their village officials and no one can identify them.
Also, some officials are unfair and only give ID cards to friends and
relatives or use the issuing of cards as an opportunity to collect
graft. Even when the refugees have ID cards, it takes a month
before they get aid. In some places, rice and other gifts are stored to
the brim of the warehouses, but they are not distributed to refugees
who are in misery. Reasons: who knows?"

For many of the refugees, the decision to leave their old home
was based on a government leaflet which fluttered down from an
airplane—an American airplane, they say, for "only the Americans
have airplanes." One such leaflet told the villagers:

The wicked Viet Cong have stored weapons and supplies in your village.
Soon Naval gunfire is going to be conducted on your village to destroy
these Viet Cong supplies. We ask that you take cover as we do not wish
to kill innocent people. And when you return to your village repel the
Viet Cong so that the government will not have to fire on your village
again.

After reading such a leaflet, most of the villagers gathered what few
things they could quickly put together and hurried away. As one

refugee later put it, "You tell us that the purpose of the bombs is to destroy the supplies of the Viet Cong—yet they can move their supplies much faster than we can move our buffalo, pigs, chickens, rice, furniture, and children. But if we do not take our buffalo, how can we make a living? If we take the time to gather our belongings, we will be killed. Most of us just hurry away without those things precious to us." Many others were escorted out by allied forces during search-and-destroy missions or starved out by the defoliation of their crops. Others left their old hamlets in fear of Viet Cong terrorism.

Typical of refugees fleeing the Viet Cong were the people of Vinh Son, a Catholic village which had fled the Viet Minh in the North more than ten years earlier, in 1954. In the North, the Communists had told them that the Americans were very cruel and that the boats which were supposed to take them south would only go out to sea, where they would be pushed overboard. The other side (encouraged by the CIA, some claim) told them that the Virgin Mary had gone south and that they must follow. Their own religious leaders threatened them with excommunication if they did not go. After arriving in the South, the inhabitants of Vinh Son were settled in the remote province of Binh Long near the Cambodian border. There they were free to practice their religion and manage their own affairs. But one evening a few men came to Father Trung, their priest, and told him that they were part of an organization to free the people from the oppression of Ngo Dinh Diem and his wicked family. They wanted to talk with the villagers and explain their purpose so that the people there could be a part of the movement. Father Trung was angry and accused them of being Communist agents. They left, promising to return. The next day, Father Trung called in the elders of the village. "We must defend ourselves," he said. "If we don't, we won't be able to pray as we wish. Our great sacrifices in coming south will be lost."

The men from the jungle did return many times. At first they came peacefully, attempting to talk to the villagers or to get food. They were driven out each time. Then they made threats. Finally they attacked, killing nearly a hundred of the men in the village. By early 1966, the situation had become still worse. The people packed what few things they could carry on their backs and began the two-day walk to Phu Cuong. Ironically, what had finally convinced them to leave was a Vietnamese government artillery barrage that killed eight people in the church—a story they were reluctant to tell lest the listener doubt their anticommunism.

When we first met them, they had been scattered to three locations in Phu Cuong. Some stayed at the church, some went to live in a fruit orchard nearby, and some had moved into an old French villa that had been hit several times by mortar shells. With us on our visit were a small group of Vietnamese students who were planning to work with the refugees that summer. The chief of the local youth and sports service took us to the camps, and we wandered through, each feeling conspicuous. Our white skin, the girls' white *ao dai*'s, and the boys' smartly tailored trousers and pointed shoes branded us all as foreigners. Only Miss Hoa seemed to have a grasp of the situation. She talked with the women, looked at the children's cuts and skin diseases, and asked the little boys to solve simple arithmetic problems. Hoa was from Phu Cuong and she seemed to feel a special responsibility for the refugees' welfare.

When we had finished the tour, we returned to the youth and sports office. Again Miss Hoa took over, proving the astuteness of the group in electing her their leader. (It had been quite a surprise for us to see a girl elected.)

"We can help," she began. "Most of the children have had almost no school. Nearly all of them have skin disease. And a simple ditch would help to keep the water from flowing into the tents at the orchard camp."

But where would classes be held? What could be done about skin fungus without soap and fungus powder? How could one dig a ditch without shovels? Clearly the solutions would not be as simple as Hoa had implied. But the students began. Miss Lan had a relative in the provincial education office. He gave the students two large blackboards and some benches. Quynh got some soap and some school kits from CARE. We remembered seeing some shovels and scrap lumber in the American surplus dump and procured them. We hauled our supplies in a truck borrowed from the Saigon live-stock experiment station.

The school opened. It was not as well endowed as it would have been in Saigon, but nevertheless children were studying. Their classroom had no roof, and when it rained the children scurried to shelter, carrying school kits under one arm and tugging at the heavy benches with the other. The airplanes overhead and the general buzz of the camp added confusion. But the teachers, university students themselves and working without books, used the one pedagogical method that they thought would have any chance of working under these circumstances—mass recitation. The tiny blackboards that CARE had provided in the school kits were especially useful in teaching the children. "Look," cried a little girl with shining eyes. "I can write duck!" She spelled out the letters for the Vietnamese word meaning duck, V—I—T, and carefully placed the proper tone mark under the "I."

Finally, the people were given land. They moved once again, carefully carrying their meager possessions—a few dishes, a picture of their ancestors, a picture of the Pope. After temporary shelters had been built, the church was erected and the hamlet was named Vinh Son for their patron saint, St. Vincent. The move to Vinh Son gave the villagers more space around their houses, but still nowhere to farm. They had to find employment either in Phu Cuong or, more easily, at the nearby American army camp. The refugees' rice payments promised by the government never arrived in any quantity. No one seemed to be quite sure why, though there were always stories of corrupt officials keeping the rice. But it was just as likely that bureaucratic red tape was not geared to a situation like Vinh Son; the villagers had come from a very insecure area of another province, and it is doubtful that their identity was ever clearly established. Nevertheless, some help in getting settled was provided by the American Red Cross, which furnished cement to make blocks for house construction as well as some rice to supplement what money the people could earn. But as in most other Catholic villages, the main responsibility for directing the work and finding the needed resources fell on the priest. It was through Father Trung's imaginative leadership and such novel projects as eel raising that the people managed as well as they did.

The Tet offensive, which brought so much sadness to Viet Nam in 1968, hit Vinh Son in a rather indirect way. The NLF troops did not enter the settlement and only one person was killed by the fighting—a child who was hit by a stray bullet. One NLF soldier even gave himself up to the people of Vinh Son because he was hungry after going three days without food. But one of the biggest problems that the people of Vinh Son faced after the Tet offensive was in obtaining rice. The police controlled the rice very closely to keep it out of Viet Cong hands. The province chief ordered that only regular family identification cards would be valid for obtaining it, since "the government is already giving rice to those holding refugee cards." But even those in Vinh Son who held these refugee cards had not received any rice from the government for over a year. Now they could not buy rice because they had no regular identification cards. Finally they had to resort to the black market and pay exorbitant prices.

The inhabitants of Vinh Son have many legitimate complaints against the Saigon government. They are bitter about the undistributed rice, but since most of them have jobs they see this not as a disaster but rather as a symptom of the corruption and lack of concern shown by the Saigon authorities. During the Tet offensive, the district chief even ordered all thirty-three of their Popular Forces troops withdrawn to the district headquarters, leaving Vinh Son unprotected. The villagers closed and locked their windows and stayed up at night to protect themselves against both attack by the Viet Cong and thievery by Vietnamese government soldiers. Some of them have received letters from relatives in North Viet Nam saying that communism and Catholicism can and do live harmoniously together in the North but that American bombing made life there unbearable. Still, Father Trung and the people of the camp cannot forget the threats and maltreatment they received from the Viet Minh in the North. Nor have they forgotten the siege by the Viet Cong while they were living in Binh Long. They cannot forget that a hundred of their men were killed.

In 1965 and early 1966, most of the refugees were, like the people of Vinh Son, fleeing the Viet Cong. By mid-1966, however, this had changed. The majority were then fleeing the massive allied offensives—bombing in the free-strike zones, search-and-destroy missions, defoliation. APC's (armored personnel carriers) criss-crossed the rice paddies, mashing down patiently cultivated rice. Saigon troops stole chickens or deftly wrenched fruit off trees as they drove past. By 1967, the use of H & I fire (harassment and interdiction) was so frequent that one White House aide privately told us that 80 per cent of American firepower was undirected. "Our buffalo will come across a shell and it will explode," farmers complained. "We spend so much time huddled in the bunkers of our houses that we don't have time to tend our crops properly," said others. "We can no longer begin work early in the morning, be-cause we will be recruited by NLF soldiers who are returning from a night operation. Even worse, we might be shot by a helicopter gunner who thinks we might be NLF soldiers."

The hamlet of Tan Tay was a tragic victim of this indiscriminate use of firepower. The peasants of Tan Tay lived by fishing and rice farming in Vietnam's most secure province, An Giang. In Septem-ber, 1967, however, they were warned by their village council that they were living in a dangerous zone and should move; the govern-ment would not be responsible for any loss of lives or property. But at the same time the council continued to issue letters of permission to fish and graze cattle in the area and to travel on the canal during daylight hours. The hamlet's thirty-three families stayed. They had been there for years, they had nowhere else to go, and, besides, such warnings were always being given out as a kind of "protection" for the village councils in case something did go wrong.

In early December, an air strike was called on the outskirts of Tan Tay. An L-19 observer plane had been shot at and the strike was called in hopes of hitting some of the VC involved. Nine villagers—four children, two women, and three men—were killed, twelve others were wounded, and the people's homes, boats, and livestock were destroyed. The survivors walked to the nearby market place with nothing but the clothes they were wearing at the time of the attack. No Viet Cong were killed.

David Gitelson, the IVS volunteer working with the people of Tan Tay, protested the air strike, particularly because the hamlet had not been sufficiently warned in advance. He also felt that more assistance should have been given the refugees after the bombing.

For example, three weeks after the air strike, the total relief had been thirty-two cans of cooking oil and thirty-two bags of wet oatmeal (the shipment had turned over in the canal). Dave also pointed out that the failure to have a medical-evacuation helicopter available for civilian casualties had probably resulted in the death of one man who died in the hospital in Long Xuyen after a three-hour boat ride; the man had been wounded in the arm. "Perhaps the essence of the matter," he wrote in a report to IVS headquarters, "is that the Vietnamese and American military don't feel any mistake has been made. When I asked a MACV senior officer in Long Xuyen whether in these circumstances this doesn't make the civilians just so much foliage to shoot through, he agreed. He said the people were lucky, that if the helicopters had been in proper strafing position, no one would have gotten out alive."

The refugees in a neighboring hamlet, upset by the lack of government concern, learned of the impending visit of an American Senator to the province and planned to register a complaint with him. Dave had promised to try to bring him to that area. But the government's refugee-service chief, learning of their plan, went to the hamlet and threatened to have them killed if they complained to the Senator. The refugees then wrote a letter to Vice-President Ky, giving Dave a copy of the letter.

A few days later, on January 26, 1968, David Gitelson was killed, allegedly by the Viet Cong. The details of his death remain unclear, however. The "VC" who captured him took him in the opposite direction from the Viet Cong-controlled area. A representative of IVS who was sent to Tan Tay when Dave's capture was reported also said that he had seen government leaflets blaming the Viet Cong for Dave's death before he was even known to be dead. Dave was known to the people in the area as "My Ngheo"—the Poor American—because of his modest clothing and the simple life he led. "My people love that man," said a Vietnamese student. "He helps my people very much."

Dave had shared the frustration of many volunteers, the frustration of knowing that one's presence, while helping a few individuals, might be used by the military to ease its conscience. Never was the frustration of the volunteer greater than when working with refugees. We found that the refugees, particularly in the out-of-the-way camps, were often forgotten once they were "brought in." There was a great deal that we could do—from involving Vietnamese students in teaching their children to making sure that there was enough food in the camps. Sometimes, however, we felt we were being "used."

One volunteer, in a remote district in Central Viet Nam, wrote to IVS headquarters of the situation in which he found himself: "It seems that they [the Special Forces] had been waiting to go on operations, but had no facilities for the refugees that would be created by the troop movements, etc. My presence alleviated this situation, and despite the fact that there were no new sources of food or shelter, it left their consciences free to create refugees as they saw fit." One day, the military called the volunteer by radio and asked if he could take care of some Viet Cong suspects. He told them that he had no facilities. The soldiers called a different station and were informed that there was a "refugee man" in the area, meaning the volunteer. The officer in charge of the operation then announced that they would "burn the whole village." The volunteer was thus saddled with the responsibility of caring for them anyway, even though he did not have the necessary facilities. "Before you came," an officer in charge told him, "we had no place to keep the refugees that our operations created. We would bring them in, but there was no food or shelter, so in four or five days they would all be gone. Then we would hear that the village we had just cleaned out was full of people again. There are orders to shoot anyone there, but we usually found that it was just the people we had 'liberated' —there was nowhere else for them to go, so they went home. Now that you are bringing food to the refugees and providing shelter [not yet built] we will be able to enforce the restrictions."

Resettlement is a traumatic experience for the Vietnamese. In their old hamlets, almost all of them were either farmers or fishermen. Suddenly they are crowded into or near the cities and towns. There is little planning in the selection of sites, and most of it is done for military and security purposes rather than with a view to economic opportunities. Many refugees have been placed along major highways and around cities and towns to "discourage" enemy attacks. In Dak To, for example, the district chief proudly told us why he had resettled several hundred Montagnards around the district headquarters: "Having the Montagnards surround the headquarters," he said, "makes it very difficult for the Viet Cong to enter. If they try to attack the town, they will have to force their way through the refugees. Many Montagnards would be killed and it would cause much bad feeling toward the VC. If they try to mortar us, many of the rounds will hit the Montagnard refugees, and it would again be bad propaganda for them."

Refugees have many causes for apathy. In the new settlements, which are often erected on barren land without the coconut trees and other vegetation to which they are accustomed, the tropical sun beats down mercilessly in the dry season and the camps become a sea of mud in the rainy periods. Inside the hastily constructed shacks, families must live together in one large room, assigned so many feet according to the number of children they have.

Refugees see relocation as temporary and often feel that efforts to build a new house or dig a well will be wasted. Another cause of apathy is that the camps are made up almost entirely of women, children, and old men. The young men are with one army or the other. This absence of husbands and fathers, unnatural in any society, results in lack of direction and failure to accept responsibility within the camps. The lethargy also stems in part from a poor diet almost completely lacking in meat and vegetables. The refugees feel that the government has a responsibility to feed and house them. After all, they insist, the government was responsible for making them leave their old village. Besides, they say, the Americans are very rich and give the government everything that is needed.

To register such sentiments, on the other hand, causes the refugees great pain and much injured pride. Yet employment is practically nonexistent and they have little alternative but to seek help from the government. They have no land for agriculture, the one vocation they know, and other jobs are often hard to find. And above all else, the refugees want to work and earn their own way. American visitors are often startled when even those refugees who are living in relatively clean and spacious housing express a preference for more squalid conditions elsewhere. "We can find work there," they explain. Competition for jobs, however, creates resentment on the part of the permanent population. The presence of the refugees pushes wages down and local people complain. Also, the in-camp refugees are not often allowed to live in the cities, and transportation costs rule out work there. A concerted effort has been made to settle refugees around such places as Cam Ranh, Bien Hoa, and An Khe, where they can find construction jobs at the American installations. This has led to accusations that the Americans create refugees so that they can have cheap labor to construct their roads and air bases. There is, however, no evidence to support this, and most American firms pay far more than the going wage.

Settling the refugees near American bases has caused a serious problem. Proximity to large numbers of American troops has encouraged the Vietnamese to pursue those occupations most disruptive to the Vietnamese way of life. Construction work separates the farm people from the land. The presence of large numbers of GI's gives young girls the opportunity to go into prostitution and encourages children to beg. By tearing the Vietnamese farmer from his centuries-old relationship with the land, with his buffalo, and with his own family, the allied forces have thus helped to create a rootless urban society. Such an unstable society not only promises little tactical support to the side that has created it, but is also likely to pay bitter dividends of social discontent for years into the future.

Much of the problem arises from the government's lack of properly motivated cadres to assist the camps. Too many government workers are indifferent or look down on the refugees. In the words of one USAID official in Thua Thien province, "The district chief won't help the refugees because the refugees have nothing to give him." Even this, unfortunately, is not always true. One district chief, for example, had to buy his job, and to get back his investment he taxed the local bars, sold the commodities that had been sent to him for free distribution to the refugees, and charged the refugees 600 piasters ($5.00) for security passes so they could get employment on the American air base.

Sometimes American advisers have stepped in and carried out the food distribution themselves. Such emergency action may be necessary; when people lack food something has to be done. This kind of distribution is usually piecemeal, however. Most Americans cannot tell one family from another and confusion breaks out. Direct American distribution, though always goodhearted, is thus frequently more symbolic than real. "They need rice, and we give them candy and toys," noted one U.S. official. The psychological gain from American distribution does not accrue to the Vietnamese government and does not help the American objective of building a government that the people will back. For the refugees, the only visible evidence of Saigon support may be a picture tacked up on the side of some building showing the province chief passing out bulgur wheat and cooking oil. How much allegiance this gains among hungry refugees who have never received government assistance themselves is certainly debatable.

One of the most prevalent themes of the Saigon government in encouraging the refugees to come to its zone has been the promise of security. "The army of the Republic is of the people with the responsibility to protect its countrymen," proclaimed a leaflet. The NLF has viciously contested this government assertion. It has pointed out over and over that the government cannot and will not provide security. The attacks on Saigon and the other cities were dramatic proofs of this. A more typical case was that of the Nam Dong and Number Five camps in Thua Thien. In June, 1967, the NLF entered the camps and told the people to move back across the Perfume River into NLF-controlled territory. If they refused, their houses would be burned down in three days. On the third day, the refugees requested the commander of two Vietnamese army companies a mile and a half down the road to provide protection. The commander replied that he had no trucks to transport his troops, but that he would send them the next day. That night the NLF entered the camps and, after giving the refugees time to pack their belongings, burned down the forty-six government-supplied houses. The peasants moved back across the Perfume River into the NLF-controlled territory, which was also a free-strike zone. The next day the Vietnamese Army commander sent his troops out to look for the new "NLF terrorists."

An abandoned village is often made a free-strike zone—which means, in the words of one GI, that "anyone seen there is a Viet Cong; if he does anything suspicious, we shoot him." Near Tuy Hoa, five woodchoppers went to get wood in their old village. As they returned with heavy loads of wood on their backs, they were spotted by a helicopter which hovered over them to investigate. The frightened peasants tried to run and hide but were caught in the machine-gun fire of a gunner who thought they might be Viet Cong. One was killed and four were wounded. Still, there is always the psychological urge for Vietnamese to return to their village to see if everything is all right—that magical pull of the land on the Vietnamese peasant. And so they sometimes go back to the old homestead, to the graves of their ancestors. Others stay permanently, preferring to risk their lives on their land rather than to become welfare cases and watch their children become beggars or prostitutes. Large parts of the ocean have also been declared free-strike zones, resulting in reduced areas for fishing grounds. That this affects even those who live inland was shown when farmers in Dalat complained that they could no longer get fish meal to fertilize their vegetables.

It is not surprising that life is difficult in a war-torn land and that the life of a refugee is perhaps the most difficult of all. What has always been open to question, however, is whether the creation of refugees is necessary in the conduct of the war. In the beginning, to be sure, there was little choice about the matter. In mid-1965, General Maxwell Taylor, the American ambassador, expressed the fear that the Viet Cong might try to "swamp the agencies of the Vietnamese government engaged in the care and handling of refugees." And so it seemed. People fled in droves from the guerrilla terrorism in the countryside, seeking refuge in the towns. There were literally more refugees than could be handled. Then, in Binh Dinh province, allied search-and-destroy operations began to generate particularly large numbers of refugees. A study group of the Ministry of Social Welfare in Saigon reported from there in 1966:

The number of refugees increases day by day. Social Welfare Service can't control because of the lack of personnel. This number will be increased and also belongs to the operations settled by us and the Allied armies in order to seize the land. For example, in Bong Son the Operation Than Phong II created about 5,000 people who took refuge in the city. These people have not received anything as of a week ago. The refugee settlements of the district can't contain all of them, for that they have to stay under the porch roofs of the school. Many families go to beg, because they miss all things.

Even aside from these physical limitations, Vietnamese officials were often reluctant to treat the refugees very well, claiming that if the refugees were pampered, they would refuse to return to their rural homes when conditions permitted. Americans, on the other hand, insisted that here was an opportunity to convert a sizable group "from a national drain to a national gain." In fact, by 1967 it seemed as though the emphasis of the American military effort was designed expressly to depopulate the rural areas, "urbanizing" the population both to deprive the NLF of its rural support and to win over the people through good deeds in the refugee camps.

Many Vietnamese officials, such as the former deputy chief of Binh Dinh province, Lieutenant Colonel Nguyen Be, had good reasons for their reluctance to encourage the flow of refugees, no matter which side was generating it. "It is a mistake," he told us in 1968, "to move the people off their hallowed land. This is a political war and it must be fought by trained counterguerrillas and political cadres, not by massive, impersonal free-strike-zone bombings from the air. If we move the people from the land, we will surely lose their support; they will resent us."

Other officials have contended that there are sound arguments favoring refugee creation. One of them cited Binh Duong province as an example: the NLF soldiers used Binh Duong as a path of entry from their Cambodian border base camps into the city of Saigon. They followed the route of the meandering Saigon River, the banks of which were rather heavily populated. If the guerrillas were the fish and the people of the countryside were the waters off which they lived, then the Saigon government had to dry up the waters to destroy the fish. It was for this reason, the officer explained, that the villagers at Ben Suc were moved from their fertile lands into the barren refugee camps farther south. The lush rice fields were left uninhabited so that the Viet Cong would be deprived of support in the form of food, recruits, porters, taxes, and intelligence—all elements of great importance to their survival and success. In addition to removing sources of real support to the Viet Cong, he added, removing the civilian population from a particular area also lifted any restraints on allied military operations. One of the chief frustrations of American military strategists was their inability to take full advantage of American technological and firepower superiority for fear of harming civilians. They had to decide whether, in view of the number of civilian casualities or displaced persons likely to ensue, an attack was worth initiating. Few American commanders were so lacking in compassion as to ignore the need to spare innocent civilians; the only question at issue was how to balance these humanitarian concerns with military efficiency. It was a dilemma, but it could be eased somewhat by removing the civilians and having a presumably open field on which to fire.

There were other ways in which the creation of refugees was thought to be to the advantage of the Saigon government. Large numbers of people under government control in refugee camps would constitute a kind of psychological victory for Saigon in terms of population percentages supporting it over the NLF. The U.S. Embassy greeted such figures with great enthusiasm, particularly when cited in voting statistics. (The fact that some refugee camps were actually under NLF control was rarely mentioned. All three camps in Ben Cat district, and by night even the new Ben Suc settlement, soon fell into this category.) AID personnel welcomed the fact that in these new concentrations access to the people was much easier than when they were living in their far-flung villages. They could more readily provide economic assistance, school facilities, and medical care. For the government, this concentration also facilitated psychological and political education, though this was generally unsuccessful except where it could be backed up by security and economic well-being for the people.

Yet, as Colonel Be and others had predicted, the creation of refugees was on the whole counterproductive, even in the military's own terms. "We must remember," he told visitors to his revolutionary development training center in early 1968, "that the Viet Cong are fighting two wars. One is the conventional war, where we can use our technological superiority over vast areas when the people have been moved; the Viet Cong are losing this war. But the other war is the guerrilla war, and this one they are winning. They are winning it by default, because we are not fighting it. By so uprooting the people from their traditional lives, we are not acknowledging the political and social bases of their struggle."

It is true that removing the people from Ben Suc and similar areas used by the NLF for resupply denied the enemy critical support. On the other hand, the movement of discontented displaced persons has frequently facilitated NLF infiltration of the new camps and, worse, of the cities. When American visitors ask refugee children where their fathers and brothers are, there are three possible answers: "dead," "in the Army," or an embarrassed silence that usually means they are off fighting in the NLF.

By placing so many people sympathetic to the NLF cause right in the middle of the cities, the government itself helped to make the attacks on the cities possible. In some parts of Saigon, the NLF brought guns and ammunition into the city before Tet in mock funeral processions. Sympathetic or perhaps just frightened refugees then buried the "coffins" in graveyards, where some of them, in fact, had resorted to building their own shacks for lack of other space. At Tet, the NLF soldiers moved in with relatives or friends, ostensibly to celebrate the holidays, but in fact to await the beginning of the attack. While the children lit firecrackers, the soldiers tested their rifles. And when the offensive began, there were plenty of refugees who made excellent guides, for they knew the location of the police stations, the habits of the policemen, and the alleyways that form the jungles of the cities.

In fulfillment of Ambassador Taylor's fears, the refugee droves who have come into the urban centers have greatly overburdened already scanty government resources. Although the VC have pressured some, it is not they who have flooded the government agencies with refugees. After all, they need the people in the countryside as sources of food, shelter, recruits, and porters. Rather, it is the allied policies that have caused the greatest mass movements. In any case, the result has been insurmountable difficulties for an already paper-thin administrative system, overloaded medical and school facilities, and relief logistics. New opportunities for corruption have been created by the enormous resources of the relief programs. The most serious result of all has been the formation of a whole new class of rootless urban mendicants.

Increasing urbanization is a world-wide phenomenon. Throughout the developing countries, and in America too, it is causing individual hardships and social upheavals. In Viet Nam, however, the nature of the urban movement has been more negative than elsewhere. People have left an area of economic opportunity for one of extremely limited opportunity or none at all. After the war, many people, the young in particular, will no doubt want to remain in the cities, perhaps to form the basis for a new industrial proletariat. Others, some sociologists predict, will return to their earlier ways of life.

What, then, will be the fate of children like Kim Quy whose profession was the outstretched palm, or of the young refugees who shined the big black shoes of the foreigners, built their airports, washed their clothes, served their drinks, or went to bed with them? What will be the fate of the old, who will die and be buried far from their ancestors' tombs, and whose last days of life will have been full of bewilderment, of chaos, of the heavens and earth in grave disorder? For the young, to be sure, life will go on, and the deceased will be venerated by succeeding generations in the Vietnamese tradition. On family holidays, the survivors, however poor, will pay their respects. They will offer gifts before the household altar. And if these survivors have nothing else to give, they will give candy and toys.

[9]

SPENDING THEIR TIME IN HELL

American Troops in Combat and Out

The girl in the pink *ao dai* vigorously shook the dice and, in a near-chant, whispered:

> "Soldier boy, soldier boy,
> Up Tu Do and down Le Loi *
> Soldier boy, soldier boy."

Then she tossed the dice onto the bar and gave a delighted little laugh. "You buy. You buy Saigon tea." †

"Yeah, I buy. I buy Saigon tea. Hasn't this country got anything but Saigon tea?"

The girl in the pink *ao dai*, sensing the mood, quickly changed the conversation.

"How many days you got?"

"Ninety-three days and four hours. That's a long time, baby."

"Where you stationed?"

"Tan Son Nhut."

"Oh, you pilot. You fly Hanoi?"

"Look, this is my night off. You come home with me?"

"No, soldier boy. I work in bar and drink Saigon tea." The girl mechanically dumped the dice onto the bar. The soldier got up and wandered out into the muggy air of Tu Do Street. A couple of girls in heavy make-up and tight western slacks were leaning against a

---

* Tu Do and Le Loi are streets in downtown Saigon especially frequented by American servicemen.

† Saigon tea is a high-priced drink which the patrons of a bar are expected to buy for the hostess entertaining them. Made to look like an exotic alcoholic beverage, it consists in reality of artificially colored water.

wall. "Hey you, you numba one. You gimme Salem?" one of them cried out sarcastically.

Meanwhile, Saigonese out for their evening stroll seemed oblivious to both the girls and the GI's. Occasionally, to be sure, they were pushed to one side by groups of distracted Americans whose careening steps showed that they had already made the rounds of several bars. But even then the strollers seemed hardly to notice.

The soldier walked on until he discovered that a ten-year-old boy was following him, tugging at his shirt. "You wanna girl?" the boy said in his high voice. "Very cheap. You come my house." The boy grabbed the GI's hand and led him on.

As they rounded the corner onto Le Loi Street, a row of old women watched impassively. They were selling black-market goods from the American PX and commissary: Dial soap, instant shaving lather, hair spray, tiny radio batteries, transistor radios, and stacks of C-rations. To them the soldiers, the bar-girls, and the little boys were all a part of the daily scene. They had even seen the black jackets with the tiger and the strange lettering embroidered on the back. Some of the GI's wore these jackets despite the hot Saigon weather because they liked the phrase that some skillful tailor had stitched in: "When we die we'll go to Heaven, for we've spent our time in Hell."

And indeed, hell was not far away. Even now the pounding of distant artillery could be heard, and yellow flares lit up the sky overhead. Helicopters puttered about, maintaining their vigil.

But the soldier who had followed the boy took little notice of anything. It was his night off.

The GI in Viet Nam has a difficult job. Often not knowing why he is there, he is never quite sure which side any particular Vietnamese is on. He never knows when or where the Viet Cong will strike next, and this uncertainty causes a tenseness and suspicion that hurts his relations with all Vietnamese. Was the girl in the pink *ao dai* a Viet Cong? How about the old women selling black-market goods? And how many Viet Cong were there among the strolling Saigonese? Suspicions are heightened through ignorance. Most GI's have their only contact with Vietnamese in bars and brothels, or perhaps with captured enemy soldiers on the battlefield. In the bars, contact is usually limited to playing blackjack and dice and to exchanging the few English phrases that the bar-girls know. To many GI's, therefore, the Vietnamese are a strange, incomprehensible, unintelligible breed—in short, "gooks."

The frustrations of duty in Viet Nam became obvious to us from conversations with the American troops. "I hope someday the Vietnamese realize all we've done for them," one GI told us after we picked him up hitchhiking to downtown Saigon. He had just finished an operation in Zone D. "It's hell out there. We burned a village. Some of the people wouldn't leave. We had to burn the village." "Were they VC?" we asked. "They were VC all right," he replied. "Black pajamas and all. They hated us—man, did they hate us." We rode awhile and then he said, "You can't tell who's who. One old woman came every day and sold oranges. We used to buy an orange from her whether we wanted one or not. One day she pulled a grenade out from under the oranges and tossed it into a tent. Some of my buddies were killed and then we killed her. A few days later we saw a kid down by the stream. We thought he had a gun and we shot him. But all he had was a fish pole. But what can you do? They all look alike. Everybody wears black pajamas. The farmers, the market women, everybody."

The Viet Cong have infiltrated at every level, including that of province chief and police chief. The GI, as a result, must be concerned with danger not only on the battlefield, but also in his everyday contacts. Using an old Chinese Communist method, the Viet Cong have on occasion sent young girls to lure marines and soldiers off the base and entice them to their death. Near Da Nang three marines saw three girls swimming nude in a stream and went to "investigate." A few minutes later one marine lay dead in the stream and the other two were missing, victims of a "seduce and destroy" mission. Similar tactics have been used in bars. U.S. military officials have warned soldiers to be careful in picking up souvenirs such as Viet Cong flags on the battlefield. Although they look tempting, they are often mined. Even street vendors occasionally become sellers of death. One method used is to place an explosive charge under the wick of a cigarette lighter. When the charge gets hot enough, it explodes. A young soldier who lost a chunk out of his face when his lighter exploded noted that he had bought the lighter at a good price from an innocent-looking old lady. These methods have not resulted in large numbers of American casualties, but they have had an important psychological effect. They have created a tenseness among the soldiers: danger may be anywhere. And they have widened the gap between the American soldier and the Vietnamese: no one can be trusted.

Distrust has other causes, not connected with the Viet Cong. In 1965, for example, it cost 25 piasters (about 20 cents) for a taxi ride from the air force gate at Tan Son Nhut to downtown Saigon's Tu Do Street. Taxi drivers found that they could move the decimal point one place to the right and charge the unsuspecting GI 250 piasters (about $2.00). The GI probably paid $2.00 for a taxi ride in New York City anyway. Often the taxi drivers would not use their meters at all, charging as much as they thought they could get. Because they could make so much money from GI's, expecially during the rush hours, the drivers began to pick up only soldiers, ignoring Vietnamese who waited angrily on the streets as taxis drove past them. The situation finally became so serious that the police had to issue orders to taxis to pick up the first person who waved them down. As for the GI's, when they learned that they had been cheated and forced to pay more than the proper fare, they often reacted by not paying the next driver anything at all. A civil servant who carried soldiers on his Vespa motor scooter to supplement his inadequate government income commented that "some pay 500 piasters for a short ride and others pay nothing, shouting at me in their strange language. But it all averages out in the end." He sipped his tea and then changed the subject. Not all Vietnamese were so philosophical, however.

For most Vietnamese city dwellers, the presence of large numbers of American soldiers in their midst has been a traumatic experience. The arrival of the soldiers caused immediate inflation, particularly in housing. When the American military moved into Can Tho, for example, rent on many of the better houses tripled in a six-month period. New construction was never fast enough to keep up with the demands of the U.S. escalation. When the Americans moved in, they rented the best houses in the most secure areas. The Vietnamese crowded together, or built in the few vacant places left. In our work in Saigon's slum area of Chi Hoa, the most difficult problem we faced was that of flooding. Refugees had crowded in from the countryside, and the only place left to build was over the canals. But after houses were built over them, the canals could not be dredged. The result was that silt and sewage became clogged in the pilings of the refugee shacks, and filthy water overflowed into the slum.

There was also the problem of garbage. The Vietnamese, being a frugal people and unaccustomed to eating foods from cans or other disposable containers, make very little garbage. Americans, on the other hand, probably make more garbage than any other people in the world, especially when they are living on army cooking. The result has been that enormous piles of refuse line the streets, causing the rat population to multiply and the incidence of plague to increase to the highest level of any country in the world. The Saigon *Daily News* once cited a wry example of the garbage problem in Nha Trang: "Only there can one find unpaved roads paved with flattened-out American beer and Coca-Cola cans."

The presence of so many American soldiers has created other kinds of problems. The numerous traffic accidents involving "foreign drivers" have been a source of ill-feeling. In Tay Ninh, for example, the province chief refused for a long time to talk with Americans because of careless driving and other incidents involving military convoys. In one case, while a convoy was parked in the town, a GI set fire to a passing hay wagon, injuring an old woman perched on the back. Around the same time, a rape attempt was made on the wife of the district chief as she walked past the waiting convoy; while a few of the GI's dragged her into a truck, others held off Vietnamese passers-by at gunpoint.

The vanity of young Vietnamese men has been hurt by the sight of Vietnamese girls ignoring them and clinging to the wealthy American soldiers. "The problem with you Americans," observed a Vietnamese friend—intentionally using a phrase originated by Britons in World War II—"is that you are overpaid, oversexed, and over here." Meanwhile, a small restaurant on Saigon's Le Van Duyet Street put up a sign saying "Foreign people not welcome," and

American soldiers in an army camp in Central Viet Nam placed a sign on their bathroom that read "For roundeyes only."

Yet for each example of mistrust, we saw an example of friendship. Many of the American soldiers take time out to teach English to small groups of Vietnamese. Doctors and medical technicians, already overworked, spend their spare time making village calls or assisting the local provincial hospitals. Still other Americans make volunteer visits to local orphanages and assist in improvement projects there. Soldiers often help to repair buildings and take care of the children. Officers overlook military rules to supply food and other materials to help the orphanages. These men, many with families in the United States, find such work rewarding. "Kids are the same everywhere," they say. "It makes us feel good to be constructive." The Vietnamese people, for their part, have seen enough armies and enough soldiers in their lifetimes to know that not all soldiers are alike and that they should not judge all Americans by the behavior of a few GI's on leave in the cities. Vietnamese friends often told us, "The military is bad, but Captain Jones is a very good man," or even, "Some of my best friends are soldiers."

Occasionally, however, we saw trust and friendship lead to a strange twist of fate. Around 1967, a fifteen-year-old boy came to a village where American marines were working with a Vietnamese pacification team on civic action projects. The boy said that his parents had been killed by the Viet Cong in a recent attack on a nearby hamlet. "We took the kid in as a sort of pet," the sergeant told us. "He used to shine our shoes and run errands. But mostly we just liked to have him around. It sort of gave us a good feeling that we could help the kid. There was so much killing going on and we wanted to do something positive." But the marines' luck seemed to change after the little boy started living with them. The Viet Cong seemed to be able to predict their moves. One night they were attacked. Six of them were killed and the Viet Cong escaped with the medicine from the clinic. The enemy had known just where the Americans slept, when the guards were changed, and where the medicine was stored. "Then we got our shock," the sergeant said. "The kid was not an orphan at all. His father was the commander of the VC company that was operating in our area. When I was told this by our intelligence agent, I was really upset. The kid meant a lot to us by then. If we had turned him over to the Vietnamese government, he would have been tortured and probably killed. But we couldn't let him stay in the camp anymore because he would just keep sneaking out information. So we made a regulation that no children could enter the camp area. The other soldiers didn't understand why I sent the kid away, but I couldn't tell them or I would have gotten myself in trouble. Besides, I didn't want anything to happen to the boy. It's just a nasty war, I guess."

It is indeed a nasty war. American soldiers have been frustrated by the refusal of the enemy, whom they call "Charlie," to fight except on his own terms. "If they'd just stand up and fight, we could get the war over," the GI's complain. On the other hand, they cannot help admiring the Viet Cong's dedication and professionalism. One unit, for example, respectfully refers to the enemy as "Mr. Charles." More ominous has been the American tendency to praise the enemy as superior to the ally. The American soldier observes what often seems to him a complete lack of interest in the war on the part of the Saigon soldiers. He sees a kind of "live and let live" policy. This has been most evident in the Mekong Delta where it has often appeared that the Saigon troops and NLF forces have reached an agreement, each group guarding its own territory and not infringing too much on the other's. To some Americans, it has seemed that the Saigon troops have even allowed the Viet Cong to expand their areas a little each year.

"It's your war, you fight it," a Vietnamese captain told us. "Sure we know where the Viet Cong are and they know where we are. But why should we kill each other?"

In the Saigon Assembly, the question whether to draft eighteen- and nineteen-year-old boys was debated. "Why should we lose the only thing we have left?" one legislator complained. "Why should we lose our eighteen- and nineteen-year-olds to fight a war for the Americans?"

At the University of Hue, we asked students if they planned to join the Saigon government. "No," we were told, "the Saigon government is corrupt. It does not help the people. We will not join."

"Would you join the Front?"

"No," the students replied, "we cannot kill our brothers." They quickly added, however, that "If more and more American troops are sent to Viet Nam, we might prefer to join the Front after all."

These have been difficult ideas for the Americans to absorb. They have been taught, after all, that they were there to help the Vietnamese fight against Communist invaders. For many GI's, anything more complicated than that was beyond comprehension. In this sense, the initial welcome of American combat forces in Vietnam was deceptive. When the marines made their first beachhead landing near Da Nang on May 7, 1965, they received a charming surprise: instead of being fired on by VC snipers and having to fight their way into enemy territory, they were met by lovely Vietnamese girls who waded into the South China Sea to greet them. Giggling, the girls placed leis around the necks of the marines and wished them good luck in their mission. Why, the soldiers ask themselves, should all this have changed? Why should their Vietnamese allies now resent them?

The task of maintaining the morale of the GI in Viet Nam has been a major one. Although the average soldier has supported the war effort, there is uneasiness about the nature of the U.S. objective, about the seeming lack of a full effort on the part of the Vietnamese, and about the impossibility of knowing which Vietnamese to shoot. Because of the problems they face, the soldiers' tours of duty have generally been kept to one year. Most soldiers, anxious to return home, always know exactly how many days they have left. One way of keeping track is with a picture of a nude girl divided into 365 parts, one of which is colored in each day. Yet the rapid turnover of men hurts the war effort and makes relations with the local people more difficult. The new waves of raw recruits have had to be hardened to the rigors of jungle fighting and accustomed to the ways of Vietnamese life as they have entered its fringes. How to bargain, how to use taxis, and how to know the right price of "Saigon tea" are all things that have had to be learned. But learning how to do things the Vietnamese way seems less important to men who know they have only 365 days to spend in the country.

Still the army has done a commendable job in providing recreational services to the American soldiers, particularly when one considers the rapidity of the build-up. The USO is almost always jammed with young GI's eating hot dogs and ice cream or playing ping-pong in the back room. Even the most remote outposts get top-drawer Hollywood movies, usually a new one every night. A tremendous feat of logistics has been accomplished in providing book and musical-tape libraries, motorboats and waterskis, and even a bowling alley. Swimming pools are also available, though in Saigon at the expense of the Vietnamese public from whom the pool was taken over. Meanwhile, it often appears to Vietnamese that the U.S. Army makes life too soft. One sophisticated Vietnamese columnist for the Saigon *Daily News* wrote in 1968 as follows:

From a strictly military point of view, not philosophical or cultural point of view, the systematic insistence that American troops in the field must be provided with as many facilities of home as possible is really ludicrous. The U.S. military command has had to solve the terrible problem of logistics to give hot meals and cold drinks to all of its half a million troops, be they involved in bloody fighting or tied up in lonely camps. War or no war, refrigerators, electric generators, air-conditioners, radio networks, newspapers, and Playboy magazines are a must all the same. You can by no stretch of the imagination figure out how many planes and helicopters and ships are needed to provide such amenities, and how many troops are used to do the numerous non-combat chores.

Presentation of medals has been another way of boosting morale. The use of medals is always an accepted and commendable practice for rewarding outstanding service. In Viet Nam, however, so many medals have been awarded that their real meaning has been destroyed. When an IVS volunteer was slightly wounded in the 1968 Tet offensive he reported that his U.S. military doctors seemed more concerned about his getting a medal than they were in treating the wound. For the U.S. Marines, in fact, giving so many Purple Heart medals caused a serious practical problem. Since a marine receiving three Purple Hearts was eligible to leave Viet Nam for good, the manpower drain soon became so great that it was decided to stop awarding Purple Hearts for minor wounds. The "iodine Purple Hearts," as the marines often referred to those received for scratches, were thus abolished. Civilian agencies, not to be outdone by the military, joined in the medal game. "At the suggestion of President Johnson," a 1968 AID announcement revealed, "all civilian employees [including secretaries] who successfully completed at least 365 days of service in Vietnam since January 1, 1962," would receive an award consisting of a large medal, a miniature medal, a lapel pin, and a certificate. For both military and civilian services, medals were usually awarded with considerable ceremony, leading many to conclude that their purpose was not in fact to commend valor as much as to afford a platform for defending the Administration's policy in Viet Nam.

Unlike other wars, and medals notwithstanding, the Viet Nam war has not produced heroes. This is not due to lack of bravery on the battlefield, for there have been inspiring examples of young Americans exhibiting exceptional valor—the pilot who flew one hundred missions over North Viet Nam; the company commander who called in artillery fire on his own position; the helicopter crew that went deep into the jungle to rescue a wounded pilot, knowing full well that the Viet Cong had set a trap. Such feats are performed every day. Still, Viet Nam has produced no Colin Kellys and no patriotic songs that have endured—a fact that not even the fanfare surrounding the Special Forces has been able to change. When John Wayne starred in a movie version of *The Green Berets*, its insensitivity shocked those who knew Viet Nam and led a Vietnamese general to ask, "Where is this supposed to take place?" The reasons for the lack of heroes are subtle. They have to do with doubts—of both the public and the soldiers themselves—about the justness of American involvement in the war; with a general inability to understand the war and its setting; and with the wish that the war—and Viet Nam itself—would simply disappear.

American soldiers in the field have been beset by a number of problems, not the least of which is a shortage of interpreters. Some units have interpreters of varying capabilities, but many operate without anyone who can speak Vietnamese. In such cases, the soldiers are severely hampered. They go into a village but cannot ask directions, cannot find out where the enemy is or even whether he has been through the area. They try to help a village in a civic-action program, but cannot learn what the villagers want. When they pick up suspected Viet Cong, they are unable to question them and must turn them over to South Vietnamese authorities. One suspect, interviewed in prison by American researchers, described his capture as follows:

The Americans who arrested me didn't say anything, they didn't ask any questions. They only tied up my hands and bound up my eyes. A few hours later, a car brought me to an airport where I had to sit on the open ground the whole night. The next day at noon they took me into a tent, took off the blindfold, and a Vietnamese second-lieutenant interrogated me. He started by asking whether I wanted to live or to die. I told him I would like to live. He asked me what I had done for the VC. I told him I never worked for the VC. He said I was lying and he beat me. I was bleeding all over. I tried to tell him the truth about the VC control over my village. But he didn't believe me. He kept beating me and telling me I lied. That night I was allowed to sleep under a tent. The next day I again had to sit under the sun the whole day and stay there the whole night. The next morning they took me to Binh Tuy where once again a Vietnamese lieutenant interrogated me. I told him the truth, but like the other officer he said I lied and he beat me. He didn't believe that I was a GVN [Government of Viet Nam] civil servant, even when I told him about the Province Chief's decision which made me a member of the Council of Notables in my village, Ordinance No. 364HC/X/QD of November 1964. He didn't even believe that I was the secretary of the Buddhist Association in my village, although I showed him a certificate signed by Venerable Thich Tam Chau that I still have in my pocket. Like the other officer, he kept beating me more and more and saying that I lied. Really I didn't know what I had to tell. Finally, they sent me to this prison.

Americans have sometimes overreacted to situations. Although their nervousness is understandable, the resultant incidents of firing into villages that posed no military threat have done immeasurable harm, actually converting local people into followers of the Viet Cong. An example of this occurred in Trai Hai refugee camp. In the summer of 1967, a short allied mortar round hit Trai Hai and unfortunately killed a woman and her child. A few days after that, someone (perhaps the woman's husband) shot at an American jeep as it drove by the camp. Although the soldiers in the jeep were unhurt, they apparently decided that the village should be taught a lesson. They started shooting into Trai Hai as they drove past. An IVS volunteer who was working there reported this to the colonel in charge of the soldiers. The colonel told him to get the number of any jeep carrying soldiers who shot into the hamlet. The volunteer, not knowing what else to do, stationed himself on a knoll overlooking the road in front of the hamlet. That same evening soldiers did shoot into the hamlet, but the volunteer was unable to record the number of the jeep they were in. Finally, the volunteer came to Saigon and reported the problem to us. We went with him to see civilian authorities in Saigon. They, in turn, suggested that the volunteer work through the provincial representative, a former military man himself. Finally, the firing into Trai Hai was stopped. But the damage done to the prestige of American soldiers was not easily repaired. How could one explain to the Vietnamese why such a hamlet had been the victim of indiscriminate fire for nearly two weeks?

Such incidents are not unusual. They occur every day to the point where one becomes unwittingly accustomed to them. A Montagnard youth living in Kontum told us in 1967 that his village had been strafed and bombed, presumably by mistake. "There are no VC in my village," declared the youth, who was a staunch anti-Communist. "The people in my village are really very sad about this incident," he added in typical Montagnard understatement. We suggested that he pass his information on to local military officials so that the incident would not be repeated. He was afraid to do this, however, and only after we agreed to accompany him did he muster the courage to risk American wrath.

At 1:30 A.M., on September 3, 1967, three helicopters flew over the hamlets of Phuoc Hoa and Phuoc An in Ba Xuyen province. One of the helicopters opened up with a short burst of automatic weapons fire and then the second delivered a longer burst. Nine houses were hit and one woman was wounded. An American volunteer was living in one of the hamlets at the time—an indication that no Viet Cong were there. It was an unfortunate mistake. More unfortunate, though, is that the American officials did not investigate and nothing was done to compensate the village for the damage it suffered. The security in the hamlets, which had been among the most secure in the Mekong Delta, deteriorated rapidly. Soon after, the volunteer had to leave because resentment toward Americans had grown and for the first time the Viet Cong were able to make inroads into the loyalty of the population.

Yet most American officers are keenly aware of these problems, and they have sincerely tried to minimize such mistakes and to discipline their troops to minimize them. They note, in fact, the rather severe restrictions placed on H & I (harassment and interdiction) fire. According to these restrictions, there must be some assurance that innocent civilians are not in the line of shooting. This allows bands of guerrilla soldiers to mix with the population and thus escape being fired upon. Still, mistakes of one kind or another can never be avoided completely, and for every GI who is genuinely grieved by them there are others who have become calloused to the whole situation. "That's war," they say. "Sorry about that."

Such callousness should not be so surprising. Modern weapons have made the act of killing psychologically easier than it was in the days of predominantly hand-to-hand combat. Although there has been a great deal of vicious close-range fighting in Vietnam, much of the activity involves pilots pushing bomb-release buttons, airborne gunners shooting from a hygienic distance at suspected enemy concentrations, and artillery men firing into "empty air." A Saigon University professor, Ly Chanh Trung, commented on these impersonal aspects of the war in a 1967 article in the Vietnamese magazine *Dat Nuoc*.

Observe the American pilots, tall, handsome, athletic, with such precision equipment as the electronic computer. They eat breakfast at some military installation or aircraft carrier; then they climb into such marvelous toys as the B-52, Skyhawk, F-105, etc., fly away for a few minutes, push a few buttons and fly back. Death is the immediate result of all this button pushing activity, but it's down there at the other end, mere dots on a map. But they have no contact with the blood or the dust; they don't hear one groan, one call for help. They have no contact with the corpses of men, women, and children blown apart or burned like a cinder down below, unless anti-aircraft rounds turn them into corpses like the other corpses. But that's the hazard of their profession which they accept when they draw their salary, as in any other profession. If they make it through their mission safely, they return to their base, eat, drink, relax, play sports, and on Sunday they go to church and listen to a sermon on Christ's Sermon on the Mount: "Blessed are the meek. Blessed are the compassionate. Blessed are the peaceful."

The instruments of war are even beautiful. The light of drooping flares is not unlike the fireworks of the Fourth of July. The jets are graceful as they arc to the plunge and then sweep upward, abruptly leaving behind a series of plops or garumphs that challenge the spectator to guess at the type of weapon dropped. Bevies of spotter planes and helicopters hovering over the scene of an airstrike seem little more than a flock of birds watching for prey. "Look out the window!" someone once cried as we were flying between Saigon and Da Nang. Another plane was bombing a village below us. It was hard to be appalled by the destruction, however, so curious were we as to where the next bomb would hit. Some of our fellow passengers argued about what kind of plane was doing the bombing. After all, it was so far away. The supreme irony, perhaps, came as we left our house one morning. "Is that thunder?" we wondered, trying to decide whether to take along a raincoat for a day in the fields. But overhead the sky was clear. "Oh good, it's only bombing," was the logical reply of the seasoned Viet Nam veteran. "There won't be any rain."

"Reconnaissance in force" is an example of the kind of antiseptic terms often used at press briefings. It describes one kind of military action in a relatively inoffensive way, making the briefing sound more like a corporation meeting than a strategy conference. The reality is different, however. An example of a "reconnaissance in force" mission was the response of the First Division to a seventy-five-man Viet Cong probe early in 1968. Evening H & I fire was concentrated in the area where the Viet Cong were presumed to be. The next morning a company or two of infantry went out to investigate the source of the trouble. As they approached the large and prosperous village of An My, only about three and a half kilometers outside the province capital of Phu Cuong, they were fired upon and pinned down. They pulled back and got permission from the province chief to call an air strike. Bombs, napalm, rockets, cannon fire, and the rattling guns of so-called Puff the Magic Dragon planes fell into the village for a whole day. The next day the infantry tried to go in again, only to be fired upon once more. Again they called in the planes. The next day they received only "scattered resistance," so with the more-or-less automatic approval of the province chief they brought in the bulldozers to finish the job. An American colonel went out on the second day of destruction, after most of the houses, personal possessions, and food stores had been destroyed, and convinced the officer in charge of the operation to save a few of the houses and fruit trees. But it was too late; most of An My had been destroyed. The military, particularly the psychological warfare experts, then faced the problem of explaining to the people what had happened. It was decided that the Vietnamese Information Service would give the province chief, who had visited the scene during the bulldozing, credit for saving the fruit trees.

The difference in outlook between the American military and Vietnamese peasants was demonstrated most acutely in the aftermath of an incident that took place one night near Da Nang. When the Viet Cong came into a refugee camp and mortared the Da Nang airport, officials at the airport responded by bombing the settlement. The bombing took place, according to the upset villagers, five minutes after the Viet Cong had left. Yet several houses were fully or partially destroyed and some of the inhabitants were killed. When the futility of the raid was pointed out to one of the officers at the air base, he replied, "Well, someday the villagers will learn that if they harbor Viet Cong, they have to suffer the consequences." The villagers, on the other hand, asked plaintively, "How can we keep the Viet Cong out? We have no guns. How can we protect ourselves?" The final irony of their dilemma lay in the probable accuracy of an American officer's observation: "Yes, and when they get the weapons they'll turn them over to the Viet Cong."

The war in Viet Nam has placed tremendous emotional strains on Americans, especially on the young enlisted men. For in Viet Nam they are being asked to make decisions that will haunt them for the rest of their lives. Controversial actions have become matters of course. In the chronological order of news dispatches, one can see the escalation of disregard for human life. In 1963 the news reports told of American soldiers burning "a couple of known VC houses"; in 1967 a GI announced, "We burned every house in that hamlet"; and in 1968 a U.S. Army major said of the destruction of Ben Tre, "It became necessary to destroy the town to save it." A Vietnamese columnist described the growing militarization of the war in this way: "The American conventional and technological warfare has put the Communist troops and innocent civilian Vietnamese in the same boat."

The war does have a dehumanizing effect on our soldiers. After it is all over, they'll talk about the victories and the unsung heroes and the girl in the pink *ao dai*. But will they forget the old woman who sold oranges and was shot after she tossed a grenade into their camp, or the kid who had a fish pole that looked like a gun? And how will the Vietnamese remember the Americans who came to fight in their defense? Some will recall the words of a Vietnamese journalist: "They come in a hurry, kill in a hurry, advise in a hurry, make money in a hurry, and leave in a hurry. They are just a huge heartless 'happening.'" Others will remember the kind Captain Jones who helped the orphanage and taught them English.

The soldier marches all day through the jungle, hearing nothing, seeing nothing. He is hot, sweaty, homesick, and irritable. Suddenly there is a tunnel before him and he hears voices inside. What can he do? What would you do? You could shout into the tunnel, "Come out with your hands over your head." But they wouldn't understand you. If they were civilians, they would crowd deeper into the tunnel. If they were Viet Cong soldiers, they would toss a grenade out. You could walk away, but you might get shot in the back. You could crawl down into the tunnel, and if they were civilians you could perhaps pull them out and be a hero. But if they were Viet Cong, you would surely be shot. Or you could toss a grenade into the tunnel. If they were Viet Cong, all right. But if you found you had killed two women and three children, what then? Not many soldiers report, "Two women and three children were killed by mistake." You might retch and walk away. And, of course, you could say, "I got myself five Viet Cong." After all, they were wearing black pajamas.

[10]

THE BIG ADVISER

Americans Try to Help

When Dr. Pat Smith opened her Kontum hospital for Montagnards several years ago, business was at first slow. The villagers were suspicious of the outsider with the strange new ways, and the local sorcerers resented her competition so much that they cast hexes upon her. Most of her patients were people resigned to death, having already held a buffalo sacrifice in an effort to appease the spirit that had caused their sickness. Eventually, however, Dr. Smith proved herself. The people realized that she was sincere in her concern for them and that her treatment was effective. Not only did the sick begin to throng to her hospital, but they came before their diseases were too far advanced to be cured. As a result, the doctor's treatment became even more effective. When old Viet Nam hands told the story of Dr. Smith, they added that even with her ultimate acceptance and success, she was still considered a sorcerer by many Montagnards. The difference, they noted, was that she had become an *effective* sorcerer.

The story goes far toward showing what foreign advisers in Viet Nam require: a lengthy period of time in which to understand the local people, their problems, and their language; enough patience and tact to gain the respect and confidence of the local people; and ability in one's chosen field and in applying it to Vietnamese conditions. The ultimate proof of success, in a sense, would be to gain the reputation of being a "fellow sorcerer" and thus to enjoy an easily understood place in the Vietnamese context and social hierarchy. Only by meeting such requirements could Dr. Smith—and the rest of us—hope to affect people's lives for the better.

Unfortunately, not enough American advisers are so well qualified, and as a result many Vietnamese have come to indict the whole effort. The respected Saigon columnist Van Minh wrote straight to the point:

With a conviction of their superiority, the Americans are obsessively concerned about "advising" the Vietnamese as well as the rest of the world. They seem to believe that anyone could be an advisor of some sort provided he be an American. Thus, there are Americans who hardly know anything about Vietnam and counter-insurgency advising Vietnamese officials on pacification, advisors who have no qualifications in refugee matters "advising" Vietnamese social workers, Americans who have no solid knowledge of Vietnamese administrative problems "advising" local administrators, and so on. The American government seems to have insisted on planting a bunch of American "advisors" in every field of activity in this country, however ill-prepared they may be.

Where has the American advisory effort gone wrong? Why have so many well-motivated American advisers found it increasingly difficult to gain acceptance for their advice? Van Minh's observations cannot, of course, be applied to all Americans, not even to the majority of Americans in Viet Nam; yet the problem is serious enough that Vietnamese wait for an American to "prove himself" before they accept his advice. Until he has established himself among his Vietnamese colleagues, the adviser will be sarcastically known as "Co Van Vi Dai"—The Big Adviser—a term used to address the Chinese overlords centuries ago.

One basic necessity for successful advising seems too obvious to require mention, yet it has never been as clear to the policy makers in Washington as it has to the Vietnamese. "What is an adviser?" a Vietnamese official once asked. "An adviser is a person who must know more than the person he advises! Most of your advisers do not speak Vietnamese and do not know our ways and our culture. They cannot eat our food, for it makes them sick. Yes, maybe they have impressive degrees and experience in America or in other countries. Maybe they know very much about their fields of agriculture or education or public administration. But do they know about our people and our country? No! How can they know? They stay here only one or two years at most, spend their free time with other

Americans, and devote much of their attention either to vacations or preparing to go home. Many are here just to make money and advance their careers. How can they advise us?"

The shortness of the adviser's stay is especially significant. The military adviser normally stays one year, the civilian either eighteen months or two years. A Vietnamese general described the typical stay of a military adviser by saying, "He takes the first three months to understand the problem, the last two months to prepare to go home, and right in the middle of his seven potentially productive months, he takes a one-month vacation." The rapid turnover of U.S. personnel creates a sense of urgency among the advisers, and this, along with pressure from Washington, causes them to prod the Vietnamese into moving faster than they would prefer to move. "We admire your efforts," said one civil servant, "but you must understand our limitations. We are limited by our bureaucracy and our traditions, both of which are slow to change." Another pointed out, "You Americans always want to change quickly. You only stay here for one or two years, and then you return to America and forget about Viet Nam. We have our lifetimes ahead of us, and we will also be here to take the consequences of whatever you or we do now. We must be more careful than you." For the Vietnamese, each change in American personnel means quite an adjustment for them, for they have to learn to live in harmony with each new adviser.

At the upper levels of the U.S. government mission, the rapid turnover may mean not only lack of continuity but even shifts in policy. In AID, for example, the replacement of Director Joseph Brent by James Killen resulted in a major shift from developing provincial authority to an almost complete emphasis on strengthening the central government. To those of us in the provinces it meant an end to the flow of materials to the rural areas while we waited for the cumbersome Saigon ministries to start working again. Each change in ambassadors meant the departure of the "old team" and the arrival of the "new team." When Ellsworth Bunker replaced Henry Cabot Lodge as ambassador, Vietnamese carefully pointed out that American criticism of lack of bureaucratic continuity in the Saigon government had its counterpart in American politics. "You see," they said, "your government is like ours. Each time there is a change, there is a complete shake-up."

Each new adviser, on whatever level, would look back over the experiences of his predecessor and observe his mistakes. Then he would proceed full of confidence that he would do better. By the time his own failings began to show, or by the time he gained a certain expertise, he was about to be transferred out of Viet Nam. Sir Robert Thompson, who headed the successful British counter-insurgency campaign in Malaya, summed up the turnover problem by noting how many cocktail parties were being given for the steady stream of arriving and departing "counterinsurgency experts." "One cannot run a war in this way," Sir Robert concluded.

The length of time it takes to get materials is another problem, and Vietnamese warehouses are filled with past advisers' dreams of improving the country. Going through them can be as exciting as a childhood search through an attic full of forgotten toys. Looking for things we could use, for example, we stumbled onto a thresher to mechanize rice threshing in the delta, rope-making machines to start a new cottage industry, tape recorders for provinces with no electricity, and a world-wide collection of bean seeds that had lost their viability.

Some advisers have managed to return to Viet Nam for third and fourth tours, but it has usually been a struggle for them to get permission to go back. The Mission felt that if someone stayed "too long" he would "put Vietnamese interests above American interests." One adviser who managed to return for tour after tour was Gladys Philpott. Mrs. Philpott was an elementary-education adviser. She knew education well—not so much abstract theories as the practicalities of getting children to learn. And she knew Viet Nam. Teachers in remote Montagnard hamlets or delta villages often talked to us about her. She knew what would work and what wouldn't. For example, she seemed to be able to sense whether a teacher could be supported by a particular hamlet. She knew the education chiefs by name and they brought their problems to her. She had come to Viet Nam because she loved the people, and she worked competently and hard to help them. This is why she gained the trust, respect, and cooperation of her Vietnamese colleagues.

Other foreigners may spend a long time in Viet Nam without ever understanding what is going on. The language problem is crucial. Few American advisers speak Vietnamese, and those who do are found only at the middle and lower levels. In 1959, according to the U.S. ambassador in Saigon at the time, only nine of the 1,040 Americans in the official establishment could speak Vietnamese: four in the State Department, three in the military, one in the Information Service, and one in the economic aid program. Through 1968, there was still nobody in the upper echelons or on the U.S. Mission Council who knew Vietnamese and could thus talk with the very people for whom policies were being made. Foreigners, whether they know it or not, are virtually helpless without the language. Although there has been, over the years, a growing emphasis on the need for speaking Vietnamese, very few Americans have really tried to master the difficult tone marks or risked "losing face" by making mistakes in front of the people they have come to advise. The advisers feel that their stay is too short to take the trouble. Most IVS volunteers studied their entire first year before feeling at home in Vietnamese. Meanwhile, U.S. government officials were deciding that the language was too difficult and were learning French instead. What they failed to realize was that many Vietnamese who spoke French also spoke English. And since only the elite spoke either of these languages, knowledge of French was of little use to an American who wished to broaden his understanding of the Vietnamese people at large. There are, of course, Americans who speak Vietnamese well: usually former members of the Peace Corps who know the importance of learning the host country's language, a few ex-IVS men who joined AID after their volunteer tours, and some young Foreign Service officers. Because they know the language, they are burdened with many of the woes of the Vietnamese people. Yet because they are young, they are frequently considered too sympathetic to the Vietnamese point of view and their evaluations and advice have usually been minimized by the policy makers.

Not knowing the local language causes all kinds of difficulties quite aside from the inability to grasp the overall situation. For example, Americans are uneasy in the presence of Vietnamese who don't speak English, and some try to avoid them altogether. The amenities of polite conversation sound silly after they are made, translated, answered, and then translated back. Small talk is thus done away with. American advisers tend to launch immediately into the business of the day, seeming abrupt to the Vietnamese. Looking straight at the interpreter as he speaks, the American often makes his counterpart feel like an outsider to the conversation. An interpreter typically summarizes several minutes of the American's speech into two short questions to the Vietnamese counterpart. The counterpart, in turn, gives a long, detailed answer, which the interpreter usually translates as "O.K." The American then demands to know exactly what his Vietnamese counterpart has said, and his harassed interpreter, not well trained in the first place, may try to reconstruct the Vietnamese counterpart's reaction. Soon the American adviser realizes the complexity of the situation and decides that in the future he will send his interpreter alone to the counterpart's office with whatever forms must be signed or to get whatever information is needed for monthly reports.

In such awkward situations, there is always the chance of incorrect interpretation. We observed an example of this when an American adviser, Mr. Doran, accompanied his Vietnamese counterpart to meet the Director of Animal Husbandry, a man who spoke excellent English. "Our ideas are very much alike," Mr. Doran said to the director. "We'll be able to work well together. I guess we speak the same language." Mr. Doran had wanted to develop a good rapport with the director and thus used the phrase "same language" in a figurative sense. But the American adviser's counterpart, who did not speak English, was also present, and Mr. Doran's words were translated, "Mr. Doran says that he and the Director will get along well together because they both speak English." Mr. Doran's counterpart remained quiet and sullen for the rest of the conversation. At the end, he was tactfully asked if he agreed with or wanted to add anything to the discussion. The counterpart smiled wanly and replied, "I agree with everything." As papers and pencils were gathered together, the adviser commented, "This sure was a good meeting. I wish they could all be like this." Since Mr. Doran's counterpart had obviously been offended by the unfortunate misinterpretation, we later tried to explain the misunderstanding to him. But he only replied, "I must learn English. It is very difficult to be a government official in Viet Nam if you can't speak English."

In addition to simple mistakes of interpretation, there is also the chance that the interpreter will deliberately mislead. Some interpreters want to project their own ideas and therefore ignore or change what was actually said. Others are in cahoots with the Viet Cong or with corrupt Saigon officials, and stories of them are well known in Viet Nam. So prevalent are such incidents, and so complex is the political intrigue in Viet Nam, that many high officials who do not speak English are reluctant to discuss their problems through an interpreter. "You never know who the interpreter represents," one high Vietnamese official told us. "He might be a spy for the Saigon government, the CIA, the police, the province chief, or the Viet Cong. Or he might talk a lot when he drinks beer. We must be very careful what we talk about with our advisers if we use an interpreter."

As if short stays and language barriers were not enough, the Americans' importation of their own way of life is often offensive to the Vietnamese. An example of this is in eating habits. Though we found Vietnamese food to be varied and delicious, others did not always agree with us. "It is sad to know that our food is not accepted," commented a Vietnamese friend, "especially since it is not always because the guest dislikes it, but because he considers it unclean. Americans would rather lose a friend than risk having diarrhea." Long before inflation and food shortages necessitated such policies, the United States was importing everything from bananas to rice to Viet Nam. New arrivals were warned to avoid such foods as lettuce and unpeeled fruits. Pills were provided for the water and to take before meals to prevent diarrhea. Simple hints were traded, such as "Put your chopsticks into the steaming rice as soon as it arrives in order to sanitize them," or "Never let your host put ice in your drink; the ice might be made from unboiled water." To Vietnamese, the spectacle of an American trying to avoid diarrhea during a meal has became either an insult or a joke. As for the Americans, they tell jokes that emphasize the unhygienic nature of local foods. According to one story that made the rounds, it is possible to determine how long a Westerner has been in Viet Nam by his reaction to receiving a glass of beer with a fly floating on top. "If you've just arrived," so the tale goes, "you'll leave the restaurant in disgust. If you've been in Viet Nam for a year, you'll send the beer back and demand a fresh one. If you've been around for two years, you'll get a spoon, scoop the fly out, and drink the beer. If you've been in Viet Nam three years, you'll pick it out with your fingers. After four years you'll just go ahead and drink the beer with the fly in it. And after five years, if you get a glass of beer without a fly, you'll send it back and demand that one be added to spice up your drink."

The American adviser's own level of living in Viet Nam does not go unnoticed by Vietnamese. Not only does he have the luxuries of the Western world—air conditioner, refrigerator, automobile—but also those of the upper-class Vietnamese—cook, maid, gardener, and chauffeur. He has an enormous salary plus hardship differential plus numerous fringe benefits. A single month's rent on his living quarters is equal to the yearly wage of a farmer or, more to the point, about double the total monthly salary of his Vietnamese counterpart. He can obtain tax-free liquor at the PX, a privilege that has fostered the saying, "Here, you can't afford *not* to drink." He can stock up on the cameras, tape recorders, and stereo sets sold at the PX for a fraction of their retail price elsewhere. At the commissary he can find all the variety of Stateside supermarkets. This luxurious living has one big drawback—it limits in a very practical way the adviser's contacts with Vietnamese. As one Vietnamese put it, "If your house is better than mine and you invite me to dinner, I cannot come because I would have to entertain you in similar fashion later. My house is very poor and I can't afford to invite you to a restaurant. Still, it is impolite for me to refuse your invitation immediately. I will therefore wait till the last minute and then send a note saying I'm sick."

Besides these differences in life styles, there is a moral question. Americans overseas, and especially in Viet Nam, are subject to tensions not felt at home. Distraction and recreation are thus necessary. Unfortunately, however, the personal life of Americans in Viet

Nam cannot be kept private. The behavior of various officials is closely observed by the Vietnamese and even reported in the newspapers. One Vietnamese journalist commented on an American party he had attended in Saigon:

I was once invited to an official party given by a top ranking official of the U.S. Mission. Virtually all the "ladies" at the party were prostitutes. I can say those Vietnamese "ladies" were prostitutes and not simply "girlfriends" of some of the male American guests partly because their *toilettes* and speeches unmistakably revealed their true nature, and partly because I took the trouble to find out afterwards that they had all been picked up in Saigon's bars. And all of them were allowed to move around and act like the most respectable ladies. One of the girls at the party was a certain Maria who could speak some French—French is a good item of snobbery among the American community here—and who swam among the guests [including the U.S. Ambassador] as Queen Elizabeth among her courtiers. Should I be married and bring my wife along, she must have been terribly shocked and felt humiliated for the rest of her life.

The fact that such an incident was reported in a Vietnamese newspaper should have caused concern among American policy makers. Vietnamese attitudes toward Americans are adversely influenced by such happenings. The Vietnamese interpret these parties and what they consider American moral laxity as insulting to their culture and disastrous to the moral fiber of their country. In all objectivity, they recognize that the problem would not exist if it weren't for Vietnamese willing to capitalize on the free-spending Americans and drag down their own culture to lower levels. The shocked guest at the American official's home pointed out that "the moral fabric of the present Vietnamese society has too many flaws. It is, according to moralists and educators, even much worse now than it used to be in the past." He was also quick to point out, however, that there would be no supply if there were no demand. "What is wrong with the American performance here is that the American life of affluence and luxury and license has been forced upon the Vietnamese and proved too much for them to resist."

In July, 1965, a scandal rocked the American Mission and the Saigon community at large. The top American public-safety adviser

had fallen in love with a Vietnamese woman by the name of Hai.
When he left her temporarily to return to the United States on
home leave, Mrs. Hai went to live with one of his subordinates who
had also come to love her. Eventually, however, Mrs. Hai's first
benefactor returned from his vacation, and she became his mistress
once again. In a violent argument, the jilted second man shot first his
boss and then Mrs. Hai, killing both. The scandal dominated both
Saigon and Hanoi newspapers for months. Vietnamese commented
bitterly, "How can you advise us when one of your public-safety
men shoots the head of the public-safety division. We should be
advising you." Nor was the event soon forgotten, for in 1968 the
saga of Mrs. Hai, a woman who had played around with Americans,
was being sung in the teahouses of Saigon.

The difficulty for the adviser is that even before he begins his job,
he is faced with the serious problems of relating to the Vietnamese.
His mode of living, and that of his fellow advisers, is too different
and too separate. The sight of Americans living in the best houses,
corrupting the morals of the youth of the country, getting the best
tables in restaurants, and having access to the best foods causes
resentment on the part of Vietnamese. To argue the right of Vietnamese to resent American affluence and the way Americans use it
abroad is academic: the simple fact is that they do resent it. Moreover, Vietnamese do not distinguish personal and moral qualities
from job efficiency. Ability is subordinated to respectability in
Vietnamese Confucian society. Thus the Vietnamese do not separate a man's work from the way he lives. As one Vietnamese noted,
"Sometimes the Americans think that our lack of cooperation is due
to VC infiltration in our ranks, but sometimes it is due to the American adviser's conduct."

Even in a technical sense, the American advisers have not demonstrated to their Vietnamese counterparts that they are more competent under Vietnamese conditions than are the Vietnamese. There
are many examples of relative incompetence, ranging from the failure of an American program to grow ramie in the highlands
(termites ate the roots during the dry season) to the idea that hamlets can be pacified with cement and bulgur wheat. Much of the

problem here can be traced to the training of advisers. Their grasp of Vietnamese culture comes mainly from exposure to a few Vietnamese intellectuals in Washington, D.C. Most of them do not speak Vietnamese when they begin work, or, for that matter, when they leave Viet Nam. Their own technical experience has been under temperate climatic conditions rather than in the tropics. One Vietnamese official, who has had long experience working with American advisers, commented that "when the United States really wants to understand Viet Nam and prepare its advisers for the problems they will meet there, they will build their training center right in Viet Nam."

In IVS we tried several different orientation programs. The most effective one for rural workers began with a one-week program in the States to acquaint them with IVS and to give them an idea of what they would be doing in Viet Nam. They then went through a ten-day program at the University of the Philippines to learn something of tropical agriculture, visit nearby villages with Philippine extension agents, learn something about the many practical uses of bamboo, and study IR-8, the miracle rice that has so much potential for Viet Nam. Finally, our volunteers spent six weeks in language study and job orientation in Viet Nam, preferably in a district town in the region where they later would work. The IVSer was expected to continue his language study after completing the initial program. This program, concentrating on practical training, seemed to make much more sense than even the improved Foreign Service Institute programs that some advisers received before going to Viet Nam.

Failure to understand Vietnamese conditions has often led to advice not compatible with Vietnamese conditions. An example of this was the attempt to change working hours. As more Americans came to Viet Nam and as traffic got worse in Saigon, some American officials began to push for a typical American workday. Instead of the two-and-a-half-hour siesta period in the middle of the day, there would be a half-hour lunch break. People could bring their lunch or get a snack at a nearby restaurant or soup stand. The midday traffic jams would be eliminated and everyone would have free time later in the afternoon. After months of listening to such suggestions,

Vietnamese resistance wore down and the new plan was accepted. The results were disastrous. Some people took the long siesta anyway, others tried to follow the new schedule but felt too tired to work well, and everyone complained. People said that the government was becoming Americanized, that it was too hot to work during the middle of the day, and that the new system was just too tiring. In less than a month, to the relief of nearly everyone, the offices were put back on their old schedules. For the Vietnamese, the chance to escape the bustle of the office and have an hour or two to meditate, sleep, or read made fighting the traffic worth while. And of course the Vietnamese, most of whom traveled by bicycle, were able to move in and out of traffic much more quickly than the Americans, who traveled in large cars.

Another case of advisers failing to understand Vietnamese sensitivities could be seen in an incident near Phan Rang on the Central Coast. A canal there was being used by farmers for the irrigation of their land. When the U.S. Air Force built its base, it too made claims on the canal, even though pipes could have been laid to extract water from a nearby river. In 1967, when the canal needed its annual cleaning out, the base commander refused to stop the flow even long enough for dredging purposes. As a result of the accumulated debris, the water flow soon slowed down so much that water was not available in sufficient quantities to irrigate all their crops. Thousands of families suffered. This turned out to be a case of advisers going directly counter to Vietnamese needs.

A more ludicrous example of insensitivity was the Country Fair concept. The theory behind it is that if a loud American band plays, if medical attention is given, and if "goodies" are passed out, then wives and children will not object to their husbands and fathers being carried away. A 1968 issue of *The Army Reporter* described such a "Country Fair." In the early morning, Operation Jamboree, conducted by an American infantry brigade, surrounded a small village. A team of Vietnamese Revolutionary Development cadres and American soldiers "escorted" the villagers to a prearranged site outside the village. All the men between the ages of fifteen and fifty were isolated, and the other villagers were assembled and "briefed." Then the military intelligence section began the search and interrogation of each member of the village, while another team searched the local houses. A medical team, including dentists, treated those in need of care, and at noon a meal was served to more than nine hundred villagers. Throughout the day, an American band played a selection of tunes; candy, soap, and souvenir prizes were handed out; American and Vietnamese psychological-warfare personnel lectured on the importance of supporting the Saigon government; and an outdoor gallery exhibited pictures of VC terrorism. *The Army Reporter* pointed out the many positive effects of the program: "The target village was thoroughly searched, and the entire population screened or interrogated, fed a hearty meal and afforded medical attention. More important, each of the villagers was given a first-hand opportunity to experience the benefits and observe the value of the allied cause in South Vietnam." According to one of the officers working on the project, "Operation Jamboree laid the cornerstone for projects of this kind in the future." Meanwhile, the Vietnamese (except for amused children) reacted differently. "How would you feel," one said, "if a bunch of burly foreigners invaded your hamlet, took away your men, and played weird foreign music to 'entertain' you."

To begin improving the adviser system we might ask ourselves how we would like to see foreign advisers behave in our own country. Would we want them to learn English? Would we resent their living above our means? Would we want them to respect our moral standards? Would we follow their advice if they knew less than we did? Unfortunately, Americans tend to set lower standards for themselves when they go abroad. A Vietnamese friend who has known Americans both in Viet Nam and in the United States put it this way:

I personally admire quite a few men and quite a few things American. But believe me, I had to learn to like them. The trouble with you Americans is that willy nilly you *force* people to accept everything and anything American. Not that you are bad guys, or arrogant, or preposterous. No, I believe that the Americans at home are more courteous, more obliging, more hospitable than most other peoples. Once you are abroad, however, you *lose* your luster. Most of you do.

Vietnamese who had formed a bad impression of the American advisory effort on the basis of the many incompetents with whom they came in contact were aghast as more and more advisers flooded their country. "This thing has gotten quite out of hand," a friend told us. "When you come here in such large numbers, you take all the initiative from our Vietnamese officials. They feel that they can sit back and let the Americans handle everything. How can you expect us to take responsibility for our own programs when you are always imposing yours upon us? How can we convince the peasant in the countryside that our government is not a puppet government when everywhere he sees Americans, Americans, and more Americans?" Vietnamese officials complained that they were being deluged with advisers. "I have one technician who has five American advisers," the director of a Vietnamese service complained. "He doesn't have time to talk to Vietnamese anymore because he is always occupied with entertaining his five advisers." "Instead of your tens of thousands of advisers," said another high official, "you should limit your number to about five hundred. That's plenty."

Certainly the number of advisers could be reduced to a much more manageable number by emphasizing quality rather than by merely "filling slots." The immediate removal of ineffective advisers should be insisted upon, rather than holding on to them as statistical evidence for Washington that "a job is being done." Certainly they should not be rewarded through promotion. Many of the surplus advisers were self-admitted adventurers or individuals who went to Viet Nam for the high pay and the easier mobility into higher positions.

The whole advisory effort had become a vicious circle. The more men the United States sent, the more Americanized the system became and the less the Vietnamese officials did. And the less they did, the more advisers the United States sent. "Let the Americans do it" was a motto we often overheard Vietnamese saying to one another. "It's your war, you fight it," said others. Both Vietnamese and Americans have resorted to tricks in order to get their ideas accepted by the other. One such trick is for the adviser to introduce an idea in such a way that the person advised will think it was his own. Another method is to ask an innocent question, the answer to which will make the respondent aware of the problem demanding attention. The Vietnamese, for their part, do not like to refuse an adviser's suggestion, for they know their refusal might cause the adviser to lose face or, perhaps worse, to destroy a good relationship. They will often agree to suggestions or programs—and then do nothing to implement them. Frustrated Americans then complain, "We'd be better off if the Vietnamese *were* our puppets as the Communists claim they are."

On a higher level, relations between the U.S. Mission and the Saigon government have always been ambiguous. Publicly exemplified by differing approaches to the Paris peace talks, their nature is generally misunderstood by both Americans and Vietnamese. The latter have always believed that the U.S. Embassy controls the Vietnamese government and should take responsibility for what it does and does not do. Americans back home have had something of the same impression—believing that faults in the Vietnamese government could be, and should be, corrected by the American Embassy through strong pressure on Saigon's leaders. This is an unrealistic view, however, largely because American influence on the Vietnamese, while great, has not always been decisive. On a lower level, we experienced this ourselves. Programs and projects we advocated, whether for organizing agricultural training courses or for establishing school libraries, were to be Vietnamese—not American—programs. There was always an element of hypocrisy in this, because so many programs proudly displayed by the Americans as "Vietnamese" were known by the Vietnamese themselves to be American in origin. Yet, many of our ideas and suggestions were turned down flatly by our Vietnamese counterparts—some for good reasons, as we later realized, others, perhaps, for bad reasons.

In any case, there was little that American advisers, high or low, could do. The official policy was that we were guests in Viet Nam and could not expect always to have our way. Many Americans, of course, have advocated an open and complete American takeover. For those frustrated by official inertia and fearful that only the NLF would profit by it, this was indeed an appealing alternative. But others have realized that the advisory effort should be maintained in reality and not as the fiction that it has sometimes seemed to be. If the South Vietnamese are ever to unite and rule themselves, this reasoning goes, they will have to learn to do so at once. The aim should then be to build permanent Vietnamese institutions—and to do it through suggestion and practical experience, not through American colonial rule.

The problem, in the end, stems from the temptation to follow both approaches. While the official "adviser" fiction is maintained, advisers on all levels feel the understandable need to "get the job done." If the Vietnamese won't do it, they will do it themselves. Few stop to ask or wonder *why* the Vietnamese won't do it, and as a result few realize that it is partly because the Vietnamese see the problems differently and partly because many of them simply lack the necessary motivation. The somewhat hypocritical position of the "adviser" has made the problem worse. And when the problem is multiplied by the great proliferation of American personnel— often ill-trained or incompetent—policy is bound to become bankrupt. Thus it is that the most sincere efforts of well-motivated men have suffered the same fate as those of opportunistic adventurers. "Do you think you've done any good here?" asked one bitter young Vietnamese nationalist. "We used to think the Americans were just mistaken in their approach," said another. "But now things have built up to such a point that we can't help believing you are more than mistaken. It seems you are being purposely evil."

Such harsh words could have been avoided—not by suppressing them, as so often happened, but by profiting by the remarks that had led up to them. "What you Americans need," a friend, at once mischievous and serious, once told us, "is a few *Vietnamese* advisers. We could really help you do your job in our country. If only you would listen to us . . ."

[11]

REPORTS FROM THE FIELD

Questionable Statistics and Official Visitors

"We're going to have some excitement for you next week," the American aid official told us one day in 1959. "A Congressional committee from Washington is coming. We want to show them your agriculture center up in Ban Me Thuot. Can you take care of the group?"

"Sure," we said. Everyone likes to have visitors and to show off his work. "How many people should we plan for?"

"Oh, about thirty," he told us. "They want to have a picnic up there. They'll only spend part of a day with you."

"All right," we said, though we could not help wondering about the seriousness of a Congressional committee that wanted a picnic. On the other hand, the situation in Viet Nam was not as serious in 1959 as it would become later.

"By the way," the aid official said. "Why don't you round up an elephant for the occasion. We can pay for that, and it will really impress the visitors."

At this suggestion, we were no longer just wondering about the seriousness of the outing. The idea of spending taxpayers' money to hire an elephant from a neighboring village seemed ridiculous. It crossed our mind that we might charge admission for rides on the elephant in order to pay the rent, but somehow that did not seem an appropriate way of treating Congressmen. In the end, and since we had been made responsible for the plans, we quietly dropped the idea.

In later years we would come to know that throughout Viet Nam there were "model hamlets," "model refugee camps," "model self-help projects," and even "model people" for the benefit of visiting dignitaries. Realizing that visitors' impressions were based on the rather isolated examples they could see in a few days' stopover in Viet Nam, the American Mission made it a practice to emphasize the "right spots." These models were not necessarily chosen because of their perfection, since continuing support was desired. But they were chosen so that local American officials would not get into trouble for not doing their job right. After a while, of course, the "model Vietnamese" got a little tired of the whole treatment. On one occasion we were asked to accompany a visiting Congressman on a short trip to the Mekong Delta. At the local province chief's house, we were offered a lunch of cold lobster, sizzling steak, and wine. Then we were taken to see a self-help school under construction nearby. We began talking to the Vietnamese project foreman and explained to him what an important visitor this was. He was not impressed, however, and said bluntly, "You're the third group of dignitaries to visit this school today." Another time, Vietnamese student leaders were having dinner with a visiting U.S. Senator, by no means the first one they had met. "How do you feel about meeting so many American Senators?" we asked one very sensitive and intelligent young man. "Well, frankly, it gets a little boring after a while," he answered, though without meaning to sound unappreciative. Actually, he should have been more appreciative, because most visitors from Washington saw only Americans when they came to Viet Nam. If they met any Vietnamese, it was usually during a few courtesy calls on government officials and an occasional student leader. "What's the point of meeting so many Vietnamese?" asked one advance man. "Because this is Viet Nam," we replied.

Plans for VIP guests did not always work out as anticipated. One embarrassing situation was narrowly avoided by local ingenuity. The itinerary for a well-known Senator had been carefully planned to include a model self-help project. The day before his arrival, when the preliminary "walk-through" was made, it was found that the villagers had decided they didn't want to make the effort to complete their self-help dam. They had completely abandoned the project. The American adviser discussed the matter with the province chief. To take the Senator to the dam site would place the self-help approach in a bad light; to change the schedule at such a late date would make the Senator suspicious. The province chief hit upon a plan. He went to the hamlet chief and "suggested" that all the people go out on the afternoon of the Senator's visit and work on the dam. We later saw a picture of the Senator surrounded by happy villagers working on the dam.

In early 1968 another prominent American toured a refugee camp named Gadsden in Binh Duong province. Gadsden was sponsored by the people of the town in Alabama after which it was named. A good deal of money and effort had been devoted to constructing a model village with separate and neatly whitewashed dwellings for the inhabitants. There was a school and sufficient wells and, marvel of marvels, a magnificent complex of pigsties in the rear. The men of a nearby American artillery battalion were overseeing the project for its sponsors in the United States. As the army major escorted the VIP around the village, he regaled him with accounts of all that had been done for the people there. A medical clinic was in session at that very moment, in fact. It was such an obviously American show, however, that members of the Senator's party began asking about the local village leadership structure, and also about the management of the pigsties. These questions were never answered, becoming lost in the plethora of good-deed statistics. The whole mood was shattered, in the end, by two separate incidents. At the pigsties, while the major glowed with pride, an old woman started berating a member of the Senator's party who happened to understand Vietnamese. "We haven't had anything to feed our pigs for weeks," she complained. "Two of mine have already died, and look how skinny this one is!" She pointed at the sow she was tending. "Things are pretty miserable here," she concluded defiantly, repeating her words for the Senator who was now at her side. The second incident occurred when the party moved on to the next refugee settlement. Upon arrival there, the Senator was promptly presented with a handful of small Viet Cong flags and propaganda materials. "These were left when the VC entered Gadsden last night," he was told.

On and on it went. Officials at corps headquarters would show maps of progress, pointing out all the new roads that had opened in their regions. When local-level personnel would express horror at the idea of traveling those "open roads," there was embarrassment up and down the bureaucracy. In the Da Nang regional center a U.S. Senator was told that the "Revolutionary Development" cadres in Quang Ngai were good. In Quang Ngai he was told they were bad. Time was also important. Visitors to Viet Nam had little way of knowing what happened to a place they visited after they left the country. An example of this occurred in the neighboring provinces of Phu Yen and Binh Dinh in Central Viet Nam. In the spring of 1967 a major pacification effort was carried out in Phu Yen utilizing enough troops to open roads, occupy villages formerly under NLF control, and remove other villages to new locations as refugee camps. During this period, visitors were shown success in Phu Yen. By July of that year, pacification efforts, and their accompanying troops, had shifted to adjacent Binh Dinh. Soon the latter became the example of success. What happened, then, in Phu Yen? Two months later one of our volunteers was warned by refugees four miles from the province capital of Tuy Hoa that he should no longer come to visit them because of the danger. And a few days later the same volunteer was advised by American officials to leave for Saigon because of the threat even to Tuy Hoa's security. Binh Dinh, too, was not a model for long. By December it was receiving similar threats from returning NLF forces.

Yet the fact-finding missions continued, each of them emphasizing progress. Secretary of State Dean Rusk had a flotilla of some sixteen helicopters for a visit to the Da Nhim Dam, a showpiece project being built with Japanese war reparations. With such an entourage he could take only a brief look before flying on to a similar model site elsewhere. President Johnson, of course, could not be expected to do much traveling on his hour-long stops because of security considerations. As a result, he visited only the mammoth American installation at Cam Ranh Bay. It was somewhat different for Vice-President Humphrey. He made one well-publicized visit to Lieutenant Colonel Nguyen Be's "Revolutionary Development" cadre center at Vung Tau. When Be told the Vice-President to his face about the evils of corruption in the Vietnamese government, it made newspaper headlines everywhere. Vietnamese were pleased that finally someone had dared to tell the truth. Colonel Be remained one of the "model Vietnamese" for VIP's because he had, by his example, become the kind of candid, top-notch person the Americans were fighting for. Yet little was done to correct any of the problems he had described to Mr. Humphrey.

There was no end to the stories of VIP visitors. Aside from the way that serious investigators were guided or misguided through a model Viet Nam, there were even more damaging accounts of "big shots" who did not hide the personal political aspects of their junkets. In early 1968, a newspaper correspondent in Saigon described to us his recent travels with Representative Joseph Y. Resnick of New York, who had brought his nineteen-year-old son and his seventeen-year-old daughter along for the ride. If the efforts surrounding such visitors were not so time-consuming and costly to the American taxpayer, this one would have made a funny tale.

Saigon planners had painstakingly devised an itinerary for the Congressman with his administrative aide. On his first day, however, Mr. Resnick threatened to pack up and leave. He objected to the canned briefings (the navy officer concerned had given the same briefing 138 times in seven weeks), he wanted to visit troops in the field rather than pacification projects and refugee camps, and his children were not granted use of government helicopters to visit outlying areas. "You've nearly ruined my entire trip," he told a flustered protocol officer. "Now my daughter won't be able to write an article for *Teen Age America*."

Continuing in spite of these setbacks, the Congressman, who was running for a Senate seat, emphasized meetings with his armed-forces constituents. U.S. government photographers snapped pictures as each soldier from his state received a good-looking sheath knife, donated by a company in the Representative's district. Each unit got a carton of Kool-Aid, also donated by the manufacturer. At one marine headquarters, an enthusiastic colonel gave a talk for the Congressman: "Got a Cong killer here," he said, introducing a lanky young marine who had shot one of the enemy earlier in the day. "When I hear a visitor is coming I tell my marines to capture a Cong for him. This Cong wouldn't cooperate," he added. "Had to kill him. Sorry." At one of the non-American installations visited by

Mr. Resnick, a Montagnard resettlement, some five hundred of the tribespeople were lined up behind warriors carrying ceremonial shields and spears. "Hello, Hello," they cheered, clapping their hands in unison. An American army captain stationed there observed this with some disgust. "These Montagnards are really getting sick of this stuff—lining up and clapping every time some VIP comes in," he said. "They don't even know what's going on. It's just one big show. And look at all those Vietnamese officials. The only time they ever come around here is when a VIP is visiting. Ten minutes after your chopper takes off, there's going to be one hell of an exodus of Vietnamese officials out of this place." The Congressman's visit to Viet Nam ended with a champagne breakfast for the Saigon press corps. "Whatever way you want to measure it," he announced, "we are winning the war and winning it big."

In late 1967 and early 1968, various constraints were placed on visiting dignitaries. It was reported that even television crews could not go out into the provinces without being escorted by a military officer. This new directive was issued after CBS had shown American troops cutting off "souvenir" ears from dead Viet Cong. When somehow Senator Charles Percy managed to sneak off in a helicopter without military accompaniment, and then got shot at when he was rather unwisely landed at the scene of an earlier massacre, the rules were further tightened. As a result, not only were subsequent VIP's closely escorted, but even members of their advance teams could go nowhere without a military officer by their side. For the timid Vietnamese in the countryside, there was nothing more intimidating than the sight of an armed American soldier. It was not surprising that they only occasionally talked freely. Yet the U.S. Mission could easily justify the close watch they kept over their visitors. "We know it's sometimes annoying," they admitted, "but we are responsible for your safety. If something happens to you, we get our heads handed to us." Meanwhile, Michigan Governor George Romney charged that he had been the object of "the greatest brainwashing that anyone can get when you go over there to Viet Nam, not only by the generals, but also by the diplomatic corps over there, and they do a very thorough job."

One visitor who managed to avoid the worst aspects of the "protectionist" or "brainwashing" policy was Senator Edward Kennedy. Having been fed the official line on a visit in 1965, he was determined to learn the truth on his trip for the Senate Subcommittee on Refugees in 1968. Four men were sent out two weeks ahead of the Senator's planned arrival, and they immediately set to work combing the country's four major regions. Instead of merely following the Embassy's suggested routing, they made special efforts to ferret out new sources of information. This was not particularly difficult, because by 1968 there were a number of disillusioned members in the U.S. Mission in Viet Nam. Even those who were trusted enough to act as official escorts for the team members were often quite candid in their criticisms of the American effort. When the Senator himself arrived for his intensive thirteen-day tour, he startled the Saigon press corps by asking for a minimum of coverage. Where other VIP's seemed to make the trip as much for the publicity as for anything else, Kennedy rightly felt that a large number of correspondents and hangers-on would impede his fact-finding mission and his ability to talk candidly with both Vietnamese and Americans in the field.

Of course, the Mission did put up some roadblocks, and the ever-optimistic "pacification czar," Ambassador Robert Komer, was especially worried that Kennedy might criticize the treatment of refugees. Komer's men, most of whom scurried around with looks of impending doom on their faces, were instructed to write full accounts of everything concerning the team members' visits. When the Kennedy people asked to meet with one young American on the official Mission evaluations panel, they were told that he was "out in the provinces and inaccessible." The man concerned was known to be candid in his evaluation of the refugee program, and it was discovered later that he had actually been ordered by Komer not to meet with the visiting Senator.

Komer was long a whipping boy for frustrated critics of the war. His brilliant mind, symbolized by the computerized approach he initiated for Viet Nam, seemed unable to understand the human problems that blocked his every turn. One small and seemingly insignificant incident illustrates his overconfidence in his own approach. When a Kennedy aide pointed out to him that his itemized regional refugee predictions for 1968 did not add up to the total he was giving out, he denied heatedly that any mistake had been made. Although the difference of 10,000 persons was only a logistical matter to him anyway, he finally admitted, upon checking the addition himself, that there had indeed been an error. "Gee whiz!" he exclaimed. "You just can't trust these majors and colonels to do simple arithmetic!" Vietnamese later commented that all this was typical of America's technological and statistical approach to the problems of Viet Nam. "These things have nothing to do with the real issues here; the American policy itself does not add up," they told us.

Senator Kennedy took the time to meet with numerous Vietnamese—not only with the yes men who filled the Saigon government, but also with respected members of the opposition. During his travels he heard an altogether different story from the one related to him by the official establishment. At one point he turned to his aide and said, "There sure is a difference between the Embassy version and the version everyone else has been telling us." Komer, however, was optimistic to the end. "He came, he saw, *we* conquered!" he cabled Washington when Kennedy left. Like the Julius Caesar he quoted, however, Komer and his computerized approach were stabbed in the back when, two weeks later, the NLF attacked the U.S. Embassy itself.

Perhaps the most tragic figure in this whole matter of reporting to Washington and in the treatment of VIP delegations was Ambassador Ellsworth Bunker. Mr. Bunker, unquestionably one of America's most distinguished statesmen, seemed genuinely disturbed by many of the nastier antics of those in power in Saigon, particularly of former National Police Chief Nguyen Ngoc Loan. Yet he probably did not know the depth of Vietnamese feelings against their government. Even Mrs. Bunker confided to a friend her fears that "Ellsworth is pretty isolated in his Embassy office." Because he was isolated (he once noted that much of his time was occupied with VIP arrivals and departures), his statements were sometimes unbefitting a man of his stature. When asked about the rising anti-Americanism expressed in Saigon newspapers in late 1967 and early

1968, Bunker responded that this was only a function of the new freedom of the press. Earnestly and devotedly, he explained to Senators and Congressmen the progress that was being made.

To the amazement of those of us working at the grass-roots level in Viet Nam, it was not until after the 1968 Tet offensive against the cities that it became generally accepted in America that the United States was *not* making progress in Viet Nam. A cartoon appeared in the Washington *Post* that showed General William Westmoreland turning "that final corner to victory" only to bump into an NLF guerrilla who had come from the other direction to occupy the same urban intersection. What General Westmoreland and the other optimists did not perhaps realize was that they had turned that corner so often that the effect was one of going around in circles and getting nowhere. The fact that VIP's were misled was thus not so important as the fact that the policy makers in both Saigon and Washington were being misled in the same way. They had come to believe in their own overly optimistic reports. It was quite natural that this should happen, and we were guilty of it for a long time ourselves. It was almost as though everyone with the U.S. government in Viet Nam had been trained to sing "Accentuate the Positive."

This is not to say that there were no hard pragmatists among the American officials in Viet Nam. There were many who were candid in admitting the serious problems they faced. But even these people, and among them many of our best friends and closest colleagues, could not help believing that dedication and greater efforts would ultimately bring off a victory. Again, this was natural. No one liked to admit that his own presence in Viet Nam was anything but useful. No one could bear the thought that he might be failing. It was not only a question of job security, but one of psychological security as well. The whole feeling was most succinctly summed up in the unfortunately too derogatory phrase, "vested interest." We all had a vested interest in succeeding. The very fact that so many VIP's did come to observe our work was a further reason to impress them with our accomplishments. An encouraging word from a Congressman or Cabinet member was not to be sneered at.

A more prolific source of information about Viet Nam came to

American policy makers in the form of reports. Although we in IVS were for the most part blissfully unaffected by the demands of official government reporting, we did have occasional experiences with the process involved. It was enough to instill in us a healthy skepticism. We knew that the problem with any developing country was a lack of reliable statistics on which to base future planning, and the AID mission seemed determined to correct this lack by sending out massive report forms for its provincial representatives to fill out each month and even each week. Because of the understandable need for statistics, we could not really criticize this. But the frustrated men who had to fill in the forms did not let their understanding keep them from venting their annoyance with the most colorful of curses. There was a time every month when hordes of Vietnamese who worked for the various American agencies stormed through the local government services collecting figures of all sorts and on all subjects. Some, of course, were available without too much difficulty. Others had to be adjusted for various reasons, as we learned at a large meeting of agriculture service chiefs in My Tho in 1965. On this occasion the new young agriculture statistics chief from Saigon seemed very upset. He had been receiving conflicting and apparently incorrect figures concerning agricultural production in the various provinces. There was a great deal of bitter discussion back and forth with the participants. Finally, one old provincial agriculture man raised his hand and asked permission to explain the problems he and his colleagues faced. Permission granted, he told the following: "The problem is that we have to estimate how much the province chief will adjust our figures before he sends them on to you. Then we have to estimate how much your office will change them. We all know this depends on what each of you wants to prove. The province chief might lower our figures in order to qualify for more relief, or he might raise them to show progress to his superiors. That explains your conflicting figures."

American reports were similarly "adjusted," or even guessed at. In one of the delta towns, for example, the Ky government organized a demonstration just before the September elections. Several army trucks transported about 250 villagers to the provincial capital. Ready-made banners were passed out and the Vietnamese Information Service took pictures to illustrate the "support of the people." An American official reported all this accurately, including the fact that the government had organized the demonstration. When the senior American adviser in the province reported to the regional headquarters, however, he said only that there had been a progovernment demonstration of 250 people.

An example of "guessed at" figures came in response to a request for "the number of bottles of beer sold in the province during the reporting period." "How on earth do we figure this one out?" an AID man, both bemused and harassed, asked us. "How about going down to the Admiral's Bar and asking him about it," we suggested. The "Admiral" was a Frenchman who had settled in Blao and opened a café that was frequented mostly by the French tea-planters of that area. Although everyone called him the Admiral, he had actually been a first mate in the French Navy. A kind, rather shoddy fellow who had heard all sorts of strange tales from his devil-may-care friends in the French Foreign Legion during the old days, he was hardly surprised by our problem. "Well, let's see," he murmured as he computed the number of cases of beer he purchased each week off the truck that came from Saigon. "That accounts for my place," he said, giving us the figures. "Then there's the café of Monsieur M. in Di Linh [the next town]. He must take about the same number of cases—no, maybe not quite as many. There are a couple of other places that also sell beer. . . ." Finally he came up with an estimate for the whole province. Then he smiled. "Let's add three bottles to that," he said, and he poured a beer for each of us. These were some of the statistics on which the war effort was based. When the Admiral died a few months later, having drunk himself to death, even this source of information was gone forever.

The problem, then, was not an insufficient flow of information between the provinces and Saigon and between Saigon and Washington. VIP followed VIP; in 1967 more than 2,000 of them invaded Viet Nam. At the same time, the American Mission in Viet Nam became known as a great center for report writing and statistics accumulation. For both tasks, the burdens on American logistics and

Vietnamese officials' time were overwhelming. Yet the net results poorly reflected the real situation. Our Vietnamese colleagues felt this most deeply. "How can your visitors learn about our country in such a short time? How can your statistics reflect the way we think, the state of our hearts and minds, if you will. Even we Vietnamese have great difficulties in understanding all the complexities of our situation."

What became most serious was that increasingly the shots were called from Washington, a Washington that made decisions on the basis of inaccurate reports and with little or no feeling for what it was like in Viet Nam. The Vietnamese were not the only ones to be appalled by this presumption of omniscience. It was resented, it seemed, by the entire American Mission in Saigon, not to mention the provinces. There were many examples of this. One of them was a spin-off from the 1966 Honolulu Conference, where President Johnson ordered AID officials to "nail some coonskins on the wall." Apparently an old Texas expression, it was explained to us as meaning that visible progress must be brought about before the President's next conference with his Saigon Mission and the Vietnamese leaders. That gave four months. The project in question, which the President liked, was to make a model province of An Giang. The idea was that if An Giang could be developed, then so could any province in Viet Nam—somewhat questionable reasoning since An Giang was by far the most progressive and secure part of the country.

On February 22, 1966, a meeting was held at the American civilian headquarters in Can Tho, the delta town which served as the center for the region including An Giang. The atmosphere in the room was one of frustration. Everyone knew that enormous sums of money would be made available, as they always were for the crash programs that were occasionally imposed upon us; but no one was quite sure that an entire province could be transformed into a subject for Presidential bragging within four months. The American presiding over the meeting confessed certain reservations about the whole business but said resignedly that we had to face up to political realities. Then he went around the room asking everyone present what he could do to help nail coonskins to the wall for the next conference. The public-works man suggested paving a road. The hydraulics man suggested repairing a canal. Someone suggested developing rock quarries, in which connection the canal and road would be vital for transporting the stone. A long discussion followed about whether the stone business would be a good one to pursue. When the education man's turn came, he could offer only a few very general observations, not yet knowing much about that province. As in all American meetings in Viet Nam, there were always several participants who had just arrived in the country and for whom it took most of their full tour just to learn the ropes. When it came to us, representing IVS, we pointed out that our organization was not the kind that was able to nail coonskins to walls in a matter of months. But we would, we added, make efforts on long-term programs. In itself, to be sure, an accelerated development of An Giang province had much to commend it—but not under pressure, not in four months, and not on the blind assumption, made at the meeting, that "the Vietnamese will go along with it."

Another example of Washington's influence and Saigon's desperation could be seen in the refugee question. Here it was not a question of whether prodding from Washington was good or bad—some prodding was useful to keep wheels turning in the U.S. bureaucracy in Viet Nam. The problem, rather, was the panicky way in which this prodding was translated by AID. In 1965 the practice of creating refugees through extensive bombing and H & I fire was just beginning in full force. The American Mission was laboring under the burden of a Vietnamese government that was not very active in refugee relief. In Washington, Senator Edward Kennedy had held midsummer hearings of his subcommittee and had found refugee care to be grossly inadequate. His interest caused a more than momentary ripple in the State Department and its overseas arm, the American Mission. It spread as far as IVS, where we were soon hearing rumors that a frightened AID would instruct us to cancel all our other programs and turn all our volunteers over to refugee assistance. This was neither a very sensible reaction nor a palatable thought for English teachers and agriculturalists whose efforts in their own fields were desperately needed. In order to preserve these interests, we were forced by the American Mission, albeit somewhat indirectly, to make up weekly reports showing how our activities were benefiting refugees. There was no lie involved—our agriculture, education, and youth work did assist sizable numbers of refugees—but the new reporting obligations and tensions distracted from our main job, to say the least. There was, however, no other way to compile the necessary statistics to help AID impress the folks back home.

A further indication of Washington's desperation over Viet Nam was the Peace Corps issue. The details have always been kept rather secret, and for good reason. Early in 1966, apparently without the knowledge of the Vietnamese government, two very high-ranking Peace Corps officials visited Viet Nam. Their trip, they said, had been instigated by pressure from VIP's returning to Washington from a tour of Southeast Asia. As members of an organization having much in common with the Peace Corps, we had been asked by the Embassy to show the visitors certain centers of IVS work in the provinces. One of the two men, the deputy director of the corps, was aware of several problems that would have to be faced if Peace Corps volunteers were sent to Viet Nam. Probably most important was the fact that such a move would cause the Peace Corps to be seen as a directly political tool of American policy—an impression it could not afford to encourage in view of its programs in other countries. We in IVS had already faced this problem, but at least our presence in Viet Nam had begun before the real war effort and heavy Americanization made everything and everyone suspect. Another problem the Peace Corps would have to face was the length of time required to build up the necessary staff expertise for Viet Nam. Finally, the Peace Corps had a reputation for unwillingness to cooperate with other American or even international groups operating in host countries, and in Viet Nam, where duplication of effort and lack of coordination were especially counterproductive, a go-it-alone policy could have been disastrous. The deputy director seemed aware of all these problems, and in any case the unenthusiastic U.S. Mission pointed them out quite clearly.

On the other hand, the second member of the delegation, the Peace Corps' regional director for East Asia, bristled with aggressive designs. He did not seem at all embarrassed over the fact that the Vietnamese government had made no requests and did not even know of their visit. (Since we could not identify the necessarily mysterious men to our Vietnamese colleagues, some suspected that they were CIA agents.) He shocked his American dinner companions one night with brash plans to "move in." "We could have a thousand volunteers in here within six months," he bragged. "Besides that, our volunteers could perhaps serve as intermediaries between the Viet Cong and the Americans out in the villages." McGeorge Bundy of the White House staff, who visited Viet Nam a few weeks later with Vice-President Humphrey, seemed to reinforce this kind of thinking. "If IVS can't do the job and raise its numbers of volunteers," he said, "perhaps the Peace Corps can." Our conception of "the job," however, was not to escalate to a thousand volunteers. Two hundred, we felt, was the largest number that could be accommodated, given security conditions and Vietnamese feelings against increased numbers of Americans taking over the country. We did not, especially at that point, share the feeling of the U.S. government that Americans could do the job if the Vietnamese wouldn't. In the end, reason won out in Washington, and the Peace Corps has maintained its integrity through not being pushed headlong into the Viet Nam morass.

The story of VIP's and reports from Viet Nam would not be complete without mention of the truly popular visitors who had something to offer other than unfounded optimism and barbed criticisms of antiwar "kooks" back in the United States. They were cheery people like Martha Raye, Edgar Bergen and Charlie McCarthy, and especially Bob Hope. They came to boost the morale of the soldiers, and when Bob Hope was in the country it was the top piece of news for the duration of his stay.

Another visitor in this category arrived in the early part of 1966 in recognition of a Bien Hoa army battalion that had ordered a lifetime subscription to *Playboy* magazine. The visitor was *Playboy's* Playmate of the Year, and she was accorded a deference ordinarily reserved for a queen. She did not have sixteen helicopters like Dean Rusk for her ceremonial appearances, but she did have six of

them earmarked for her use—earmarked indeed, as each was deco-
rated with *Playboy's* famous bunny symbol. We happened onto the
small Tay Ninh airstrip just after she had disembarked for a visit to
the great cathedral of the Cao Dai sect. (The cathedral was justly
well-known and had been visited by notables as diverse as Martha
Raye and Edwin O. Reischauer before the *Playboy* signature was
added to the guest list.) A number of eager U.S. enlisted men were
awaiting the Playmate's return to her craft, speculating in the in-
terim as to how she would enjoy the colorful temple with its enormous Cao Dai eye which represented the ever-present, ever-seeing
God. "Boy, when she gets into that Cao Dai temple, that ol' one eye
will pop right out!" said a sergeant. Another soldier was annoyed
because he had to return to his office and could not wait quite long
enough to see the girl. "This is going to be a bare miss," he said,
fully intending the pun.

The idea of a "bare miss" went far in explaining the American
problem in Viet Nam. Many of the visitors and many of the reports
tried hard and faithfully to represent the facts and the situation as
they saw it. Yet they missed the mark because statistics were bare of
meaning. Although much in the reports was true, they did not
represent the situation as it really was. When policy was based on
such a misrepresented situation, the results were understandably disastrous. Reports and visitors always emphasized the tons of food
commodities or cement that had been distributed, or the number of
"enemy" that had been killed. But these were not what the Vietnamese themselves emphasized. Of course they appreciated the food
and cement, and death to them, as to all human beings, was abhor-
rent. Yet to die for a cause was noble, and Vietnamese perceived the
cause differently from the way the Americans perceived it. "Look
at our different understandings about freedom," said one Vietnamese acquaintance. "By freedom, you mean civil liberties. But we
mean national independence and social justice. Now we have neither
of these, but because we are not Communist you seem to believe we
are 'free.' "

And so the Vietnamese continued to despair over the American
way of running their country. "Perhaps we are too different," they
said, "and that's why you never seem to understand us." They were

right, of course. In fact, when an American began to defend a Vietnamese point of view, his fellow Americans would tease him. "You've been away from home too long," they would say. "You're beginning to think like a Vietnamese." But the truth was that until more Americans thought like Vietnamese, all the statistical reports and all the VIP tours and all the program gimmicks from Washington would have little bearing on the situation.

[12]

"LOOK UP, WALK STRAIGHT, SMILE"

A Troubled Generation of Students

"Dollar, dollar, how you wander, from the one hand to the other. . . ."

We were all sitting in a circle, secretly passing a one-piaster coin from person to person and singing the ditty.

". . . Is it fair? Is it fair? To keep poor Peter standing there!"

Peter was standing in the center of the circle, trying to determine who had the coin at any given moment. He was allowed three guesses, but it was very difficult because our Vietnamese friends at the Voluntary Youth Association work camp were so clever about pretending and acting as decoys for each other. Ba adjusted his fingers before closing his hand into a fist in such a way that it was clear he had just been passed the coin. Then he giggled and made obvious efforts to pass it on to Cau. When Cau giggled, Peter, who had been spinning around to keep track of everyone, pointed the finger at him. Cau laughed heartily and opened his fist. Nothing was there. Everybody went into gales of laughter. Peter had been fooled, and the coin was way on the other side of the circle.

After everyone became tired of that game, the evening's leader, Cat, announced the next one: "Cai ten, cai ten." That was a good game for us because it was all in Vietnamese and we had to be on our guard in order to respond properly. "Cai ten" meant "the name."

"The name, the name," someone called out.

"Whose name?" the group demanded.

"The name of—Bob," the same fellow responded.

Bob jumped, and everyone looked at him in hopes of a slip-up which all of us could laugh about. But he quickly regained his composure. "The name, the name," he shouted.

"Whose name?" the group flashed back, still wondering whether he could get through the whole sequence.

"The name of—Chi!" he yelled. Everyone cheered. But not for long, since then it was Chi's turn, and so it went on until everyone had been called on in one way or another.

For Vietnamese students prior to 1963, these games and songfests were the equivalent of American beer or even pot parties. For them nothing was required by way of stimulation but a willingness to drop all inhibitions. Then the boys would clap giddily, jump up and down, roll around on the floor, impulsively put their arms around friends, and go wild with laughter. The girls were more restrained, and when the young men ganged up on one to get her to sing a solo of warbling Vietnamese song, she would at first show nothing but modesty and reluctance. "But my voice is so bad," she would plead. Yet this was mostly a matter of form for the girls, and eventually— after the game of coaxing had been played out—they would sing beautifully and with full flourishes. The cheerfulness, real appreciation of the fun of life, and *esprit de corps* of these youths were truly impressive.

But not all their activities were as frivolous as the evening recreation sessions. The main efforts of the Voluntary Youth Association were in carrying out work projects and seminars. In spite of their emphasis on social-welfare problems, even these were occasionally interfered with by the Diem government. As the only independent, nonpolitical youth organization in the country, the Association was, in fact, under considerable suspicion. "The government allows us to have work camps and seminars only because they think this will keep our minds off the problems of the country," one of the campers explained to us. "By being very strict with us, they know that we will be careful and not risk losing what little freedom we have. Even the number of participants in this work camp was limited by the government because they are so suspicious. They're afraid that if too many of us gather in one place we will demonstrate against them. It is all very foolish because the more they limit our freedom, the more we dislike the government. Someday all the students will rise up at once, but the time is not right now."

This five-day project, however, involved nothing more controversial than the construction of a bicycle shed at the boys' high school in Can Tho. It had started out very auspiciously when our arrival in the Mekong Delta town was celebrated with a large welcoming banner, gracious speeches, and a long table with soft drinks and small cakes neatly arranged on it. As at most work camps, we were accommodated in a large room at the school where we set up cots borrowed from the army. Wire was strung across the room so that we could hang our mosquito netting. We did our cooking outside over small charcoal pots, and each participant took his turn. When our turn came, we decided it might be interesting for our Vietnamese friends to savor the joys of American cuisine.

Early one morning we went to the big market in town, along with those responsible for the lunch. The shopping proved to be a lengthy ordeal, since each purchase required a good deal of bargaining with the vendor. While our Vietnamese colleagues purchased the enormous number of small items for the many different dishes that they would serve at lunch, we searched for the limited number of items we needed for dinner: beef for the hamburgers, French bread, green beans, potatoes, and fruit for dessert. Beef was much more expensive in Viet Nam than in the United States, and we quickly became concerned that our allotted $4.25 would not be enough to feed the twenty-three persons expected that evening. Potatoes weren't available that day, and we had to settle for sweet potatoes. That afternoon, while the others worked in the schoolyard, we chopped the beef by hand for ground meat, cut up the sweet potatoes into something approaching a cross between French-fried potatoes and potato chips, and sliced through long loaves of French bread to form hamburger buns. We were unable to duplicate an American flavor, however, and despite last-minute attempts by some of our Vietnamese friends to bring the food into line with *their* traditional menu, the dinner was a disaster. A few of our colleagues were kind enough to compliment the cooks for their "hard labor," but off in a corner we saw them sneaking a little rice into their bowls from a secret pot they had been preparing on the side.

Meanwhile, the work project was taking shape. The tall grass had been cleared from the schoolyard and lines staked out to show the dimensions of the cement floor we were to prepare. Next, ditches had to be dug, and with both heat and humidity in the nineties the task was not an easy one. The worst problem, however, was not the heat but the fact that we had too many foremen. Minh was supposed to be in charge, but it was by no means clear that he knew anything about building bicycle sheds and everyone else contributed his own ideas, mostly in a good-humored way. Fortunately, the confusion allowed many occasions for rest stops while the decisions were worked out. These stops turned out to be wonderful times for joking and fooling around. Like the tea breaks, they grew longer and longer, and so, at the end of the fifth day, it was hardly surprising that the bicycle shed was not yet completed. But we had at least started it, and eventually it was finished by others.

A few weeks later we met Dinh, one of the girls who had been at the camp, on a street in downtown Saigon. "Several of our friends have been arrested by the police," she whispered. We asked for details, but she excused herself. "This is not a good place to discuss such things," she explained, and hurried off. It was only after the *coup d'état* of November 1, 1963, that we heard the full details of what had happened. They were in stark contrast to the fun-filled days at work camp. Phi, who was big for a Vietnamese and particularly jolly too, was among those arrested. Another was Cau, who had been walking innocently down the street when he was picked up; a very serious and restrained person, he was hardly a rabble-rouser. Almost all who were arrested were beaten. An exception to this was Hanh.

Hanh was one of the student leaders of the Saigon University demonstrations that followed the pagoda raids in August, 1963. Many students spent those days moving from house to house, staying with various friends overnight, in order to avoid arrest. Hanh himself had been considering going elsewhere to sleep on the night he was arrested, but at the last minute he decided not to. This proved to be a mistake, for at midnight there was a knock at his door. "At first," he said, "I thought of trying to escape by climbing onto the back balcony and then onto another building. But I knew that the house was surrounded by armed troops, and so I asked my little brother to open the door and admit the police. They immediately placed me under arrest and took me to a secret villa not far from your own IVS house. There I was subjected to intensive and frequent interrogation and isolated in a tiny cell for some ten days. But I was not beaten, perhaps because my uncle is a high civil servant. After the first ten days, in fact, I was transferred to another prison and treated quite well. The police placed me with other students who also had highly placed connections, and they allowed us to play volleyball and sing songs. The prison staff even included a doctor who gave us injections of fatty materials; I think they were intended to make us gain weight.

"After my release, and in the remaining days before the November *coup d'état*, my house was placed under strict surveillance and I was on probation. My parents immediately told me I must not participate in any youth or political activities again. They were very upset because they had not been able to find out where I was imprisoned; for a while they even thought I had been machine-gunned to death."

Five weeks later, when Hanh told us the whole story, there were still a number of secret villas in the Saigon area where undiscovered prisoners were awaiting release. The repressions of the Diem regime were thorough indeed, and nobody knew their full extent until after the coup.

In the early years, IVS volunteers worked with student groups to a rather limited extent and mainly as work-camp participants. The reason for this was that of all the student groups active in the Diem period, only the Voluntary Youth Association was independent and devoted solely to social-action projects. After the coup, however, there was a great upsurge in Vietnamese youth activity, most of it a direct result of both their new sense of liberation and their newly found political and social responsibilities.

One of the first groups to emerge was the National Voluntary

Service (NVS). It was an outgrowth of the Voluntary Youth Association, whose members had long recognized a need for young Vietnamese to work in the countryside. As a kind of domestic Peace Corps and sister organization to IVS, NVS sent out teams of five for relatively long stays in rural Viet Nam. Working in public health, agriculture, and education, these teams were thoroughly trained, well motivated, and quiet and unassuming as they went about their work. Because they stayed in their villages for long periods, they came to be well received by the local people. We felt a particularly close bond with the NVS people because we shared their basic outlook and believed that our presence in Viet Nam had had at least some influence on their early founding. Whenever we could, we gave them material and moral support. But we purposely avoided any overt participation in their activities, for that could have been the kiss of death for their young volunteers. We knew that NVS's strength with the rural people was based on its independence from governmental or American control. The NVS preference for relative anonymity, however, eventually contributed to its decline. Over the years, the government mercilessly drafted most of the leadership cadres until only a handful remained to continue the organization's mission. Besides, the nature of the program, requiring participants to volunteer for several months, did not attract most young people. The political activism that had helped to overthrow Diem had awakened them to the knowledge that they had tremendous political power, and they intended to use it.

But if the students' role in toppling the Diem regime was viewed with respect by the post-Diem governments and by the Americans, their subsequent political activities were not. In fact, a kind of double standard was used. The wickedness of the Diem government, and particularly of the Nhus, was almost universally recognized in the last part of 1963; therefore the students were right to demonstrate against it. But the U.S. Mission had publicly endorsed the governments that followed as if each was the ultimate in perfection. Therefore, student demonstrations against these governments were wrong and had to be discouraged. The fact that the majority of students, and of the Vietnamese people as a whole, saw no greater good in these regimes than in Diem's was a fact lost on the Americans. It became American policy to think of students in terms of two groups: the "good" students, who either demonstrated in favor of the regime currently in power or avoided political activism altogether; and the "bad" students, who demonstrated against the government and especially against American policy. Unfortunately, most of the Saigon governments during the post-Diem period were altogether blind to the constructive potential of youth and did not encourage the social-action interests of the "good" group. The generals saw even there the possibility of a threat to their own power, and they preferred to compete with each other for the direct control of certain groups which would support them politically and which they could use for their own purposes.

In the immediate post-Diem period, various groups of students submitted eighteen projects to the new government, outlining possible roles for youth in the national development program. All were rejected. The students were frustrated and disappointed at the thwarting of their good intentions. In 1964 they were urged by General Khanh to demonstrate against the French, as a warning against General de Gaulle's proposals of neutralism for Viet Nam. They poured onto the streets with anti-French banners and tore down the French war memorial. But their anti-French feelings did not last long. "After all," they told us, "the French aren't even here. How can we blame our problems on them?" Soon they were demonstrating against General Khanh himself. Khanh's plan had thus backfired, and his ultimate fall from power, like Diem's, was due in large part to student power. Once again, the students tasted the fruits of political success. Yet, the fact of so many being injured or killed in the demonstrations had a sobering effect upon them. Many felt that their political activities had been detrimental to the national cause. "We want a role in building our nation rather than just in overthrowing governments," they told us.

One year after the November 1 "revolution" that toppled Diem, IVS and the Voluntary Youth Association cosponsored a youth leadership seminar–work camp at Vung Tau. We invited friends and colleagues interested in student activities from the various provinces where we were working, along with some of the leaders from Saigon. When everyone gathered at the local high school, where we

camped on mats spread on the floor, we were pleasantly surprised at
the diversity of the groups that were represented: the High School
Movement for Social Action, the Voluntary Youth Association, the
Boy Scouts, religious groups, and what would become the mammoth Summer Youth Program. There were serious young political
activists, bubbling work-camp participants, and older teachers
whose age placed them outside the limits of the "youth" definition.
Yet all were deeply committed to the constructive potential of student activities. One of the older leaders summed it up in a discussion
period: "In this part of our country, particularly, we are involved in
a very complicated war. It is not only a military but also a cultural,
social, and economic war. Military power alone will not win this
war. We have to go to other frontiers—those of poverty, ignorance
and disease. And it is in this prospect that the Vietnamese youth,
born in war and always suffering the sorrows of war, have to struggle and find out a meaning for their lives."

The week-long seminar–work camp brought many problems to
the fore. Our colleagues complained that "the older generation does
not understand us"—the familiar issue of generation gap. One elderly national leader, when discussing the role of youth in the development of Viet Nam, limited himself to the observation that
"young people must be disciplined not to spit in the streets." Most
older people believed that the students' place was in the home or in
school. Students, they felt, were too idealistic and inexperienced for
the harsh realities of this world. Politics should be left to politicians.
There was truth in this, as later events would prove, but there was
too much chaos in the country to expect students to calmly pursue
their studies. "There is a war," one student told us. "How can we
study while our country is being destroyed? After all, we will be
the new leaders of Viet Nam. We have a stake in the future of our
country."

The outdated French education system was still another hin-
drance to the development of youth activities and leadership in Viet
Nam. Because the purpose of education during the time of the
French had been to meet the needs of colonial administration, the
select few who made their way through the exclusively urban system found themselves trained in a manner largely irrelevant to the

revolutionary realities of their country—particularly to its predominantly rural society. The gap in understanding between educated and uneducated, and between urban dweller and tiller of the land, became increasingly great.

"The children in primary schools chant their daily lessons and learn them by heart," one of the seminar participants observed, "but they do not know the significance of what they are repeating. The high-school and college students earn their diplomas by memorizing the professor's lectures. The diploma itself provides for a stable, privileged position in society. But nothing is demanded by way of creative thinking. The teachings of the great philosophers are repeated intact on the examinations. The student does not have to analyze problems or even understand the meaning of the great philosophers for present-day Viet Nam. There must be a thorough revolution to bring the system into the context of modern national development."

We once noted to a friend in the Faculty of Letters that many student political leaders seemed to be classical philosophy majors. "That's natural," he replied, "the philosophers are the ones who know how things should be." But others realized that philosophy was not practical politics; nor was it always relevant to twentieth-century technology, economics, and social revolution. These people felt that as a result of foreign, elitist, and old-fashioned influences on their education, they were ill prepared for modern development. One of our students described his very practical motivations in becoming an agriculturalist: "Eighty per cent of Vietnamese people earn their living by agriculture. And almost all are poor. They work hard with old tools, with their buffalo, and with their sweat. They don't have money to buy a transistor radio to listen to the theater every Saturday. They are frightened by the Communists and the government, too. They are victims of backwardness and war. And they are Vietnamese, as I. And so, I have the duty to help them; and so I am studying agriculture."

The November, 1964, floods in Central Viet Nam gave the Vietnamese youth their first opportunity to prove that they could be an important factor in large-scale social assistance. Up and down the coastal lowlands, typhoon rains had killed five thousand people and left many more thousands homeless and destitute. The call went out for help to relieve the sufferings of these survivors, and it was the students who responded most vigorously and most enthusiastically. Even before they saw how the government would react, the students made known their desire to help. In Saigon, Hue, and other cities in between, they lined up to register their names to join the relief effort. They collected masses of clothing and money through their own benefit theatrical performances and regular soliciting. Some six hundred volunteers were selected by student leaders for work in the afflicted areas.

Sponsored by a government committee for flood relief, the students first confronted the problem of transportation. Since both flood waters and Viet Cong guerrilla activity prevented movement by road, airplanes had to be found. Fortunately, the American military agreed to provide such airplanes. At first this created some difficulties. One group of students who had been promised a plane to Qui Nhon arrived at the Saigon airport only to find that the plane was not yet ready. Impatient, and not knowing enough English to speak diplomatically, they demanded action of the American sergeant responsible for dispatching passengers. The sergeant became angry at their apparent impudence and tore up the manifest. "Whose planes do you think these are, anyway?" he asked. "Well, whose *country* do you think this is?" the student leaders countered. As a result of this embarrassing confrontation, it was decided that an IVS volunteer should serve in an intermediary role and check off the names of departing students as they boarded their flights. For students it meant greater ease of transportation, and for the American military it prevented incidents and seemed to assure them that no Communists would board their planes.

Once in the provinces, the chief difficulty was in working with local government officials. For most of the urban youth this was their first glimpse of local administration in action. Perhaps they expected too much. The whole flood-relief effort was widely billed as the government's chance to prove its responsiveness to the people. Yet the government's response was not satisfactory, and the students found examples of corruption and ineptitude everywhere. They could not help being depressed. Being compassionate toward their own people, the students often wished that they could help the poor who were suffering in the most distant hamlets. But they dared not go there, both because of the guerrillas and because giving aid in such areas was forbidden by the government. The students, whether they liked it or not, were dependent upon government and American support, both for relief commodities to distribute and for transportation assistance. At the local level, they found themselves obligated to cooperate with district chiefs who often preferred to keep commodities within their own grasp, resenting the students who cut off their sources of profit.

The government officials, for their part, were not always happy to see the students come. They already had their hands full, especially since some Viet Cong were believed to be among those fleeing the rising waters. Efforts had to be made to keep NLF sympathizers from getting any of the relief materials and from propagandizing the people. The military situation, too, was frequently tenuous. To have a hundred or so students arrive thus created an additional burden. One U.S. aid representative was particularly open in his criticism. "My God," he snarled, "don't we have enough problems here without having to put up with your city slickers out for a lark?"

But the students were there, and there was a lot to do. Soon they were involved in the distribution of relief goods and in providing manual labor to help rebuild roads and houses. When they first arrived in the district or village where distributions were to be made, they were usually provided with lists of needs drawn up by the local leaders. But as Yen, the group leader in Binh Dinh, put it, "We found the hamlet people complaining that in government distributions only the relatives and friends of the hamlet chief receive the relief commodities. So we tried to make our own survey of needs—an objective survey. But then the hamlet chief and other leaders and local soldiers threatened us with guns and grenades if we didn't distribute to them. What could we do? Life here is very different from life inside the classroom."

The student leaders faced problems with their own group members, too. Some, it developed, *had* simply joined for the lark and were either not up to the work or not sufficiently disciplined for it. In cities like Qui Nhon, and through no fault or provocation of their own, they sometimes got into trouble with the town "cowboys," the roving bands of urban youth. One night we had to rescue a few of the younger Vietnamese volunteers who were receiving harsh treatment from the local toughs.

Yet the students did much good, and they worked hard amid difficult circumstances. Rolling up trouser legs, they sloshed through the flood waters to aid the stricken and perform needed services. City boys came to know what life was like for the majority of the population. They learned to understand the difficulties of their own government in dealing with the problems of the country people. The experience was thus helpful both to those they aided and to themselves. For the most part, they showed a fine sense of responsibility and genuine kindness toward the people they helped. Still, it did not entirely divert them from political interests, as the government and the Americans had hoped. They continued to feel that if the government was not good, it must be changed.

The flood-relief successes were not forgotten. Significant numbers of youth had found a new sense of purpose whereby they could contribute constructively to their society. Thus, even during the extreme political instability of late 1964 and early 1965, student leaders were planning new forms of social-action assistance. The new plan, formulated in cooperation with some of us Americans, soon emerged as the "summer youth program." Its goals were several: to provide the youth with a role in the building of Viet Nam; to give young Vietnamese an opportunity to learn more about their country, and particularly about the problems their government faced in rural development; and to encourage young people of different regional and religious backgrounds to unify and develop responsible leadership. Some in the American Mission added one other goal; though it remained largely unspoken, student leaders knew what it was: to encourage social-action work camps in order to "keep the students off the streets," and thus remove a significant source of political instability.

Perhaps partly for this reason there was some criticism of the

American role in the program. Direct outside participation seemed an insult to national pride. Yet it was difficult to stir up support for the students within the Saigon regime. The Vietnamese government was both unable and unwilling to accept financial or political responsibility. It took three months just to grant tacit support. In midsummer, in fact, Prime Minister Ky abruptly decided to cancel the program. It was not until junta colleagues taunted him with the reminder that he was always talking about social revolution, and that this was his chance to practice it, that Ky changed his mind. Even the American Mission would probably not have supported the students had it not been for the active interest of a few Americans and the continual fear that the students would "take to the streets."

Support of the diverse political and religious leaders was another problem. Certain Buddhist groups refused to participate until major structural and leadership changes had been made by the student organizers. Even though activities could have continued without their participation, the goal of unity was a compelling one, and the students strove to achieve it through skillful negotiation and compromise. In time they succeeded, and Buddhist groups were among the most active. Their achievements culminated in the construction of an enormous orphanage in Saigon.

In Central Viet Nam, not only were Buddhist-Catholic divisions still sharp after the winter's political tensions, but student leaders in Hue were unwilling to cooperate with the Saigon leaders, citing organizational disagreements and a high and potentially corrupting "administrative budget" as two areas of particular concern. A deeper reason was probably the typical Hue regional pride that made them reluctant to be subservient to Saigon for anything. Most people who knew Hue had told us flatly that such a program could not be carried out there. The rector of Hue University pointed out that his students were very independent-minded and that it would be difficult to unite them, especially for an American. "The students here are very sensitive about American participation in such projects," he warned. The temporary American vice-consul also expressed doubts, summarizing his views by wishing us good luck. One had the feeling that most adults were afraid of the students in Hue.

Our first meeting with the students themselves was set up by a former Student Union chairman who was then president of the Buddhist student association. To our surprise, since we had understood that all of Hue's youth groups would be represented, only members of the Student Union itself showed up. They recounted their complaints of the Saigon program. They also informed us that the regional government representative had granted them a substantial sum of money for social activities from the estate of Ngo Dinh Can, former President Diem's wealthy brother. Thus they did not see any urgent need to join the national summer youth program. We appealed to them, however, to consider the advantages of a unified movement for all groups in the noble undertaking of helping their nation's poor. We were aided in this by General Thi, the popular corps commander, who had already become an ardent supporter of the summer youth program. To answer the students' administrative criticisms, we suggested the formation of a semiautonomous center for the program in Hue. By operating under its own budget (though within the national guidelines), Hue could function more efficiently than if it constantly had to wait for communications to pass between it and distant Saigon. We further suggested that five provinces in Central Viet Nam group together under the Hue center, also to facilitate administration. Such an arrangement seemed to please the Student Union leaders.

Finally we noted that IVS could assist in liaison between the two centers, as well as with the sponsoring American authorities. Being third parties with no religious or regional bias, we could rather easily move among the various factions within the region and then between Hue and Saigon. The role of serving as intermediary with American authorities could, however, result in embarrassing predicaments for us as independent IVS volunteers. It meant that to the Vietnamese we would inevitably be seen as "representatives of the money" rather than as complete equals in work camps. At the same time, some American officials also mistrusted us. Still, such a role was unavoidable if the program was to be carried out at all.

The preliminary interest of the Student Union members led to a second meeting a few days later. There was still lack of full representation of all Hue groups, and we pointed out that implementation of the program depended upon unity. That afternoon we visited the president of the Catholic student association to urge him to participate in the social action program. "Helping the poor people in the countryside should have nothing to do with politics," we pleaded when Dinh expressed his anxieties over working with the Buddhists. "That's all very well to say," replied Dinh, "but you must realize that here everything is politics." Finally, however, he agreed to attend a meeting the next day—on the condition that we would be there.

At eight o'clock the next morning, representatives were finally in attendance from all of Hue's nine different youth groups: the powerful Student Union (controlled to a considerable extent by the Buddhist hierarchy), the Buddhist university student association (whose leader worked and lived with the head of the Student Union), the Catholic university student association (our fearful friend), the Buddhist and Catholic high-school organizations (which largely followed their university counterparts), the "Buddhist Family" (a kind of religion-sponsored boy-scout group), the boy scouts and girl scouts, and the Voluntary Youth Association (a branch of Saigon's nonsectarian work-camp outfit). The atmosphere at the meeting was friendly, though at first the Catholics looked a bit nervous and the scouts and Voluntary Youth seemed somewhat skeptical. It was clear that the Buddhists were the strongest element represented, but they had assured us that "there is no reason to mix politics into this program." To emphasize their interest in a nonpartisan effort, the Hue central committee elected officers in a manner that did great justice to the principle of accommodation among various factions. Kiem, the boyish head of the Student Union, became chairman; an older Buddhist Family leader assumed the essentially honorary position of vice-chairman; Dinh, the Catholic student head, became secretary-general, a post involving considerable powers over daily business; and Mrs. Dan, a middle-aged girl-scout leader, was named treasurer. Mrs. Dan, who was full of good humor and motherly advice, was also so tough on her occasionally free-spending younger colleagues that she became jokingly known as "the tiger lady."

Still, Dinh had trouble convincing his "constituents" among the

Catholics that they should participate with the Buddhists. It was as one young Buddhist had mischievously said: "They just hear our names mentioned and they hate us at once! They can never forget the past." One afternoon, soon after the third meeting and election of officers, Dinh came to our house and announced that it would be impossible for him to continue. "Why don't you at least give it a try?" we suggested. "If you do not join, Hue can have no program at all. That will mean no one can carry out their projects to help the refugees and the poor people. If it is not possible for everyone to unite in such an important task, it is unlikely that we can gain support for such a program at all. This is a good opportunity for you to fulfill your desires to help the people. What are you afraid of, anyway?" After hours of our talking back and forth, Dinh agreed to discuss the matter further with his fellow Catholic student leaders.

The next day he returned to see us. "You have convinced me to participate in the program," he said. "My group members, however, do not agree to work with the dangerous Buddhists. Therefore, I will join as an individual member and not as representative of the Catholic students' association." This was better than nothing, certainly, and we expressed our gratification. A few days later our patience was fully rewarded, for the Catholic association, upon seeing how smoothly the central committee was functioning, reversed its decision. Joining the program as a group, it named Dinh as its official representative and then undertook the construction of several brick refugee buildings near Phu Bai airport. The crowning point of the new unity took place a few weeks later when Dinh, the Catholic, found himself acting as the official committee envoy to a Buddhist work camp inauguration. "I did feel a little strange surrounded by all those monks," he admitted sheepishly.

The summer vacations were nearly half over by the time the leaders from the other provinces in Central Viet Nam came to Hue in order to have their projects approved and funding granted. In Quang Nam province, the youth leaders had planned to compete with local government authorities in providing refugee housing. Their coordinator was a young political activist seeking recognition (as we became good friends, we called him "Napoleon"), and the projects he submitted were especially grandiose. Many were carried out by local religious groups. They were all well executed and set a good example for the provincial authorities to do more for their refugees. In Quang Tri, the plump and jolly dentist who coordinated youth activities made an initial request for some $30,000. When we noted that this amount seemed outlandish, (it was later cut to about $1,500), he weakly replied that "we need more because our province is on the border with North Viet Nam." As an interesting sidelight, the dentist once showed us his rustic office. Commenting on a phonograph with a huge collection of American records, we learned that this was his equivalent of anaesthesia for pulling teeth. "If I play music," he explained, "the patient doesn't feel a thing—it's the modern method." Although we did not ask him to pull any of our teeth, his devotion to social welfare was clear. "It took me an extra four years to get my diploma in dentistry," he told us. "I did not study well like the others because I was always so preoccupied with social-work projects as a student."

The Quang Tin group, like that in Quang Nam, also concentrated its efforts on working in refugee camps. What was especially impressive here, however, was the dedication of its leader. Committed to social action and the training of youth, his work involved considerable personal sacrifice. We learned only later that he was responsible not merely for the support of his own family of twelve, but also for four other families of relatives—all this on his meager teaching salary. One of the Quang Ngai leaders was similarly impressive. He was about forty years old, although age never really mattered in the youth program because in Vietnamese we all referred to each other as "brother." He had fought with the Viet Minh against the French for a time, and in the process had lost some of his fingers on one hand. The loss was made all the more obvious because he was an excitable man, and in frequent fits of desperation over government corruption and the state of Vietnamese society, he would flail his arms about wildly. "There is no hope for us," he would say over and over. "Our society has become filled with corruption and rottenness. We try here and there to do some small projects to help the poor and suffering people, but it is all so minor."

Yet even as the shooting war escalated, capturing headlines

around the world throughout 1965, a new spirit of mutual aid captured the spirit of the young. The tenor of the times was capsuled in the title of the student newspaper *Len Duong*—"Hit the Road." Throughout the summer, and in all the country, about 8,000 young people participated in social-action activities—united in one program, working in cooperation with government authorities, achieving much of practical value for the rural people, and perhaps above all, popularizing the idea of social service among the young.

"To the country!" became the call of the youth as city boys and girls shed their white shirts and long dresses, cast aside their pointed shoes, and worked under the hot sun with their compatriots in the rural areas. Teams of students dug wells and drainage ditches; built outhouses; repaired roads; helped construct schools, medical dispensaries, and refugee housing; distributed medicines; and provided recreation for children. "Leeches suck our blood, our muscles ache, and the sun is hot," said one Buddhist youth improving a country road. "But we're having a wonderful time." An old man with wispy beard and dressed in the traditional black gown of Viet Nam nodded his approval of the city boys' work. "They help us very much," he said simply but sincerely.

The students had been the first to admit their need to better understand the rural people of their own country. The gap between rural and urban areas was a deep one. To "create mutual affection between the villagers and the city breed" was one of their chief stated goals, though they also admitted selfish purposes in wishing to discover "new feelings" in the countryside. The students realized that to achieve these goals, good will and action were not sufficient. "The important thing is that we should mingle with the provincial life," their handbooks noted. "We should be careful in our deportment, even in our speech and action, and amuse ourselves in a natural way. In the past there were people who went to the country with dandy clothes and gaudy jeans, in wide contrast with the plain black suits of the country people. We should mingle with the inhabitants' daily life: repair their garden, kitchen, house, and share their meals. Acting with all our good will and capacity, we all wish for some results. The very deep affection we leave behind us will be our pride. When taking leave, the waving hands, the country matrons' greetings will be sweet souvenirs to us. 'When will you come back?' is a question each camper must hear when leaving the country."

While "Len Duong" was the theme for young urban youth helping their rural compatriots, its opposite, "Xuong Duong," meant "March Down the Road"—in other words, "Demonstrate!" The neat turn of the phrase seemed almost designed to summarize the dual types of student activism up to that time. In the summer of 1965, official American observers thought that finally a way had been found to stabilize the government by keeping the students busy with social-action projects. When the leading junta generals visited Hue once in July, a small demonstration was organized to press certain demands, but afterward the students seemed satisfied. "They said all the right things," one commented, "but of course we must wait to see if they follow through with the right actions." When we asked how long the new government would be given to produce these right actions, the answer was hedged: "We cannot foretell." By August, it was beginning to seem as though the traditional summer season of demonstrations might pass unmarked. But our predictions were premature, for tranquil Hue soon buzzed once more with political intrigue.

At first there were only hints of dissatisfaction. They came in response to a new government draft order which appeared to call all professors and teachers into the army. If implemented, it would force the closing of the university and the high schools. Then we began to hear rumors about all-night meetings and planned demonstrations of protest. At one point, a meeting was announced not only on the draft, but on the "role of foreign troops in Viet Nam." We knew that this was the kind of topic that frequently gave vent to anti-American views, and certainly the American presence had been under criticism for some time. Jokingly, we asked Kha, the vice-president of the Student Union in Hue, what had been discussed under the "role of foreign troops"—had they considered the Filipinos or the Koreans, or what? He replied with a grin: "Yes, Filipinos and Koreans . . . and so on."

A few days later we had just completed a summer youth program meeting when Kiem, the Student Union president, came in. "A student struggling committee has been formed," he announced. "We shall work for the downfall of the Thieu regime so that the people can elect a popular civilian government." We followed Kiem outside to the steps of the Student Union building where one of the more theatrically minded strugglers read us the new pronouncement. Hue would not be quiet again, and we wondered how it all would affect the summer youth program.

The next morning the whole front part of the Student Union was alive with unaccustomed activity as students plotted the downfall of their government. Our summer youth activities office in the rear seemed inconsequential amid the competition. Kha was sitting at a desk to one side, translating some manifestos into English for the international press. He confided that he was not in full agreement with the movement. "But I cannot quit," he said, "or they would think me a coward. Could you help me with the translations?" And so the movement continued. After a time, however, it developed that support outside of Hue was not substantial enough. The government, in addition, toned down the objectionable draft law, undercutting the protestors' arguments. The leaders decided to wait for a better time. Meanwhile, the summer program continued, though less efficiently than before.

As the 1965 program was drawing to a close, student leaders were already making plans for continuing their activities throughout the school year and into the 1966 and 1967 vacations, too. They wanted to make certain changes in procedures, as did we. Most important for them was to channel the assistance through their own government, rather than accepting aid directly from the Americans. They had in some instances been open to the charge, which they resented greatly, of being subservient to the United States. Channeling assistance through the Saigon government, however, proved to be extremely cumbersome and unreliable. As a result, the 1966 program, though successful in the end, was further delayed in its beginning. And in 1967 and 1968, there was no program at all. The powers in Saigon had regressed to the point where they were too involved in election preparations and political manipulations to take any chances on supporting "risky" student activities.

There was, to be sure, one work camp held in Quang Tri province in 1967. This was in Cam Lo, the northern resettlement area for persons who had been forced out of the demilitarized zone under the pressure of war activities from both sides. Students from Saigon and other cities traveled to Cam Lo and built over eighty refugee houses. In spite of difficult working conditions, rocket attacks, and intense heat, they planned to go on and construct a school. But the government abruptly cut off funds even for this minor project, and the students, resentful and with no more resources, were forced to return home.

The large-scale work-camp approach to student activities had many obvious shortcomings, as youth leaders were quick to point out. Some young leaders felt that the large camps, while well motivated, were too frivolous and publicity-minded. Lasting for only short periods of time, they were more in the nature of an amusing diversion than a serious nation-building effort, the critics said. Besides, the large programs, with their administrative costs, transportation problems, and living allowances that were sometimes above the subsistence level, added up to a luxury that Viet Nam could not afford. Yet in terms of giving large numbers of students the opportunity to participate in constructive projects and to begin to understand the rural people, the summer youth program succeeded. It publicized the ideals of active social consciousness in a traditionally family-oriented society. And it gave impetus to further efforts on the part of young Vietnamese.

Two developments that grew out of the 1965 summer experience were the "New School Movement" and the District Eight project. The former was intended as a response to the lack of extracurricular activities sponsored by the public high schools, a lack which constituted one of the Vietnamese education system's primary failings. Each province, to be sure, had its own youth and sports service, but its duties were confined to sponsoring very occasional athletic tournaments. Student social-action leaders now began to formulate a plan for the New School Movement, which was directed at developing democratic institutions, social cooperation, and leadership at an early age within the system itself. Its leaders believed that the schools were not just places for spreading classical learning. They had, in addition, the responsibility for teaching their students to become worthwhile citizens. This meant that the students should elect their own student governments and plan their own social-action and extracurricular activities under guidance from their teachers. Miraculously, the Ministry of Education in Saigon gave support to the program, even assigning talented teachers to work on its implementation. Many teachers and students throughout the country hailed the idea, though the older and more conservative ones feared the new plan would pose a threat to the recognized school power structure. In the end, however, the conservatives need not have worried. The New School Movement turned out to be a short-lived affair. With the next change of cabinet in Saigon, and the replacement of the good and understanding minister of education, the program was canceled, and the teachers were either drafted or transferred to hardship posts in far-off provinces. Officially sponsored youth programs were once more left in the hands of the largely impotent local youth services.

The other development was very different. A kind of "new politics" program for Saigon's Eighth District, it began when a group of energetic young leaders got together and asked then Prime Minister Ky for permission to try an experiment in self-help government in one of Saigon's poorest sections. Ky agreed and appointed the men to positions of authority in District Eight. At the time they took over, the situation there was desperate. Refugees had been pouring into the area and setting up crude shacks over fetid canals and in stinking graveyards. Some huddled in a huge, dilapidated warehouse with only enough room for one bed per family. Since they came in by single family groups, without their old village organization intact, they were without established leadership—an impediment to community development. But the young leaders changed all that. Through patient attention and the ministrations of young social-action workers, they organized the people in the district to build thousands of new houses, to clear out the old graveyards, and to construct needed public buildings such as a school and a market. Medical students offered assistance in their special field, giving inoculations and minor treatments. Agriculture students helped to organize cooperatives, and so on. Two years later, the district bore no physical resemblance to its former state.

Even more important were the changes under the surface in terms of self-government. The young cadres had been trained more in the skills of communicating with the people than they had in what were really less essential technical or construction skills. Local and religious leadership had been sought out and encouraged to develop, and a new community spirit was born. The people came to feel a stake in their own government as it was seen to operate at their level and respond to their needs. The reduction in the number of NLF cells operating in the area was almost a direct by-product of all this. While forty-five active cells were reported in 1965, virtually all had been eliminated within the first fifteen months of the new program. The whole effort was considered so successful that the young leaders were invited to institute a similar approach in Districts Six and Seven.

The success of the project was not without its pains, of course. Police corruption continued to be a problem, as did the drafting of the best administrative cadres into the army. But the leaders could do little about these things, and they knew their strengths. When anyone asked Liem, the manager in charge of the District Eight project, what the difference was between their program and ordinary district government, his reply was to the point: "The difference is that we show the people we care about them. We are always out talking with them and working with them, not sitting in our offices or taking bribes. We also give them responsibility. It's all really very simple: we just try to respond to their needs." If people like Liem and his colleagues could govern the country, we often felt, Viet Nam's problems would have been solved. It was remarkable what could be done when the right people were given the opportunity. In those dark days of the Viet Nam war, these efforts were like a ray of sunshine.

The success of District Eight did not last, however. In the May, 1968, NLF attacks on the city of Saigon, there was severe fighting in this area. As much as two weeks before, district residents had reported to Vietnamese and American government authorities that guerrillas were infiltrating into their district. The people's confidence in their local administration had led them increasingly to inform on enemy movements, but in this case no action was taken. When the attack finally came, allied military forces responded brutally. American helicopter gunships and airplane strafings laid waste to the thousands of valiantly built houses and public buildings of District Eight. House-to-house fighting, said the commanders, would have been too demanding on allied manpower, even though a relatively small number of guerrillas were involved. District Eight, as a result, was crushed and devastated, the will of its young leaders nearly broken.

Yet many of them continued their work as did other young people throughout the country. After the various urban attacks, and even while they remained in a kind of daze from it all, large numbers of students joined again in relief efforts. Their work was not always encouraged by the government because of the fears of Viet Cong infiltration into student ranks. Still, Saigon's youth worked day and night to help those in need. Young people from Da Nang journeyed to Hue to help their suffering compatriots there. They split up into teams of five and assisted poor families in putting back bricks and tiles, burying dead bodies, building temporary shelters, and organizing sanitation and health activities. "Though our work may sound good," said one, "it is still much too little in the face of the destruction and misery of our people. But given our abilities, we just don't know how we can do more."

The youth of Viet Nam are intense and nationalistic. Often their frustrations are directed at American policy. "End immediately your interference in Vietnamese internal affairs; withdraw immediately arms, ammunition, and men support for the repressing Thieu-Ky troops in Central Vietnam; help concretely the Vietnamese to regain the National Sovereignty, free of any kind of pressure from any foreign power," they wrote the "American Government" in 1966. In 1967, the Inter-University Council became more specific in a letter to President Johnson. The text of the letter was as follows:

Considering that the intervention of the United States of America in Vietnam after the 1954 Geneva Agreement has led the Vietnamese people to believe that the Americans are replacing the French Colonialists. The American Policy has not helped the Vietnamese People in any way, but it has only dragged on the Vietnamese into a bloody and fratricide war.

The Vietnamese people, principally in the countryside, have been living in misery, and because of the American intervention the country has been split and its struggling force reduced.

On behalf of the students in particular, and the Vietnamese people in general, we request Mr. President and your government:

(1) to end immediately the American intervention in the Vietnamese internal affairs, and to let the Vietnamese people to settle their own problems.

(2) to end immediately the bloody war in Vietnam by a halt of the bombing in the North in order to progress to negotiations for Peace.

(3) to assist sincerely by economic, social, and cultural developments in the South, and only in these fields.

If Mr. President and your government continue their policy of supporting the individuals without consideration of the Vietnamese people's aspirations, we will consider the United States of America as an aggressor instead of an ally fighting for Independence, Peace and Unification of our country.

The feelings of young Vietnamese are deeply influenced by the fact that they have never, in all their lives, known peace. One young man described this in an English composition:

I was born in 1946, just as the first Indochina War was getting started. My father died fighting with the Viet Minh. I don't know how. The war has been going all my life and there is no end in sight. The draft call for young men born in 1946 has gone out, and in September I'll certainly be drafted. I was born into a war, I have always lived in a war, and perhaps next year I'll finally die in it.

Our Vietnamese student friends face no end of dilemmas, and their attitudes at times are understandably schizophrenic. Late into the night they sit around in circles, brooding over songs of the heart by Pham Duy or, more recently, over the melancholy verses of their young idol, Trinh Cong Son. "A Mother's Fate" is one of their favorite songs:

> A thousand years of Chinese reign,
> A hundred years of French domain,
> Twenty years of civil war,
> I pass to you a mother's fate,
> A sad Viet Nam is a mother's fate.
> . . .

A mother's fate, a heap of bones,
A mother's fate, a hill of tombs.

. . .

A mother's fate is barren land,
A mother's fate is burning hands.

As they sing, someone plays background guitar music. Occasionally one of the girls wipes her eyes with her handkerchief. Then they sing the refrain.

You must live with open hands;
I hope you remember your race;
Don't forget our Viet Nam.
Please come soon, I wait for you;
Far away I dream of truth;
Children of all fathers, forget all hate.

Yet the students do not always brood. They feel the urge to struggle for something better. "We plan on struggling," one of them said, "because we want to see a better Vietnamese society—a society having no privilege for anyone—a society in which the rural people and the urban people don't look at each other as strangers. There should be no more hindering, suspecting; rather each person must strive to do his best to increase the people's standard of living—in brotherhood and in respect for all human values. Youth and students want to build such a society, to use their own talents and powers, without any intention to be involved in any politics. We would like to be soldiers, but only to attack such enemies as poverty, illiteracy, illness, and the distressing situation that has prevailed in our land over eighty years of domination."

Thai is a friend whose story exemplifies the frustrations of his generation. He was active in political movements ever since the overthrow of Diem, when he was elected president of the Saigon Student Union. In the summer of 1964, his magnetic personality enabled him to organize demonstrations of up to 20,000 against the Khanh government and its demands for dictatorial powers. He seemed surprised himself at the political power he commanded in such situations, even defying the obnoxious Khanh to his face. Yet, when the floods struck Central Vietnam, Thai was one of the primary leaders of the student relief effort. In 1965, he served as editor of *Len Duong*, and his articles were frequently critical of both the Saigon and Washington governments. "Will South Viet Nam dare to have a regime growing from the people that will make social reforms with determination, as well as heighten the poorest people's standard of life and realize social justice?" he wrote. "The more Washington authorities decide our foreign policy, imposing conditions for war and peace on Vietnam, the more the Vietnamese people will lose their prestige toward the nation itself and toward foreign countries. We need a government elected by the people, endowed with power to voice the thought of a nation holding its sovereignty both in internal and external affairs, and chiefly to make final decisions as to invitations of foreign troops to participate in Vietnam's warfare."

As the American military effort intensified, Thai's frustrations, needless to say, continued to grow. An architecture student, he began to think of using his skills not only for buildings, but also to construct a better society. He read widely and thoughtfully during this period. When the Struggle Movement broke out in March, 1966, Thai worked with labor groups. On May 1 he led a labor demonstration of 52,000 against the U.S. Embassy. It was hardly surprising when he was arrested by the national police soon after and held in solitary confinement. On at least two occasions he was placed in a metal drum filled with water and beaten with a lead pipe. In November he was taken to the "center for political reindoctrination," a prison near Bien Hoa where 800 suspected Viet Cong were being held, mostly without trial. Also in the prison were provincial officials who had fallen out of favor with their province chiefs and some fifty intellectuals who had been engaged in antigovernment activities. It seemed strange that Thai should have been imprisoned with Viet Cong cadres, for he could not help being impressed by their discipline, spirit, and perseverance. Two members of the Viet Cong who had been educated in the United States impressed him particularly. Thai spent much of his time in prison studying Japanese, encouraged to learn the difficult language because of his interest in Japanese architecture. Finally he was released so that the government could draft him into the armed forces. When his preinduction physical examination revealed that he had tuberculosis, he was sent home to recover for three months. "He got TB in prison," his sister said, "but now it is lucky for him; he won't have to go into the army."

At home, friends who met Thai after the Tet attacks on the cities found him obsessed by the woeful plight of his compatriots. He wanted desperately to help them, but did not know how. His leadership talents were extraordinary, but the government in its fear suppressed them, offering him a choice only of prison or the army.

Other young Vietnamese, finding themselves in the same predicament as Thai, have thought long and carefully about their futures. Most feel the need to make a firm choice to support one side or the other in the conflict. Among the new crop of young nationalist leaders, many have joined either the Front or the Front-supported Alliance of National, Democratic and Peace Forces. For them, this seems the only way they have of working for the country. The Front has extremely well-organized programs for youth and students, and it gives them considerable responsibility, authority, and feeling of belonging. Other young people continue to waver in the middle. One, in complete despair, has gone to work for a bank, opting out of the political scene entirely.

Among the older leaders who took part in the summer youth program, some have joined the Saigon government to serve in the education ministry or in refugee affairs. Others had visions of forming an independent youth force to objectively supervise the 1967 elections, though this plan never got off the ground. Some actually ran for the Legislature in 1967, hoping to institutionalize youth activities from within the power structure. But very few won seats. Among those who did were two young activists from the District Eight project. Many student leaders have been drafted into the military, and sometimes they have continued their interest in youth activities while on leave. The military careers of a few have taken more ironic twists. One friend who was deeply involved in student politics, notably in some of the movements with anti-American undertones, confessed with some embarrassment that he was in the military language school. "What are you studying?" we asked. "English," he answered sheepishly. "I'm to become an interpreter for the Americans."

What has happened, then, to the one group in Viet Nam that held out hope for the country's future long after all others had fallen into despair? What has happened to the promise of those who had offered to build up the nation anew? What has happened to the youth of Viet Nam?

Hope has still not been totally extinguished. When disaster strikes, whether in the form of floods or rocket attacks, the students can still be counted upon to rally first to help their compatriots. Yet, in a country where everything is either of the government or else subject to the government's blessing, independent-minded youth are indeed in a frustrating position. As an independent force, they are respected by the Vietnamese people at large. As a government tool, they feel their freedom and effectiveness stifled. The governments in Saigon have never thoroughly learned this lesson. For short periods, it is true, the regimes have been responsive to the youth. Yet these "eras of good feelings" have been short-lived and not "good" enough. Many of the most talented student leaders have, like Thai, been suppressed and actually prevented from serving the country. They are never trusted quite enough. New leadership thus has little opportunity to develop unless it switches sides and follows the NLF.

As for the Americans, they too have many lessons to learn from experiences with youth groups. One is simply to take the students seriously and to recognize them as a significant force on the national scene. It is important not to alienate them after the manner of the American who shouted at a top youth leader, "I don't want a bunch of do-gooders running around the province like boy scouts." Another lesson is to understand the students' need to function independently, and not under the total control of either their own government or that of the United States. While the American Mission was until recent years quite effective in supporting youth activities, it was too often with the "keep them off the streets" mentality and with a certain devious desire to manipulate the direction of their activities. For this purpose, youth leaders were identified and ranked in some mystical order of prominence by certain Americans—an action that might have been taken by any government's intelligence and political operations but nevertheless resented by the Vietnamese. What was particularly resented was that the names of some ardent nationalists appeared in American dossiers as "pro-Viet Cong" simply because they would not bend to the will of the Americans. It was the old technique of distinguishing between the "good" students and the "bad" ones. Finally, the necessity for *quiet* American support should have been learned. The students needed and wanted some American guidance, but not too much. It is always important in working with the particularly idealistic and sensitive young people to use great tact and to support them without taking over their programs altogether. One of the greatest compliments we received came when a student leader praised us as individuals for our *"subtle* support." To the extent that so many of the youth programs did succeed, it was because the Vietnamese carried them out on their own initiative. This is a lesson that could be profitably applied to the entire American mission in Viet Nam.

The young people of Viet Nam still offer the country's best hope for the future. They have been, and still are, our own personal sources of inspiration. From the fun-filled days of work camps to the trying ordeals of life in war, we can never forget their sincerity, their dedication, and, not least, their accomplishments. Their humble devotion is perhaps best reflected in a letter from a friend. "Young people like me seem to be so upset with their impotence to the war of which they are so acutely aware," she wrote. "We want to do many things but with a very vague idealism of helping poor people. . . . So far, what did I do?—a few workcamps, a few patriotic song performances . . . , but look at the whole; blood, death. . . . We can't decide our own fate. The non-communist revolution that I expected seems to die away now, the modern nationalism seems faded. Around us, guns, B-52, Phantoms, heavy trucks, noisy helicopters, barbed wire. . . . I don't want to sit at school to ponder the philosophies of Darwin, Emerson, Zen, though they are necessary, while my people get killed more and more. . . . I got to heal their pains, stop their crying, help them look up, walk straight, smile. That's all I want, just little things like that."

[13]

THE CHOICE

Appeal of the NLF

"I was a young man then," said General Thi, telling of his capture by Viet Minh soldiers. "I had used all my money to buy some new clothes. Then our train was stopped by the Viet Minh, and they saw my clothes and accused me of being rich. They asked me for some clothes to support the Liberation Army. I explained that I had none. But they persisted. I was so young then—that was in 1945—and after awhile I hit one of the Viet Minh soldiers. He was very angry and they beat me up. Then they took me to their prison camp in Quang Ngai province.

"Life there was difficult. We did not have enough to eat and they made us work very hard. Only the rich men whose families bribed the guards got enough to eat. There were many prominent men there. At first I was very proud to be in prison with such famous people—former province chiefs, the head of the railroad, and many others. Although I became disillusioned when I saw how selfishly some of them behaved, others were strong and had my respect. The Viet Minh tried to break their spirit. I saw them put salt in one man's eyes. Another man, who was very well educated (he had studied in France), was imprisoned because he refused to make ammunition for the Viet Minh. He told them he had studied to build bridges and canals, not to destroy. He was shot. These were the brave men. Every day we saw some led away and others commit suicide. When we awoke in the morning we often saw bodies hanging from the beams of our barracks. It was very cruel in the prison camp.

"The girls who guarded me were always friendly and even joked

and laughed. Because I was young, maybe they liked me. But they
were well disciplined. When I asked them for food, they never
forgot their duties. They refused to give me more than my very
small share. The director of the prison camp was not an educated
man. He was a simple peasant, and often we were asked to write
letters for him. Still, he had been given great responsibilities. The
Viet Minh were clever to use simple folk in this way and also to
discipline the girls so well."

As General Thi continued his story, he kept coming back to the
Viet Minh of those days and the Viet Cong of today. It was their
terrorism and cruelty that stood out especially. Yet there seemed to
be a certain nostalgia as well. "Perhaps I would be with the Viet
Cong now," he said, "if I had not seen the way they treated the
people who opposed them, if I had not witnessed their treatment of
the Catholics and of the Cao Dai."

The resentment that many Vietnamese feel toward the Viet Cong
is founded neither in anticommunism nor in a positive desire for
democracy. Their feelings are much more related to their own personal experiences. Those who have seen Viet Cong terrorism, or
whose families have been victims of it, have deep feelings against the
Viet Cong. Others, whose families have been the unfortunate victims of American bombings or Saigon Secret Police terrorism, react
with equally strong feelings against the Americans and Saigon.
Many try to avoid association with either side. Yet this is not always
possible. For most Vietnamese, the overwhelming dilemma of their
lives is the need to make a choice. But how is a choice possible
between two evils? "I am very upset about all the bad news of my
country," said one man who had fled the North when Ho Chi Minh
took over in 1954. "I am angry with both sides: the shameless
inhumanity of the VC, and the shameless corruption of the nationalist side."

For some there was escape. After parts of Hue were occupied for
nearly a month by the NLF in early 1968, a friend concluded that
"we cannot live in Hue without belonging to one force or the other.
When the VC come, we can't defend ourselves and will be taken by
the VC like many of our other student colleagues. I hate the VC,
but I can't live under the corruption and incapability of the Hue

authorities. That is why I decided not to stay in Hue anymore. I will go to Da Nang and teach."

But few Vietnamese are as mobile as our young friend who moved to the comparative safety of Da Nang. For most, this kind of escape is impossible. They are stuck with having to choose. They can make their choice in the form of indifference or apathy, and that is what many have done. They cooperate with both sides—with one by day and the other by night, with the one that is stronger at the moment. Still others, however, are not satisfied with this middle way. For a variety of reasons, they feel obliged to choose, in an active sense, one side or the other. Some have chosen the Saigon government and become the "good guys." Others have joined the NLF and have thereafter been known as "the enemy."

One evening in the summer of 1967, an IVS volunteer was chatting with a Vietnamese teacher friend at her home when three or four of the lady's students came to visit. They were startled to see an American, but soon overcame their fears. "We've come to say good-bye," they told their Vietnamese teacher. "We're leaving tonight." Their teacher knew immediately what they meant. They were going to join the Front. "*Why* are you joining?" the IVS man asked. "We must fight for our country," they answered. "We must fight the Americans who have taken away our sovereignty. We must fight them because their presence is destroying our native land, physically and culturally and morally. To fight now is the only way to prove our love for our country, for our Vietnamese people."

The NLF holds a considerable attraction even for Vietnamese who do not go so far as to join their ranks. "There is so much about them to admire," friends would tell us. "They are well disciplined, very ingenious, and many are true nationalists." Few denied that the Viet Minh had been cruel or that their successors, the Viet Cong, are also cruel. Yet the fact remains that when it comes to making a choice, the NLF are often picked over the Americans. Both sides, after all, have contributed to the suffering. "Communists want to save us from colonialism and underdevelopment," commented Thich Nhat Hanh, one of Viet Nam's leading monks, "and anti-Communists want to save us from communism. The problem is that we are not being saved, we are being destroyed. Now we want to be

saved from salvation." Our friends would note that at least the Viet
Cong terrorism was planned and directed at specific individuals or
for specific propaganda reasons. "But the American and Saigon government bombings are so random, and mistakes are so often made,
that death becomes arbitrary and senseless," they said.

Another factor favoring the NLF is that "the Viet Cong are
Vietnamese like us." The Americans, by contrast, are identified as
foreigners like the French before them and the Chinese before the
French. "We are against the VC because they are controlled by
Communists," said many of our friends. "Yet it is sometimes difficult for us to imagine them as being our enemies. When we
see VC prisoners we must think twice. After all, they look just
like we do, they speak the same language, and they share many of
our aspirations. It is only too bad that they are controlled by Communists." The knowledge that the enemy soldiers are Vietnamese
has frequently led to reluctance to kill them. A Vietnamese Air
Force pilot once told a friend that he dropped his bombs over the
ocean rather than fulfilling his bombing missions over North Viet
Nam. "I can't bomb my own people," he explained. For the same
reason, many Vietnamese, particularly those from some of the Buddhist groups, advocated an end to bombing in the North. "It doesn't
help," they said. "We must bomb China. That is the source of the
trouble." Such statements do not reflect profound knowledge of the
dynamics of the war so much as they do the centuries-old hatred of
the Chinese overlords and a deep love of fellow Vietnamese.

This love has manifested itself in various ways, not all of them
containing any particular political logic. One occasion that we could
never forget was an emotion-charged observance on the border between North and South Viet Nam. It was held on July 20, 1965, to
commemorate the signing of the 1954 Geneva Accords that divided
the country into two parts. Before the days of escalation and battles
in the Demilitarized Zone, the border between North and South
Viet Nam was very quiet. The deep blue Ben Hai River meandered
from west to east as it marked the division. It could be traversed in
only one place, where there was a green wooden bridge right out of
a fairy tale. Nothing more than a red and white barrier pole prevented one from mounting this bridge. On each side of the river,

however, were tiers of loudspeakers blaring propaganda across at each other, along with huge signs proclaiming either "Get the Americans out of the South" or "Get the Chinese out of the North." For a time there had also been a kind of competition to see which side could raise the tallest flagpole and hoist the largest flag. Each side continued to make its pole higher and higher until finally they tacitly agreed to stop at the same height. On the south bank, a huge yellow flag with red stripes billowed in the wind, while immediately across on the north side there fluttered an equally huge red flag with a yellow star.

The commemoration in 1965 was sponsored by the Student Union of Hue University. Emotions first became charged at dusk when a horde of students rushed out onto the bridge, stopping at the halfway point. Against a yellowing sky, the young "voices of freedom" chatted with northern border guards. When they withdrew from the bridge for an evening program, the voice of a student spokesman wailed through the microphone. "We are commemorating a Day of Shame for Viet Nam," he shouted. "We should be crying!" As midnight approached, the students took torches and formed an awesome procession in the darkness. Pacing the banks of the Ben Hai River, they fervently sang their patriotic song, "Viet Nam, Viet Nam!" At exactly midnight they surged again onto the bridge. "Long live Viet Nam!" they cheered, and then burst into song again. Throughout, the impersonal loudspeakers from the North droned on with their propaganda and one could not help feeling the dilemma of young nationalists in a divided land. Different governing systems, perhaps, but one nation. Regional differences in outlook, yet one people. "Nam Bac Mot Nha," said a sign over an archway on the northern bank of the Ben Hai—South and North: One Home.

As more and more Americans came into the South, the NLF theme of foreign intervention seemed more and more credible to the average Vietnamese. "The VC are so much like us that they are a most elusive enemy, like a ghost; but the Americans are so obvious," said a Vietnamese friend. "Even though I believe in the American cause and am against the VC, it is very difficult to convince others of the VC danger." The NLF took many positive steps to increase their credibility with the Vietnamese people as a whole. They involved the peasants in their cause in very subtle ways. When they collected taxes, for example, they did so by establishing a daily contribution of rice. Every day when the women cooked a meal they were obliged to set aside a handful of rice which would be collected regularly by the Front. When weapons needed to be made, there were tasks for even the old men to perform, to involve them in the cause. Anyone, for example, could whittle the spikes which were placed as booby traps on paths used by the Saigon troops. Anyone could carry messages and feel a part of the liberation force. The average man, in fact, could become a hero. This fact was reflected in NLF films and propaganda. The case of Nguyen Van Troi demonstrated it well. Troi placed a bomb under a bridge over which U.S. Secretary of Defense Robert McNamara would pass on one of his visits. When he was caught, he remained proud of his cause to the very end. "I have committed no crime against my people," he shouted as he was bound to the post at which he would be shot by Saigon authorities. "The U.S. imperialists are our enemy. They have come here to sow death. . . . Long live Viet Nam! Long live Ho Chi Minh!" A simple workman by origin, Troi was easy for Vietnamese to identify with—much easier than the elitist officers of the Saigon Army would have been.

In addition to involving the people in their cause, NLF cadres appealed to local needs and desires. The desire for land ownership was only one of these. Refugees would note that in NLF-controlled areas the guerrilla soldiers often helped poor widows in harvesting their crops. If an NLF soldier took a chicken, he would leave the farmer with a receipt which was supposedly redeemable after the war. Such methods not only contrasted with the notorious practices of stealing on the part of Saigon troops, but they also gave the farmer a stake in seeing the war ended on terms favoring the NLF— for only then could the farmer collect on his IOU. The NLF built up its support little by little and with great patience and wisdom. The extent of its infrastructure amazed even the Vietnamese. It was not until the 1968 Tet fighting, for example, that associates of Hue's energetic and highly competent boy-scout leader learned the full story about this man. He had been a local NLF leader for fourteen years. "I just can't believe it," a colleague said later. "We had no idea. He's such a good man."

One of the NLF tactics involved a subtle use of timing. When the power line was put up connecting the Da Nhim Dam with Saigon, much of it ran directly through NLF-controlled jungle territory. Throughout the construction period, no sabotage was attempted. When the job was completed, however, and the Saigon population had begun to enjoy the electricity, the wires were cut. The Saigon authorities then played directly into the hands of NLF propaganda. Although a schedule had been established enabling all districts of Saigon to receive electricity for equal amounts of time, influential residents complained and insisted on certain priorities for themselves. The poorer sections of the city thus went without power. Americans, wedded to electricity for their air conditioners, refrigerators, and stereo sets, took the hint and prepared for the worst. They built noisy generators outside their homes, further irritating the Vietnamese, who resented this added din in the streets. Meanwhile, the NLF, confident of eventual victory, could plan on later repairing the cut lines at little costs to themselves.

The NLF concentrated on translating its actions into effective propaganda. Each soldier was considered a member of a propaganda team with a personal responsibility to impress the population. If leaflets were to be passed out, they were distributed by hand rather than impersonally dropped by plane. Their slogans sounded Vietnamese, whereas the Saigon efforts seemed to be coined by Americans. ("Keep the Chinese out of the North" was an example of this; no Vietnamese needed to be told to keep the Chinese out of his country.) Political messages were conveyed in subtle ways, frequently through the traditional form of Vietnamese *cai luong*, or folk opera. Vietnamese love *cai luong;* to the country folk in particular it is a rodeo and a circus and Rodgers and Hammerstein all in one. The Saigon government, by contrast, imported television as a "psywar" device. Electricity was virtually nonexistent in rural areas, however, so the audiences were automatically limited. In addition, many sets never found their way beyond the district chiefs' houses, since local officials often claimed that installing sets in a public place risked damage or theft. Finally, for those who did get to see television there was an identification problem. Featured on the screen were smartly dressed Saigon stars; but they might as well have been Martians, for the common people could not identify with those from such a different level of society. Further complications arose when popular American westerns were shown. Most Vietnamese, it turned out, sided with the Indians rather than with the cowboys.

There were other ways in which the Saigon side compared poorly with the NLF. Saigon's lack of responsiveness to the people was probably the most important factor explaining the NLF's growth. Four-lane highways were built when the people needed irrigation ditches. Grotesque bronze statues were constructed in the cities when people in the countryside lacked enough rice. Land taxes were collected from land that the Viet Cong had distributed free of charge. And corruption was so bad that Vietnamese often joked that if the Americans wanted to win the war, they should drop money and luxury goods over the NLF-controlled areas and over the North—the reasoning being that officials there would then become as corrupt as those in the Saigon government. Corruption in the Saigon army was particularly widespread. A Hue resident gave the following examples which occurred during the Tet, 1968, fight for the city:

"(1) A performing group from Radio Hanoi came to Hue and took only three wind instruments from the National Conservatory of Music; they left a note to that effect. But when the Republic of Vietnam military came, they stole or destroyed all the instruments.

"(2) Most of the people who came as refugees lost all the things from their houses during the time when only the Saigon military had permission to move about in those areas.

"(3) Outside the city there is still no security now, and the people don't yet have permission to return. Most of the animals and tools of these people have been stolen by the pacification teams when they went on operations with the American military."

In cities like Vinh Long, the Saigon troops were so flagrant in their disrespect for property that military trucks were backed up to store fronts and the merchandise was loaded and carried off in mass. One of the most influential statements to come out of Vietnam, released on January 5, 1968, by the Council of Vietnamese Catholic Bishops, was in response to just such actions. To them, moral decadence was one of the most disturbing aspects of the war:

How can Peace truly exist if the responsible people have simply their "flowery promises," if the laziness, dishonesty, corruption, and robbery exists in all social classes, if there are still many who live luxuriously or indifferently among millions of war victims or even take advantage of this war to impoverish their wretched fellow men?

Much of the difference between Saigon and NLF troops is simply a matter of discipline. NLF discipline is not foolproof, as was shown by the excessive killings during the occupation of Hue. Yet their people have been trained in such a way and inspired by such leadership that they have learned to control themselves relatively well. An IVS girl who had once been a prisoner of the NLF for two months testified to this. One of her NLF "hosts," she said, had rescued an American pilot whose plane had been shot down. The fury of the Vietnamese was such that he genuinely wanted to kill the American invader. "But I knew that I must not," he told the girl, "and so I didn't." Discipline mixed with thoughtfulness was exhibited again on the IVS girl's release. Representatives of the Front guided her and her Quaker friend to a farmer's house within half a mile of the main highway. (From there, they could easily find their way next morning into territory controlled by the Saigon government.) Although the NLF men asked the farmer to put the girls up overnight, they took care not to endanger him to possible Saigon reprisals. To this end, it was emphasized to the girls that the man was not with the NLF. What was more impressive was that to avoid any material imposition on the poor farmer, the NLF men gave the girls a little pail of rice for their breakfast next morning. Saigon troops, unfortunately, are rarely so considerate of the people for whose allegiance they are supposed to be fighting.

The NLF have of course met many difficulties, too. One of the key aspects of guerrilla warfare, for example, is "living off the land." Wild fruits and vegetables are important sources of food and the NLF has applied strict rules to preserve the supply. In the case of wild manioc, severe punishment is dealt to anyone who does not replant the cuttings after digging up manioc roots. Still, such poor and irregular sources of food have not been adequate. A dependable food-supply system has had to be worked out with the local population, and the NLF has not always succeeded in this. Transportation of regular supplies is difficult because of air strikes and the perishability of the food. Storage is difficult because villagers sometimes disclose the locations of the reserves to Saigon troops. Occasionally, the people have not felt as great a responsibility for NLF property as the cadres thought they should. One captured document expressed concern about the failure to respect NLF rice supplies. "A recent check," it said, "revealed that a great amount was lost, as certain families had used our rice for chicken feed. At Hoa Loi, one of our units had entrusted 20 bushels of rice to one family. That family used our rice to feed its chickens; as a result only about 14 bushels were left." The experience showed, among other things, that the people in NLF areas were as human as those under Saigon control. It also showed that without the people's support, neither side could succeed.

Although ideology is secondary to everyday experience, one phrase does elicit considerable reaction among Vietnamese. That phrase is "social justice," and it helps to describe an integral part of the NLF's appeal. "Maybe we would be no richer under Viet Cong rule," said one of our friends, "But at least everybody would be *equally* poor. There would be no wealthy exploiters like we have now. We admired the Viet Minh for their austerity and we admire the VC and the government in the North for it now." Then he went on to tell the story of Saigon's streets. It helped to point out the wish for social equality. "Take Cong Ly," he said. " 'Cong Ly,' in Vietnamese, means 'justice,' and it so happens that Cong Ly Street is a one-way thoroughfare. This is very symbolic: Justice in Viet Nam is a one-way street. It is only for the rich and the powerful.

"On fashionable Tu Do Street, the French tried to prevent overcrowding by forbidding bicycles. All nonmotorized vehicles, and thus the poor people, have had to detour around. 'Tu Do' means 'freedom.' Thus, freedom in Viet Nam is only for the rich.

"Our situation is summed up by the name of a third street in our capital city—'Thong Nhut,' which means 'unification' in English. On one end of Thong Nhut Boulevard is the zoo. On the other end is the presidential palace. Viet Nam, you see, is unified by two monkey cages!"

The story of Saigon's streets, while frivolous on the surface, contains a serious moral in terms of which way uncommitted Vietnamese will turn. If justice and freedom are qualities unknown under the various Saigon governments, and if national leaders are likened to the monkeys in the Saigon zoo, then disaffection with the regime is a very real problem. "But which way can we turn?" Vietnamese ask. "To the NLF?"

The key to NLF success has been its ability to capitalize on this political dissatisfaction. The military effort has been much less important, and it was only with American escalation that the war took on a predominantly military cast. The dividing line is of course a hazy one, since NLF terrorist tactics have always had a military element to them. But essentially the Front has aimed at political goals, at impressing the enemy and the neutral general public with NLF strength, or at striking at the enemy's most hated partisans, such as corrupt local officials. "The party guides the armed forces in all fields," NLF cadres are taught. The political basis of Liberation Front tactics explains why American troops have been unable to combat them effectively. The Americans have been aiming at an entirely different problem. Where the NLF stresses traditional values and progressive advancement, the Saigon authorities have deferred progress and stressed military repression. The Americans have tried to make improvements and to make the Saigon government more responsive, but in 1967 even they placed their civilian effort almost entirely under military supervision and control. The effects of this approach have been self-defeating in many cases. One American volunteer, who was helping refugees from an NLF area, was told that those he was assisting were the families of the enemy. His giving them food amounted to giving aid to the foe. When the volunteer replied that he was in Viet Nam to help people regardless of their political beliefs, particularly when they happened to be women and children, he was ordered to leave the country. But the fate of the American volunteer and his humanitarian concern is not the point of the story. More important was the loss in terms of an opportunity for effective psychological warfare and a political response to a political war.

For most American officials, both the nature of the war and the identity of the enemy have been something of a mystery. It has been a strange and difficult war to understand. It has never even been clear what the enemy should be called. The term "North Vietnamese" does not fit the combatants, since so many are native southerners. The term "Viet Cong" is not very apt either. Coined in 1956 by President Ngo Dinh Diem, it means literally Vietnamese Communist. For Diem's purposes it was quite a convenient way to refer to any opponent of his government, since calling them Communist entitled Diem—particularly in American eyes—to imprison vast numbers of his enemies; since Americans could not know how many of these "Communists" were actually anti-Communist nationalists, Diem was safely assured of continuing American support against these "Viet Cong." The insurgents themselves, however, greatly resent this term. In 1960 they formed the National Liberation Front,* and they now address each other not as "dong chi"—comrade—but as "nguoi cach mang"—revolutionary. A Saigon foreign minister once noted in private that only 5 per cent of the "Viet Cong" are actually Communists, though he hastened to add that this 5 per cent is a controlling minority and forms the leadership nucleus.

What, then, are the remaining 95 per cent? Some Vietnamese estimate that 20 per cent are nationalist South Vietnamese who sincerely believe they have been fighting for freedom and independence; many had fought the French for similar reasons. The rest, and at 75 per cent the vast majority, are simply products of circumstances, finding themselves in the Front because of family connections or an urge for adventure, because they were drafted or kidnapped, or because they became disillusioned with the alternatives. When these persons are asked about communism, they respond with blank stares. "For a thousand years we fought the Chinese," one said. "After that the French came and we defeated

---

* Actually, its precise English name is "National Front for the Liberation of South Viet Nam."

them. Now we have to fight the Americans." And so, perhaps inevitably, they support the NLF—sometimes by joining its army, sometimes by carrying supplies or guiding units into the cities, sometimes by providing storage space for food and weapons, sometimes by feeding hungry guerrillas, and sometimes simply by not reporting NLF activities to government agents.

With all the talk about communism, most Americans have been unaware that at one time the United States supported the NLF, or rather its predecessor, the Viet Minh. "The first time I ever saw an American flag," reported one ex-prisoner, "was in a Viet Minh prison camp. The Viet Minh were really proud of the support they were receiving from the United States." This was in the last days of World War II when Ho Chi Minh's nationalistic guerrillas formed the only active resistance against the Japanese. They proved most valuable to the allied war effort by providing intelligence and by rescuing allied pilots who were downed behind Japanese lines. In exchange, the United States provided weapons and assurances of assistance to the independence movement. President Franklin D. Roosevelt was especially interested in self-determination for the peoples of Indochina. In 1945 Ho Chi Minh, before a cheering Hanoi crowd, made an appeal for American support by reading familiar lines from the Constitution of the newly declared Democratic Republic of Viet Nam: "All men are created equal," he began. "They are endowed by their creator with certain inalienable rights, among these are Life, Liberty, and the pursuit of Happiness."

But the friendship between the Americans and the ragged Viet Minh guerrilla bands was short-lived. America turned her attention to Europe; her loyalties went to NATO and thus to France. "If there is anything that makes my blood boil," said the American General Douglas MacArthur, "it is to see our Allies in Indochina . . . reconquer the little people we promised to liberate." But by 1954, some 80 per cent of the cost of the French war in Indochina was being underwritten by the United States itself.* Ho Chi Minh's soldiers were no longer the faithful allies who gathered intelligence on the Japanese and rescued American pilots. They were now seen

* George McT. Kahin and John W. Lewis, *The United States in Vietnam* (New York: Dial, 1967), p. 32.

as Communists, a perversion of mankind that had to be "contained."
To be sure, Ho Chi Minh was an avowed Communist, and few
doubted in later years that the real power behind the NLF was too.
But it was also a case of the same nationalism at work once again.
What motivated Ho to support America against the Japanese now
motivated him to oppose America for supporting the French.
Therein lay the dilemma—and the difficulty for the Vietnamese of
choosing sides.

By 1968, however, nationalism seemed to be winning out. Because
the NLF stressed traditional values, it appealed to the natural sentimentality of the Vietnamese people and attracted them. There was
something romantic about joining the Front and fighting alongside
one's brothers against the foreigners. Not only was it historically
logical, but—consciously or unconsciously—it could not help appealing to the true Vietnamese spirit, a spirit expressed in "Road
Sabotage," a 1948 Viet Minh poem by To Huu:

> The cold moves from Thai Nguyen down to Yen The
> and the wind rages through the woods and the Khe Pass.
> But I am a woman from Bac Giang who does not feel the cold,
> who feels nothing but the land, the land.
> At home we have yet to dry the paddy
> and stock the corn and chop the manioc;
> at home we have quite a few children;
> still, I follow my husband to sabotage the road.
> Lullaby, my child, sleep well, and wait.
> When the moon fades, I will return. . . .*

One has but to read the letters of NLF or North Vietnamese soldiers written to their loved ones back home in order to realize the
sentimental view these men have toward their mission and toward
the war. The same romantic vision may be seen in the propaganda
that paints rosy pictures of approaching victory. "The country-
selling regime of Saigon is collapsing," claimed one leaflet in 1968.

* From "'Road Sabotage" by To Huu, translated from the Vietnamese by
Nguyen Ngoc Bich and copyright © 1967 by the Asia Society, Inc. The poem
is included in an anthology of Vietnamese poetry edited by Nguyen Ngoc
Bich, prepared under the auspices of the Asian Literature Program of the Asia
Society, New York. It was first published in *The Hudson Review*, Vol. XX,
No. 3, Autumn 1967.

"The American imperialists are in a stalemate situation without any way out. . . . Let all true patriots unite closely with the entire people and march forward to win glorious victory for the Fatherland." Doubtless, many joined the Front simply to be on the winning side. It was logical enough that the foreigners would not stay in Viet Nam forever.

And so it is that Vietnamese have been forced to choose one side or the other. Sometimes their choices mean the separation of families, and often a whole village will find itself torn apart. Some of the young people, unwilling to kill their brothers on either side, cannot make a choice. Sometimes they hide in the slums of the large cities, where they are occasionally picked up by the police as draft dodgers and sent to military training camps; in a few weeks they may desert the army and return to their hideouts once again. These young men are not just lazy. They have suffered much in their hearts and minds. "We may smile on the outside," they say, "but inside we are crying." The agony of choosing was expressed very well in a letter from a young Vietnamese who was himself about to "disappear":

Maybe this is the last letter I send you—because I must make the choice, the choice of my life. I am pushing to the wall. To choose this side or the other side—and not the middle way!

I can no more use my mouth, my voice, my heart, my hands for useful things. All the people here have to choose to manipulate guns— and they have to point straightly in face of each other. One side the Vietnamese city people and Americans, another side Vietnamese rural people and Communists and Leftist minded people.

What have I to choose?

But all things are relative now—I can't side even with Americans or Communists. But you have no choice. Or this side or the other side— With Americans, you are accused of valets of Imperialism, of pure Colonialism—You are in the side of foreigners, of the people who kill your people, who bomb your country, with the eternal foreigners who always wanted to subjugate you for thousands of years. . . .

No, it's a desperate situation. I want so desperately to be still in jail— It don't pose before you a terrible problem: to choose. . . . I can't keep quietly, I can't have a peaceful mind in these days.

I can't become a mercenary in this kind of puppet army. Americans in uniform are not my friends at all. They're just foreign troops in my country. Furthermore, I can't carry the gun and kill my people, Communist or not. They're all my compatriots that I learn to love, to encherish.

No, I can't, physically and mentally.

I met many of our friends. They're so desperated.

A–, he dropped by to see me, he said he could not fire in the battlefield without blooding in his heart, he can't help crying for his own dilemma.

B– said desperately, "Maybe he side with the VC, against these militarists!?"

Many of my friends in Hue must have to choose—or prison in this side or some kind of "desperate collaboration" with the other side—

I want quietly to do my things well—to build a new environment for my country. But you can't do it without the choice of a political system. Not with foreign domination—Chinese, French, Japanese, or American. . . .

[14]

"WE, THE VIETNAMESE PEOPLE, CAN MAKE IT"

The Postwar Prospects

Hoa grew up on a small farm in the Mekong Delta where her father grew rice, coconuts, and bananas. Her family was poor, and it was only because a somewhat better-off aunt and uncle in Can Tho accepted Hoa to live with them that she had been able to go to high school. When she graduated at the top of her class, her energy and fluent English helped her to get a job with an American organization in Saigon. Then, with the money she earned, she was able to go part-time to the university.

Bright and strongly nationalistic, Hoa represents the hope of Viet Nam. Yet, like most other young Vietnamese, she is torn apart by the situation. She is concerned about the pressures of change and talked with us many times about its effect on friends. "Some want a complete change," she said; "to leave all the traditional values behind and westernize Viet Nam entirely. These people are increasing in number because they are the results of the present Vietnamese education—the leftover of the French—which serves only the urban elite and is very unresponsive to the mass. Most of the students are very knowledgeable about European culture, but the understanding of their own people and culture is very limited. Consequently, they can only be civil servants but never good leaders who are urgently needed in Viet Nam today. Another group is the tradition-preservers. Their knowledge of the national heritage is very intensive but not up to date because their schools are considered obsolete and therefore forgotten. A few tried to bring the importance of a study of Asian heritage to the public but they received a very indifferent attitude from the government and the students. The rest defend themselves by sticking blindly to the old traditions and withdrawing completely into their shells."

Hoa would work for hours at the local hospital, helping to change bandages, talking to patients, writing letters for those who couldn't write, and through her cheerful smile encouraging others. Hoa had a gift of being able to lead by humble example, and unlike many of the other young leaders, she was not proud and did not try to develop a political following. She emphasized the importance of what each individual could do: "Some can make only the smallest contribution in terms of the whole, but that contribution should be the greatest in terms of what one has to offer of oneself. However, I have had the best chance to be in contact with many people. I set up groups of my friends to study and work together. After a few small accomplishments, a sense of 'community' has been felt among us."

Out of her work came the realization that "the world is not all peaches and cream or a big bowl of rice." She grew up in the period of Vietnamese efforts to throw out the French colonial power and establish independent rule. But "the word 'self-determination' was only heard; it never resulted in the peoples' true longings," she once wrote. "I have witnessed the tremendous destructiveness of Western imperialism and communism to Vietnamese society. The vast gap between a small minority of urban war-profiteers and corrupt government officials on the one hand, and the large majority of oppressed farmers on the other, has constantly impoverished this little Viet Nam. Socially, the overflow of Communist collectivism and Western individualism has traumatically broken down the family structure which is the basic unit of Vietnamese society. If there is no remedy, Viet Nam will inevitably be collapsed. Its survival depends entirely on its people. We must cure the ills of our own society."

Being active in student projects, working in the slums, and joining student groups to assist in the refugee camps put social pressures on Hoa herself. "I found myself being torn apart," she told us. "On one hand I want to be a 'good girl' in a traditional Vietnamese family, and on the other hand I must be an active social citizen in this critical period of Vietnamese history. I have unlocked the narrow family confinements to walk firmly in the larger environment of society. Doing this hurt me very much, because I could not fulfill my filial duties toward my dear parents whom I love so much."

Hoa sees the answer only through some kind of revolution, though preferably not through a Communist one. She sees the continuation of the Americanization as further eroding society and the Saigon government as just an extension of the Americans. After the NLF urban attacks in February, 1968, she joined other students in helping the homeless. But she came to feel that even the young, who once were the reservoir of strength and dedication, had been compromised. "I worked with the other students to build two hundred new houses for the Saigon refugees," she wrote us. "The longer I stay with the Saigon students, the more I get discouraged. This situation is just a miniature of Viet Nam—full of corruption, political ambitions. I feel sometimes practically hopeless. I know I should not be this way but I can't help being realistic and honest with myself."

Hoa felt that she should follow the path of many other Vietnamese patriots such as Phan Boi Chau and Ho Chi Minh. She wanted to leave the country and join movements abroad so that when the opportunity afforded itself she could return and make a real contribution. Quite without trying, she developed a small following among the students, and it was then that she began to find herself "watched" by the government. In late March, 1968, she wrote:

At home, I am knowledgeable of the situation but don't know what to do. I can't speak what I want, though it is constructive and true. I am pushed down more than ever. If I am put in jail, it wouldn't do any good because you know too well what the fate of a Vietnamese political is like. No one knows him; the people call him a communist regardless of what he is. I do not want to waste my young age in a dark prison. If I can't help my country effectively at home, I will do it abroad.

But because the exodus of young people had become too great, the government had stopped issuing visas to most applicants for scholarships aboard. Hoa had neither the right family connections nor enough money to bribe the appropriate officials. But unlike many others, Hoa did not join the Liberation Front, nor did she try to escape the realities of war by working at an excellent wage as an interpreter. Instead, she chose to work in a provincial hospital, philosophically shrugging off disappointments by noting that "things never turn out the way we want them to. We have to accept life as it is. No one knows what is going to happen."

While a concerted effort has been made to control the young leaders and to prevent "troublemaking," little has been done to provide an atmosphere in which young men and women like Hoa can reach their full potential. We saw these people emerging from the high schools and universities and from all levels of society. The tragedy was that rather than being encouraged to develop their natural leadership abilities, many were singled out as "potentially dangerous." Some were imprisoned, some managed to leave the country with scholarships for study abroad, some escaped into the jungle and joined the NLF, and many, thoroughly disillusioned, went to work for the Americans. "We work for the Americans whatever we do," they told us. "We might as well do it directly and get paid your high wages for it."

South Viet Nam is a land rich in both human and natural resources. Its potential for development is great. Rice paddies stretch for miles in the Mekong Delta, and virgin timberlands, open grazing lands, and some of the world's best rubber terrain dominate the Highlands. The economic potential of the narrow coastline of Central Viet Nam is more limited, though the sea is rich in fishing areas and fishing could become more profitable as the fleets are motorized. There are also some valleys in Central Viet Nam that, with irrigation, would offer good agricultural potential.

Even with so much natural richness, however, the present situation in Viet Nam offers few grounds for optimism. A quarter to a third of the population has been relocated at least once; many have been moved several times, causing a feeling of instability and rootlessness. Defoliation, indiscriminate bombings, and simple neglect have destroyed much of the agriculture. The results of defoliation, in particular, may never be overcome, since the soil, newly and mercilessly exposed to the sun, may be hardening permanently. The education system suffers from lack of teachers, overcrowded conditions, and continual political interruptions. The sudden return to civilian life of up to a million South Vietnamese soldiers threatens massive unemployment. A sudden end to American economic aid could, if not replaced by some other source, cause widespread starvation.

It is true, as Hoa said, that no one knows what is going to happen in Viet Nam. The Vietnamese have long dreamed of an end to the war. Yet no one can predict what an end will bring—what kind of government, what form of foreign assistance, or what type of economy. One thing seems clear, however: American participation in South Viet Nam's affairs will be more limited than it has been in recent years. In many ways this will be good for Viet Nam, since the whole effect of the American takeover has been to make the Vietnamese lose their sense of self-reliance and self-respect. The massive American aid programs, rather than providing chances for self-improvement and advancement, have been handled in such a way that the majority of benefits have accrued to a few—the corrupt ones and the opportunists. The Americanization process has gone all the way from the study of American geography at the expense of Vietnamese geography in the high schools, to the reliance of Vietnamese pacification workers on American payment and support. On the military side it has gone from Americans writing psychological-warfare leaflets to deciding which Vietnamese villages to relocate. It is tragic to find Vietnamese who can name the American states and their capitals but cannot say where all the Vietnamese provinces are located. It is common for Vietnamese to condemn this trend bitterly and at the same time to try to take advantage of it by obtaining scholarships to the United States, by procuring high-paying jobs with American firms, or by getting draft deferments for working as interpreters. American dominance was cynically described by the popular Vietnamese newspaper *Song Chu Nhut:*

If the American is the main director, actor, audience in the Vietnam tragedy, we, the Vietnamese, are all very honored to play unimportant roles such as prompters, clowns—playing as wicked and poor persons—both on the stage and in the audience.

Because of this all-encompassing American presence, many Vietnamese have become apathetic. They have come to see the war as a continuing state of existence, with the country occupied by foreign troops for an indefinite period. They have lost sight of their own role in the future. When students at Saigon's teacher training college were asked to list fifteen occupations in an English examination, almost every student included launderer, car washer, bar-girl, shoeshine boy, soldier, interpreter, and journalist. Almost none of the students thought to write down doctor, engineer, industrial administrator, farm manager, or even their own chosen profession, teacher. The economy has become oriented toward services catering to the foreign soldiers. These are the best paid and most secure jobs. In 1968 there were over 100,000 Vietnamese civilians employed by the U.S. military alone. Employment with the Americans has a certain snob appeal. Because of much higher pay (secretaries working for Americans earn double the wages of teachers or agricultural extension agents), they can afford to live better and dress better. Even more important for the young men is the security of working in an American office—security in terms of minimizing police searches which threaten induction into the army. Vietnamese employees in American offices make up one of the largest groups of well-trained people in the country, and while the American need for competent personnel is clear, the consequent loss to Vietnamese government makes the policy somewhat self-defeating. The ministries of agriculture and education, for example, have both made informal complaints. "How can we carry out our work," one ministry official complained, "when so many of our most able people are hired away by the Americans?" At the same time, some Vietnamese secretaries complain about not having enough to do with their new employers. "I type a letter a day, sometimes two, but mostly I make my American boss feel important because he has a private secretary," said one attractive young lady.

True economic development can only come when the people are intimately involved in the effort and when there is an abundance of trained local technicians. Up to now the Vietnamese have been largely excluded from developing their own country. For example, much of the valuable research being carried out in Viet Nam by Americans is classified and not even available to Vietnamese. Some of the material is of a sensitive nature, yet much is not. A report we once made on fertilizer requirements for delta rice was immediately classified and then made unavailable for our own use, since we were not properly cleared for these materials. A great deal of information on such subjects as skills available among refugee populations, on sociological problems, and even on various agricultural practices is unavailable because of overzealous classification. To the Vietnamese, of course, this secrecy makes the whole American effort appear as a kind of cloak-and-dagger effort threatening their sovereignty. The Americanization of Viet Nam makes them feel useless and irrelevant in their own country. In the United States, when we once attended a meeting on urban development, someone asked, "Where are the Negroes?" In Viet Nam we often attended planning meetings on national development policies and asked, "Where are the Vietnamese?"

Vietnamese need to be given the political freedom to express their ideas and the opportunity to rise according to their own merits. In the past, thousands of Vietnamese have gone abroad either in search of an easier life or because they have not found any constructive roles for themselves at home. We asked one noted Vietnamese economist living in Washington, D.C., when he planned to return to Viet Nam. "I would return right away," he said, "if my government asked me to and gave me a chance to assist my country in a challenging job. How, in such a case, could I refuse?"

The importance of Vietnamese talent abroad is often underestimated. Not only is there a wealth of political leadership in various forms of exile, but some of the country's best doctors, agriculturalists, economists, physicists, historians, and teachers have joined the "brain drain" to countries where their efforts seem more appreciated than at home. There are, for example, more Vietnamese doctors in France than in South Viet Nam itself. Many of these people will never return to Viet Nam again. They are comfortable where they are. Yet others do wish to return and are only awaiting a better day. One of these self-imposed exiles expressed his position in these words: "I would like to go back to Viet Nam to help my people. But what can I do? I would be drafted into the army immediately. I would be in the position of having to kill my people. I am an agriculturalist. I am trained to make things grow, not to destroy. If my government would ask me to come back to help my people to grow rice, even in the dangerous zones, I would gladly return."

Attempts have been made in the past to lure the exiles home, but the government has never been able to guarantee that they would be offered jobs in their own areas of specialization. The well-trained teacher with an M.A. or Ph.D. degree from some American university (usually at American expense) may end up as an interpreter or English teacher, jobs that do not adequately satisfy his expectations for helping his countrymen. Often, in fact, the Ph.D. becomes a foot soldier, and while there is indeed some social justice to this, there is little wisdom in terms of allocating precious human resources. The same problem exists for the many young people who have been trained for various vocations in Viet Nam. Many of them too are drafted as soon as they graduate. While no one can deny the military's need for manpower, it is also true that success in the Vietnamese context—where the struggle is essentially a social, political, and economic one—depends on strong civilian services. "I am quite worried by the draft obligations of this province," observed an American agriculturalist working in the rich rice-producing province of Kien Giang in 1968. "The hydraulics chief and the agriculture chief are being drafted along with numerous key civil servants. If this continues there will be very few people left in the civil service who have the experience or ability to keep the various services moving at all, let alone smoothly. . . . It has the effect of paralyzing the administration." Certainly there are solutions to the problem, and one was suggested by our self-exiled agriculturalist friend. To overcome the inevitable criticisms that these technically trained men were not drafted because they had "pull" or were rich, or because they had American connections, they could be assigned to crucial civilian jobs in the less popular rural areas. There they would be exposed to dangers too, and the skills they have learned are vitally needed.

What will happen when peace finally comes? For many of our Vietnamese friends, the current exigencies of war and survival have kept them from thinking so far ahead. Yet plans are being made and discussed by some of the very competent Vietnamese economists.

Many questions are bandied back and forth: What might be the role of foreign aid and capital investment? What kind of import controls should be established? To what extent will the state control the economy? What will be the economic relationship of North Viet Nam with South Viet Nam? These are questions that cannot be answered until a political solution has been reached. Yet some attitudes have emerged on at least two of these issues.

The accumulation of sufficient development capital, for example, is always a problem. Vietnamese have not forgotten that during the French colonial days most of the capital investment and profits were almost completely dominated by the French. Rubber production and manufacture, rice-wine distillation, beer brewing, and coal mining were monopolized by foreigners at the expense of the poor Vietnamese. More recently, the American presence, while not dominating capital investment, has increased public resentment of foreign involvement in Vietnamese national affairs. It might then be expected that the Vietnamese will be cautious about accepting aid and direct foreign investment. Although interest in American postwar aid has already been expressed by both the NLF and North Viet Nam, it has been on the condition that such aid be granted without any strings attached.

As for imports, stringent regulations have been recommended for luxury goods such as cars, refrigerators, Honda motorcycles, air conditioners, and television sets. Some commentators have noted that an emphasis on austerity and on productive types of imports, such as machinery and fertilizer, is necessary. The present import program, said one Vietnamese journalist, "is far from meeting the basic necessities of the majority of the Vietnamese people. Luxury items such as beauty products, perfume, television, cars, etc., have in fact sustained a 'dolce vita' of a wealthy urban minority in complete disregard of the broad masses which have been living in austere conditions without adequate supply of food and clothing." One consideration in any commercial policy adjustments, however, will necessarily be the interests of the Chinese community in Viet Nam. With a population of well over a million, and with a great deal of control over commerce and the national economy—power that commands both respect and resentment on the part of the ethnic

Vietnamese—the Chinese could be rather easily mobilized into a strong political force were their vital economic interests to be affected.

A peace agreement will certainly not mean an end to problems in South Viet Nam. For one thing, there is a strong likelihood that there will be no sudden, immediate end to fighting. Even if a cease-fire is declared by both sides, there are many bandit groups that have grown up over the years, posing as guerrillas and taking advantage of the inability of the police forces to cope with them. Policemen themselves have sometimes profited from their positions to "tax" the local population and pocket the money collected. Such bandits may well continue their activities until a new government is strong enough to root them out and guarantee security in the countryside. This will not be an easy task, since firearms have become widely available during the war and many have undoubtedly been secretly stockpiled for later use.

Once there is peace, however, and once the foreign presence has been reduced to less overwhelming proportions, the Vietnamese will face the task of reconstructing their society and developing its human resources. It *will* be a *Vietnamese* task, and whatever form the emerging peacetime government may take, the task will remain the same. It will involve consolidation of separated families, back-to-the-farm campaigns for rural people, light industrial development and job training—especially for soldiers released from military duty, new opportunities for Montagnards, special development projects and education reforms.

The first priority will inevitably be the encouragement of a new dedication among the Vietnamese people and a rebuilding of their source of strength—the family. War-weariness and despair must be overcome and a new sense of direction felt by the people. It is especially among the children that efforts should be directed. As families have been torn apart, the children have trickled into the cities by bus, sampan, troop transport truck, or foot. They have established themselves on street corners, begging enough to buy a shoeshine kit, or perhaps going under the wing of a slightly older boy who helps them. Their lives are centered around these street corners where they eat, sleep, beg, shine shoes, and play Vietnamese chess. As new boys come from the countryside, the old-timers take them into their custody, pass down their shoeshine kits, and then graduate themselves into picking pockets, petty thievery, and smalltime gangsterism. Some are caught, but most pay off the police. Those who do go to jail learn new tricks. In 1966, 4,000 juveniles were convicted, the Minister of Social Welfare told us, but because of lack of space only 250 of them were put in the juvenile delinquent home. The rest ended up in regular prisons with hardened adult prisoners. Time plays cruel tricks, and the children's stealing, once an act of desperation to overcome hunger and loneliness, has become a way of life. Tomorrow is not something to believe in, and everything—food, money, and friendship—must be used today before it somehow escapes.

Those of us who worked with the juveniles, however, found that the hardness of many of them is only on the surface. In Da Nang the IVS volunteers opened their homes to some of the shoeshine boys. One of them described these children: "Brought up on the street, they talk the language of the bars and the brothels; they are at the same time innocent and wise to the ways of the world. They are twelve and thirteen and maybe fourteen years old. They work from eight in the morning till twelve at night, shining shoes, and conning money any way they can. There are many ways. But these boys manage to stay within the law, and their discipline and characters are unspoiled. If I loan them money, I can expect it back. If they are given something to eat here, they prepare it and clean up afterwards in a way that would make any social worker pleased. They are generous and share equally among themselves and with us. If they buy something for themselves with the little earning they get from shining shoes, they buy something for us also. They wash themselves and their clothes frequently and with care. Their personal habits are excellent. They are a band and indeed a little family unto themselves, and their emotional solidarity is amazing. Sure there are fights and little scrapes, but they are quickly passed over and brightly forgotten."

The challenge is to prevent permanent damage to this future generation, and the answer lies partly in re-establishing their family ties. Efforts contrary to this, well-meaning though they may be, will be a disservice to the individuals and to Viet Nam. Many of the children on the streets have one or both parents still living. For these it might be helpful to establish centers which could trace down missing parents and children. It would be a long, tedious job with as many heartbreaks as successes, but in Viet Nam, with its very close family system, the location of even an aunt, an uncle, or any other relative may provide the needed home for the child. Such centers could hopefully be established in every major town and concerted efforts made to register both lost children and lost relatives. As families are reunited, day-care centers might be established to allow parents to work while their children are being cared for. In the numerous cases where parents cannot, for health or other reasons, financially support their children, material assistance and the guidance of social workers may be required. There are precedents for such efforts in the very useful and humanitarian work of private groups such as the American Friends Service Committee in Quang Ngai, the British Save the Children's Fund in Qui Nhon, and the Foster Parents Plan. A by-product of similar efforts in the future could be the relief of overcrowding in orphanages. Since better alternatives would be available for many of the children who now end up there, orphanage facilities would be required only for those whose families could not be found or who were known to have died over the years of war and suffering.

Large-scale adoptions by foreigners of Vietnamese children are not the best answer to these problems. The tragic pictures and stories of children lost and orphaned by the war have drawn worldwide attention to their plight. The problem of "Amasian" children —children with American fathers and Vietnamese mothers—has also induced sympathetic reaction. But the difficulties here are not as great as might be expected. First of all, there are not many Amasian children. Venereal disease has been very prevalent among the prostitutes and the American military has encouraged the use of contraceptives, thus preventing the large number of mixed-blood births that might otherwise have occurred. Then too, light skin is appreciated among Vietnamese, as experience with Eurasians (usually French-Vietnamese) has shown. (Vietnamese girls, in fact, go to great lengths *not* to get sunburned.) "White Vietnamese" children have thus experienced very little or no discrimination to date. In the case of "black Vietnamese" children, the problems are greater and there is discrimination.

In general, the natural reaction is for families abroad, especially Americans, to want to adopt Vietnamese children. While sometimes this is most desirable, often it is not. Aside from the fact that some of these children still have living parents or relatives who may return to reclaim them, there is the problem of older children who would react to the great differences in cultures between Viet Nam and America with a psychological shock. In 1967 we received a call for assistance from the Minister of Social Welfare. "Two women have just arrived from the United States," he said. "They represent a group of women who want to take two thousand teenage Vietnamese children to the United States for three years and then send them back to Viet Nam. These women have no understanding of our culture and the difficulties these children would have both in adjusting to life there and then readjusting to life again here in Viet Nam. Perhaps as chairman of the Council of Voluntary Agencies, you could explain why this would be so difficult." Explaining to the women why they should not take children from the slums and refugee camps of Saigon and inject them into affluent America was not easy. They had come to help, they complained, and "everybody gives us the runaround." The government of Viet Nam did not want to give a direct no because the women had letters of introduction from some American Congressmen, and they were afraid of political repercussions. Eventually, however, the women were persuaded of the possibly disastrous effects of such a plan on the children they wanted to help. They returned to the United States without any children.

In addition to re-establishing the strength of the Vietnamese family, special efforts will undoubtedly be required to assist the rural people. Since both the economic and social strength of Viet Nam lies so much in them, and because the war has caused them particular hardship, it is they who must be given better opportunities in the future. But how does the Vietnamese social worker get the bar-girl, now earning twenty times the farmer's wage, to return to the farm and plant rice? How can the thousands of children who now roam

the city streets be taught a new scale of values—that is, the traditional Vietnamese scale that their parents practiced in the countryside? How can the Montagnard soldiers who were taken from a
slash-and-burn agriculture be convinced to return to their villages,
now that the provision of a rifle has given them a new feeling of
equality with the Vietnamese?

Nothing will be easy. Yet many Vietnamese foresee the need
for a "back-to-the-farm" campaign. Viet Nam, after all, is a predominantly agricultural country. Formerly one of the world's leading rice exporters, it has in recent years been forced into a position
of importing. This trend should be reversed for a return to both
economic and social stability. A primary inducement for farmers to
return to their land is the opportunity to own it. Land ownership
should be regularized and justly shared among those who till the
soil. For most Vietnamese, and particularly for the refugees, a back-
to-the-farm movement would mean a return to their old land, which
they already owned and worked. Here assistance—presumably from
abroad—would be needed in providing food (it would be nearly a
year before the first rice crop could be harvested), seed, fertilizer,
water buffalo, and farming equipment. Farms, if they aren't used,
deteriorate quickly. The tiny dikes that separate the rice paddies
will have to be rebuilt, the irrigation canals dredged, fruit trees
replanted, and houses rebuilt.

It should be made clear from the beginning that the peacetime
government is not the same "handout" government that produced
the present class of mendicants in Vietnamese society. Thus, there
might be a charge of so many workdays of labor for each item
distributed by the government. These days of labor could be supervised by the hamlet and village councils and used to provide the
locality with needed services: a road into the hamlet, an irrigation
canal, a building for a school, or new trees to prevent erosion in a
wind-swept area. Insofar as possible, these activities should be concentrated in the slack agricultural periods so that they would not
interfere with times for rice planting and harvesting and so that
surplus labor would not be wasted.

The new homesteaders would provide the government with an
excellent opportunity for extension work. When the rice seed was

distributed, it could be IR-8, the miracle rice from the Philippines which produces two to five times the yield of local rice. Demonstrations on the use of fertilizer and insecticides could be organized. Enthusiasm and morale could be kept high by local contests in everything from rice production to rat extermination, with local people being the judges. The advantages of a return to the rural areas are, first, that it would make use of native skills and emphasize South Viet Nam's greatest natural resource, her rich, productive land; second, that it would reduce congestion in the already over-populated urban areas; and finally, that it would give meaning once again to the traditional values of the Vietnamese people, closeness to the land and close family ties.

On the other hand, it must be recognized that there are many who will not want to leave the cities. If an imaginative program is not developed for these people, the future government will be faced with an uncontrollable army of street wanderers, petty thieves, gamblers, and dope peddlers. What is needed is a good balance of job training, job provision, and a strong police force dedicated to helping the civilian population rather than to spreading terror. At the end of the war there should be a large number of soldiers who have received at least some training from which a postwar urban economy can benefit. Thousands of soldiers have learned to operate various kinds of military equipment, some of which—automotive vehicles, construction machinery, and the like—can be converted to civilian uses. The military facilities which will no longer be used after the war will include everything from barracks to airports to deep-sea ports. Some of these may have to be abandoned, for maintenance would present staggering problems. Some, however, could form the basis for industrial development in the postwar period.

Jobs for those who do not want to go back to the farms could be in cottage or light industries and in the processing of raw materials from the agricultural sector. The advantage of small cottage industries is that by making use of family labor they help to keep the family together. At the same time, they require neither large investments nor great technical skill. The advantage of processing agricultural raw materials lies in South Viet Nam's richness in agriculture as contrasted to North Viet Nam's mineral resources. An example of one kind of cottage industry that might be investigated for Viet Nam is the manufacture of rice bags. For although Viet Nam has traditionally been a large exporter of rice, it has never produced enough rice bags. Kenaf, a fiber similar to jute, grows well in many parts of the country and could be used for this purpose. Furthermore, the Vietnamese have had considerable experience in home weaving, an activity with the additional advantage of being able to employ people who have become partially disabled by the war. Examples of other cottage industries that could be expanded or developed include lacquerware, bamboo work, pottery, mat making, and on a somewhat higher level, food processing. In any case, it would be helpful if a corps of individuals could be trained soon so that teachers will be available either for on-the-job training or to teach courses in the various skills required when the war ends.

For the Montagnards in the Highlands, some guarantees of political autonomy, a bill of rights, and clear property deeds to their lands are all important. One area where the Montagnards could contribute significantly to the national economy is through beef production. Raising cattle fits well into their traditional seminomadic pattern of life, and there are vast expanses of grazing land available for this purpose in the Highlands. The most limiting factor in the past (outside of security) has been the inadequacy of marketing facilities to absorb any increase in their output. Since many of the tribal people don't speak Vietnamese and are not familiar with bargaining practices, they are at a disadvantage in the market place. Perhaps the greatest economic service a peacetime government could provide would be to set up cooperatives under Montagnard management. Such cooperatives would assist the tribal people by buying their produce at a reasonable price and by stocking both the traditional items, such as salt, cloth, and brass gongs, and the new items which the Montagnards will want to buy.

The overabundance of certain skills will cause frustrations during the postwar period. Some of the highest paid people today, such as interpreters and bar-girls, will be in little demand after the war. Some soldiers, while not well paid, may have no civilian skills or may not want to go back to the rural areas. The establishment of employment centers manned by persons skilled in job counciling could thus help to guide many of these people into productive employment. In the case of soldiers, it must be recognized that they will be anxious to get home and resume their old lives or to begin anew as soon as possible. A solution must be worked out for them that makes use of the manpower in the army, allows the soldiers to feel productive, and yet does not overburden the new economy. A program similar to the American GI Bill could, if financial support were available, absorb a small number into immediate training programs to prepare them for new careers. But in any case the release of the armies will have to be well planned, for the sudden return to civilian life of a number approaching a million young men would create employment and morale problems far beyond the capabilities of any job-counciling service to handle.

Some of the personnel released from the demands of war could conceivably be channeled into the Mekong River Development Plan. The Mekong dominates life in Viet Nam's populous delta. Its watershed, exclusive of the area beyond the Chinese border, covers a total of over 300,000 square miles in Thailand, Laos, Cambodia, and Viet Nam. Yet its waters remain untamed, and the people along its banks live in fear of floods half the year, while the land goes idle for lack of water the other half. As the Mekong flows to the South China Sea, its great potential for irrigation water, electric power, and transportation is virtually untapped. Preliminary work for increasing utilization of the river has been carried out by the United Nations Economic Commission for Asia and the Far East (ECAFE), but the political instability of the area has prevented substantial work in harnessing this valuable resource.

Another endeavor that could have a major impact on Viet Nam's economy is the Phan Rang Valley Project. The Phan Rang area has some of the best agricultural land in Viet Nam, but lack of water has left it parched and poverty-stricken. Availability of water from the Da Nhim Dam, which was constructed under Japanese war reparations, could provide the necessary ingredient to make this region one of the most productive agricultural areas of the country. A wide variety of vegetables, such as onions, garlic, beans, and corn, as well as watermelons, tobacco, cotton, and rice, could be grown there. Fishing is also an important local industry which, along with the exploitation of limestone, salt, and high-quality silica sand, could be profitably expanded. A new asset of the Phan Rang area is the nearby Cam Ranh Bay port facility, making the Phan Rang–Cam Ranh region potentially one of the most important commercial centers of the country.

Although government initiatives will surely be required in the early stages of postwar economic life, individual Vietnamese will to some extent find their own ways to adjust to the new situation. One of the principal areas in which the government will have a clear-cut responsibility to lead, however, is in the field of education and in a complete revamping of the current system. Vietnamese are the first to admit that both the quality and quantity of their present education are inadequate. The present system is a deteriorated version of the pre–World War II French structure. Where the French in France have since somewhat updated their own schools, the Vietnamese have not—or at least not enough. Even the French teachers who were in Viet Nam have mostly left by now because of a nationalistic move which recently placed their schools under Vietnamese direction. (Americans who applauded this step did not realize that it was meant as an antiforeign—and thus also anti-American—effort.) Under the old system, and partly because classes are too large and crowded to permit individual attention, children learn by rote or by the "shout and holler" method. They are not trained in problem solving. Teachers who can sometimes barely read and write themselves struggle to teach these classes of up to a hundred students, while the military has drafted qualified teachers at the rate of 3,000 per year. According to 1968 U.S. government figures, 20 per cent of the Vietnamese population between twelve and seventeen years of age are in school, and literacy (according to the UNESCO standard of ability to read and write something in any language) is about 63 per cent for the whole population. The universities are overcrowded; Saigon University's Faculty of Science, for example, has 6,000 students, and facilities for only 400. Because of the difficulty of the examinations, which are largely based on outdated mimeographed copies of the professors' lecture notes, few can graduate. Of the 8,000 students in the Saigon Faculty of Law, 381 took the exam and 95 passed it. To serve the needs of

South Viet Nam's 17,000,000 people only about 1,700 university students graduate annually.

The overall emphasis of education has been on liberal arts at the expense of such important fields as agriculture, engineering, and the sciences. The professors, instead of becoming involved in the development of one university and its students, are usually part-time instructors. They have regular jobs in one of the various ministries or they form part of the corps of "flying professors" who commute between Can Tho, Saigon, Dalat, and Hue, giving hurried lectures in each before rushing on to the next. New graduates of the teacher training colleges are assigned according to their grades. Those with the highest grades are assigned to Saigon, and the lower the grade the further away and the more remote is the assignment. This system of rewards and punishments, which was intended to inspire prospective teachers to study harder, directly affects the educational level in the more remote areas. Many of the teachers, not wanting to face the shame of teaching so far away, don't go—and the rural areas then have too few teachers. Both students and teachers protest this system, but to no avail. Nationwide meetings of educators are occasionally held and improvements are suggested. But very few are ever implemented. After the war, higher priorities should be placed on educational change, with more emphasis on developing those faculties which can supply the technicians—agriculturalists, educators, and administrators—who are most needed in a society undergoing revolutionary changes.

The answer does not lie in training more Vietnamese students in the United States or in Europe. Not only is the subject matter not adapted to Viet Nam's needs, but living abroad inevitably removes a Vietnamese from the reality of his country's problems. A Vietnamese social worker in Saigon's slums commented on those who return from such study. "The Vietnamese who have studied abroad form a second diplomatic corps. When they return home, they must have a TV set, a refrigerator, and a car. They gather together among themselves in the Vietnamese-American Alumni Association and speak English. They speak of Viet Nam's problems in an intellectual sense, but do little about them. They have no contact with their own people." Much of this is true. Even the most understanding among the foreign-trained Vietnamese are reluctant to work where electricity is not available and life seems dull.

Part of the problem has been in the selection and compensation of students who go to the United States. The tendency has been to select those who are already the most Americanized, without carefully studying the reasons of these people for wanting to go. One philosophy teacher said he was going to the United States to study about poultry. "Why?" we asked. "I hate chickens," he replied frankly, "but that is not the point. I want to go to the U.S. I have never traveled. But I can't get a scholarship to study philosophy. I'll change when I get there." The same year this man received a scholarship, one of the most able young Vietnamese in the country, who graduated at the top of his university class and was already active in the social problems of his country, was turned down. In addition to the matter of selection is the fact that the scholarships given are overly lucrative. Most Vietnamese live in the United States far better than they could in their own country and better than many of their American graduate-student associates. In the long run, this ease of living does the foreign student more harm than good; it makes the readjustment to Viet Nam that much more difficult.

For Americans, an end to the war will likely bring sighs of relief and a feeling that the problem has been finally solved. For Vietnamese, however, the "Viet Nam problem" may never be solved. The Vietnamese will have to rebuild their country and find a new way for their people—a way that will bring about modernization with minimum additional upset to social values and traditions. In order to do this, they will need to establish a consensus as to priorities and methods. In this, however, they are likely to have great difficulties. To many Vietnamese, unity is a problem of far greater concern than social and economic reconstruction. "With peace we can easily develop our country," said one. "But how can we ever have peace? Our people have always been so divided."

Although accommodation seems necessary among all the factions —the Saigon authorities, the NLF, the religious groups, and the sects—decades of war have raised tensions to very high levels. Reconciliation will be difficult and, whichever group might come out strongest in an accommodation, the loss in lives may well be great. Vietnamese fear this. Many of our colleagues who have been associated with the Saigon government are understandably afraid of what will happen to them if the NLF should gain the upper hand. Yet in the years since 1965 they have come to see that they are increasingly powerless to resist the eventuality of an accommodation government, and some have come to feel that they might be better off even under NLF rule than under continued wartime conditions.

The long-term questions in Viet Nam are more than social and economic. The main questions are whether such disparate forces as the Communist elements within the NLF and the militantly anti-Communist northern Catholics can ever live together in peace, or whether any single group can gain enough power to unify and rule all of South Viet Nam. Some have suggested that a more moderate third-force grouping might play the key role in reconciliation, but the question remains whether such a group would be able to bring together seemingly irreconcilable extremes. Pluralistic society and accommodation government are admirable in theory, but are they —given Vietnamese realities—possible? It is worth repeating that the Vietnamese share many common cultural traits, but they have united most effectively only in the face of foreign invasion. Without a common enemy, what will the Vietnamese rally around? Is it possible for the South Vietnamese ever to unify into a viable society, let alone to take the next step of gradual rapprochement with their compatriots in the North? These are the hard questions that will have to be answered by all the Vietnamese people, not in idealistic pleas for unity, but in the form of decisive choices and active commitments. They are the fundamental questions that lie at the heart of the country's problems.

In the end, it would seem that the very aspects of Vietnamese personality that have sown division within the society have also allowed the Vietnamese people to maintain their identity throughout the centuries of Chinese, French, and now American presence. The same independent spirit that divides some Vietnamese from others has also contributed to their national strength and ability to overcome their problems. The future will be decided by people like Hoa, who pulled herself up from a simple life in the rice paddies to organize students for work in the refugee camps. These people will be put to a hard test, but there is at least some reason for hope. "I still keep working to rebuild Viet Nam in our 'own' way," Hoa wrote us in 1968. "I am probably very idealistic, but I believe that we, the Vietnamese people, can *make* it."

[15]

THERE *IS* A LESSON

What We Can Learn from Viet Nam

For children in Vietnamese refugee camps, the past is hazy and they seldom talk about it. For them the new life is full of fascination. "It is more fun here in the camp than in our old village," they say, defying the opinions of their indulgent elders. "There are more people and there are more things going on!" The airplanes overhead are a source of special wonder. "Is that what you will use to return to your country?" they ask us, pointing to a jet bomber. "Is it very far to your country?"

"Yes, it is far," we tell them. "You would have to go for more than twenty hours in a jet plane like that, directly and without stopping." The youngsters gasp. "Why do you come so far to Viet Nam?" they ask. "In your country everyone is so rich, and here life is so poor."

"We come to help your people," we say.

"Oh," they reply. But they do not understand.

It is often difficult for Vietnamese—whether young or old—to understand the nature of American help to their country. It has been equally difficult for Americans to understand. "What are we to make of all you have told us?" we have been asked over and over again. "What conclusions should we draw from the American experience in Viet Nam?" "What lessons can we learn for the future?"

One of the great tragedies of the Viet Nam war may indeed be that with all the lessons that could be learned, Americans will learn the wrong ones. To some, the constantly increasing anti-American feelings among Vietnamese have been interpreted as "lack of gratitude for all we've done for them." For others, the conclusion is, "We can't trust Asians," or "Why spend our hard-earned tax money for people who live half a world away and who aren't even interested in helping themselves?" Such feelings of frustration seem to have resulted in a swing of the pendulum in America, from a position favoring a large degree of foreign involvement to a new desire for isolationism. Extremist views have become fashionable as some advocate increased military spending and militant responses to world problems, while others entertain the glib assumption that Americans can best serve the interests of other peoples by leaving them entirely alone. Meanwhile, enlightened foreign aid has run into the gravest of difficulties in the United States Congress.

Such reactions, given the physical and emotional stresses to which we have all been subjected over Viet Nam, are understandable. Yet the lessons of Viet Nam lie elsewhere. This is not the place for us to delve into history and to suggest whether or not the United States should ever have become involved in South Viet Nam. Insofar as we ourselves supported the broad outlines of U.S. policy until mid-1965, it is difficult for us to blame our country's policy makers up to that year. Their dilemmas were real ones, and they did not have the benefit of hindsight that we have today. But this *is* the time to attempt an objective reappraisal of what went wrong once we were there, with the purpose of avoiding more Viet Nams in the future.

American failures in Viet Nam have been, essentially, failures in communication and understanding. Too few, if any, Americans have understood what the Vietnamese were thinking and feeling. This is perhaps not surprising, since most Vietnamese are themselves unable to clearly articulate the full ramifications of their culture and of their desires for the future. "We need a good plan," they often say, but this sounds vague to us. The Vietnamese admit that they have brought many of their problems on themselves. "We are a hard people to save," one told an American journalist.

But the fault is more ours than theirs, for it was our duty to understand before we intervened in such great force. Convinced of the nobility of our mission to help them—a mission they can appreciate in principle—we blinded ourselves to the fact that we were soon bear-hugging the Vietnamese to death. Influenced and guided

by the ruling and urban elite, we forgot the common people. We
have, to be sure, doled out material riches, the products of our own
booming economy, yet relatively few of these riches have filtered
down to the poor people who need them most, and too few of them
have even been relevant to their real needs. The unloading of American wealth in Viet Nam has served to widen the gap between rich
and poor in a time when the people are crying out for social justice,
dignity, and the preservation of their own Vietnamese spiritual
values.

By the same token, refugees have often been unconvinced that
they are being served to best advantage when Saigon or U.S. troops
bring them from their homes under Communist control into the so-
called free areas. To many—though certainly not all—it is better to
enjoy either NLF rule or the spiritual peace of their ancestors' land,
even if physically the land is shaken by terrorism and mired in
poverty. It is better to stay at home in a thatch house, surrounded
by family, than to leave for a crowded cement house in an alien
setting.

But we Americans have never fully realized these differences.
Because of the language barrier, most Americans cannot talk with
the people or understand them. Americans are not blind, but in Viet
Nam they are both deaf and dumb. Because American understanding of the people has been so limited, the tactics devised to assist
them have been either ineffective or counterproductive. They have
served to create more Viet Cong than they have destroyed.

The American Mission has failed to acknowledge the distinction
between superficially stable governments and popular, responsive
governments. Within Viet Nam, there have always been progressive
and popular personalities and groups: the Struggle Movement forces
and the student groups, for example. In the military and in the
Saigon government itself, there have been competent leaders. But
during the course of American involvement, most seem to have
been shunted aside and branded as dangers to national stability. The
American government has stood by a series of military dictator-
ships, all of them detested by the majority of the Vietnamese people. It is hardly surprising that the stability of such regimes has
proved illusory.

The entire emphasis on military force has proved to be a mistake. Bombings and defoliation may indeed prevent the Viet Cong from grouping and moving about with complete freedom, but they also cause farmers to turn against Saigon and the Americans. The various pacification programs may indeed have been sound in terms of bringing improvements to the countryside, but their implementation has depended on dedicated and sympathetic personnel, an ingredient too frequently lacking in any effort considered an "American program."

Most serious of all have been the war's dehumanizing effects on both Vietnamese and Americans. It is often said that all wars bring suffering and that the Viet Nam war, unfortunate as it has been, was unavoidable in a world of power politics and competing ideologies. Yet the fact remains that much of the American war effort has been unleashed not against any enemy, but against innocent peasants. The enemy has been elusive, and it is seldom clear just who or where he is. To kill the enemy, it thus appears that one must kill the entire population. To the Vietnamese, it has come to seem as though their original reasons for fighting are no longer valid in the face of such destruction of their social values. To the average American GI, the long-term effects of such a cruel experience are hard to estimate. For those in the air who push the buttons that drop the bombs, the blood and terror of the innocent who are killed accidentally must weigh heavily, if remotely, on their minds. The full impact of their experiences may affect values in America itself for years to come.

It is too late to correct these mistakes and still salvage Viet Nam for America. But it is not too late to learn from them for the future. Because of our experience in Viet Nam, we have often been asked to answer the impossible questions concerning the problems there. We do not claim to have any ideal solutions for Viet Nam or for American policy. Indeed, there are no ideal solutions, and it is easier —and safer—not to answer such questions at all. Yet they must be dealt with, and choices, however fraught with peril, must be made. The general guidelines we offer here will be argued or considered presumptuous by some, and found self-evident by others. Still, we present them in the form of an outline of our own conclusions based on what we have seen and experienced as American volunteers and devoted students of Viet Nam.

What seems most clear to us is that, whatever the military role of North Viet Nam, the major issues of the war have been in the South—especially in the degree of responsiveness of the Saigon government to its people. In the South, it would seem wiser for the United States to give diplomatic support to the leaders who best respond to the needs of their people rather than to those who fulfill uniquely partisan Free World interests. Because of the divisions in South Vietnamese society, such leaders will be hard to find or define in terms of general acceptability to all factions in the country. In the end, such a suggestion may be tantamount to American acquiescence in a Communist-influenced government. If this is so, it will not be because the Communists alone are capable of responding to the needs of the Vietnamese, or because they represent a majority of Vietnamese; it will be because the anti-Communists have to a large extent forfeited their opportunities in that country.

Much has been made of the broader consequences for the rest of Southeast Asia and for American foreign policy if Viet Nam should show any turn toward communism or even if anything less than total American military victory—by now impossible—should result. There are compelling arguments concerning the threats to Southeast Asia by Communist-inspired liberation movements and by China. Yet Vietnamese history suggests that the emphasis even under a Communist government would be a primarily nationalistic one. Reunification with the North would probably come in stages, beginning with the passage of mail back and forth, proceeding to cultural, trade, and personal contacts, and culminating in some form of political union. It seems to us likely that, given its traditionally anti-Chinese orientation, a strong and independent Viet Nam could prove an ideal buffer protecting much of Southeast Asia from China.

Similarly, it would seem that an American setback in Viet Nam would not constitute proof that wars of liberation can always work. In Viet Nam, because the guerrilla cause had a historic claim to the nationalist banner, the insurgent side was especially favored. The same is not necessarily true for other countries. The best defense against successful internal subversion is responsive government. If a government cannot fulfill this basic requisite to protect itself from such an attack, then neither can outside power help it. The domino

theory, which holds that if one nation in Southeast Asia falls under
Communist sway, the others will topple in turn, would thus seem
to apply only where governments are not sufficiently well founded
in themselves, and in Southeast Asia the fate of only Laos might be
said to depend directly on that of Viet Nam.

Finally, all the above suggests to us that Viet Nam, while important, is not critical to American interests. As a nation, perhaps, we
"lose face" in retreat, but no Chinese, no Russians—none but a few
million struggling Vietnamese—are likely to gain by our loss. The
importance of Viet Nam should no longer be based on its emotional
symbolism as a test for Free World principles. Its importance now is
as a source of learning for better policies in the future.

If America's chief error in Viet Nam has been a failure to fully
understand the situation and the people, then the most important
lesson must be to improve our learning processes. Perhaps it is true
that we cannot think like Asians or ever know them completely. But
the image of an inscrutable Orient is also a myth. We can, in other
words, vastly improve our communicating skills, and we must not
hide from the necessity of doing so in this very small world.

We must begin with more careful selection of our representatives
overseas. The jobs and the tensions are such that neither those who
fail to make the grade in America, nor those who seek only high
salaries and career promotions, can be faithful to the needs. We
must insist on intensive language and area training for all our personnel who serve abroad. Our country's riches could be more use-
fully devoted to thus improving the quality of these people than to
increasing their numbers. Vietnamese have often pointed out, in
fact, that twenty poor advisers are worth nothing, while one highly
motivated and well-trained individual is worth everything.

Once qualified personnel are sent to a country, they must stay
long enough to develop a familiarity with the situations involved.
One way of improving their understanding of the ordinary people
would be by requiring aid advisers, for example, to spend at least
one day a week working with the people at the lowest level of their
specialty. If they are agricultural advisers, they should spend a day
planting rice or harvesting sweet potatoes; if they are education

advisers, they should teach a class of English at the local high school; and if they are military advisers in a place like Viet Nam, they should go on military operations with a host-country unit, sleeping in the same quarters and eating the same foods. All these activities should be carried out in the local language with no interpreter. If nothing else, the dedicated Americans, by their participation in such activities, would be more easily distinguishable from the less dedicated. Yet a day of this kind of activity would give any adviser an unparalleled understanding of the local culture and the actual situation in his field of specialty. He would become more aware of social injustices and of exploitation of the common people, while also recognizing some of the practical problems faced by his counterparts at a higher level. He would gain a better idea of why certain things are not done and at the same time would get ideas for things that might be done.

In addition to recruiting and training more qualified overseas personnel, American aid must, as a whole, be more judiciously controlled for optimum economic advantage. Those who receive our aid must meet us halfway—in terms of economic policies, not in political allegiance—and they must be willing to help themselves. There are both moral and political problems in this, since any controls can be interpreted as intervention in the affairs of other governments. Furthermore, a refusal to grant aid to unresponsive regimes could mean that the people of a country, not always to blame for their government's faults, might suffer needlessly. Yet, the Viet Nam experience has shown that aid to unresponsive governments is not only useless, but self-defeating and perhaps unjust as well. We can use our funds better in other countries or for other development projects; certainly there are in the world more than enough potential aid recipients that adequately fulfill the necessary criteria. Our enlightened discretion might even serve as pointed suggestions to the unresponsive that they should reform. Governmental responsiveness to its own people and a willingness for self-help should thus be the chief criteria for dispensing American aid abroad.

Our criticisms of the American aid mechanism must not be misunderstood. It is fitting and right for the United States to assist the developing countries of the world. The globe is too small, and man's ability to help other men is too great for us to neglect such duties. America must increase its already generous contributions to other peoples. Given our apparent outpouring of aid, it often comes as a surprise that the United States is actually one of the more miserly countries in the industrial world. While our government, according to AID, gives 0.57 per cent of the national income in foreign economic assistance, six other countries, less rich than our own, are giving a higher percentage; *nine* countries give more than the United States in terms of official and private aid combined.

Part of the problem is that the United States has overemphasized military aid. Budgetary approval for tanks and jet fighters seems easier to obtain than the smaller sums required for better vegetable seeds and schoolbooks. Some will say that America cannot be defended with seeds and books. Yet Viet Nam has shown that the most basic struggle of man is for social and economic improvement. It was at least partially the Saigon regime's failure to satisfy demands in these fields that led to the NLF's use of force. It was this same failure that helped the NLF insurgency to neutralize its opposition through apathy and even to gain active supporters for its cause. To respond to social and economic goals at their roots would thus seem wiser than waiting for war to erupt. The challenge is being faced now in Thailand and in other developing countries. A deeper American commitment to development aid is not only morally right, but in the best interests of a more peaceful world.

Still, America, though it can take the lead, cannot singlehandedly solve the world's problems. To attempt this is to invite the resentment of other nations. We have come far in recent years toward international cooperation. But we have not come far enough. An international approach to the solving of political problems and an international approach to economic development assistance must be still more wholeheartedly encouraged. Even in an age of rising nationalism, efforts should be made to avoid fragmentation and to move toward greater cooperation. In the political field, the Viet Nam experience has taught the lesson pointedly: international consensus is important to the success of any nation's behavior abroad. In Viet Nam, America has enjoyed little enthusiastic support from either its European allies or from the United Nations as a whole. In the economic and social arena, the lessons have emerged as well. Organizations like the World Bank and the International Development Association have been subject to relatively few political problems in their urging of economic reforms in developing countries. Their projects, though limited, have enjoyed remarkable success. Yet the U.S. Congress has failed to make more than a paltry contribution to these international groups. "Why should we spend our money to send some Swede to work in India?" the Congressman's constituents might ask. The prerequisite for a new American dedication to international aid is thus an aware American public responsive to new currents of thought and new realities in the world.

Perhaps the best place to begin is with the youth. In 1961 the Peace Corps gave fuel to the natural idealism of young people both in America and overseas. Since that time, tens of thousands around the world have joined in voluntary service activities. More recently, however, a sense of disillusionment has set in, as many feel unwilling to join in or accept any effort geared to advancing the parochial national interests of specific countries. They rightly feel that such an approach is becoming morally outmoded. A Vietnamese student showed the not uncommon cynicism about American aid and its handclasp symbol: "Are you trying to shake our hands or are you trying to grab something?" he asked.

A more genuinely international approach provides an attractive alternative. It would not prevent wars and it would not solve the world's problems overnight. Nothing would. Yet it could serve as a basis for understanding among peoples of different countries who know too little of one another. IVS found that the small international element of its Viet Nam team contributed significantly to the effectiveness of the whole program, not only because people from other countries brought with them valuable skills in tropical agriculture and community development, but also because they enabled Vietnamese to see IVS as a group of individuals without any vested political interests. There is no reason why an international peace corps could not be formed, giving young citizens of all the world an opportunity to serve their fellow men in nonpartisan and united development efforts. By insisting on nationally and culturally integrated teams, it would be easier to avoid the "white man's burden" approach. Advisers would be in a position to learn from the advised, and all would be enriched by the exchanges of skills and ideas that go along with teamwork.

Naturally there would be many difficulties in implementing such a plan. The challenge must be faced by more than the American government and people alone. All governments and all peoples throughout the world must face it too, and private groups and foundations must do their part. Yet the will and the spirit are abundantly available and Americans could do much to promote their success. We Americans have been most generous in our concern for others, and we have been pioneers in the field of international cooperation and assistance. Yet the times call for us to improve upon our own efforts, and to do this we must learn from the best thoughts of other peoples in other nations. As our Vietnamese friend put it, "We could really help you Americans—if only you would listen to us. . . ."

Opting out in despair is not the answer. The world moves on and we are all a part of it. Nor does the answer lie in militant or ideological responses to what are fundamentally human problems.

For years in the future, historians will piece together the story of Viet Nam and of American involvement there, and the temptation may be to fix the blame on one group or another for all that went wrong. We do not believe that America's role reflects any fundamental perversion in the American character, or that Vietnamese actions reflect any in their own. When all is said and done, there are no villains in this story; there are only ordinary human beings who have somehow been pushed—or plunged themselves—into a dilemma. In the desperate effort to get out, something has happened to them—and to all of us. The errors committed in Viet Nam are thus based in human faults that became exaggerated. But they are faults that can be corrected.

In order to correct them we must begin with a more humble understanding of this world and of the aspirations of its diverse peoples. We must hear their voices and try to put ourselves in their position. Only when we make this effort can we begin to respond honestly and effectively and learn some of the lessons of Viet Nam. For in the final analysis, the lesson of Viet Nam is that "our enemy is not a man; if we kill the man, with whom do we live? Our enemy is inside each one of us."

Appendix

TEXT OF LETTER TO PRESIDENT JOHNSON,

September 19, 1967

[Simultaneously with the signing of this letter by forty-nine IVS members, Don Luce and three other staff leaders resigned from their positions so that they "could speak out freely" on what they "saw and felt." The letter and resignations, coming from persons so close to the Vietnamese and so close to the implementation of American policy, made a deep impression in government and nongovernment circles—and in the world press—for months thereafter.]

Dear Mr. President:

As volunteers with International Voluntary Services, working in agriculture, education, and community development, we have the unique opportunity of living closely with Vietnamese over extended periods of time. Thus we have been able to watch and share their suffering, one of us since as early as 1958. What we have seen and heard of the effects of the war in Vietnam compels us to make this statement. The problems which the Vietnamese face are too little understood and their voices have been too long muffled. It is not enough to rely on statistics to describe their daily concerns.

We present this statement not as spokesmen for International Voluntary Services, but as individuals.

We are finding it increasingly difficult to pursue quietly our main objective: helping the people of Vietnam. In assisting one family or one individual to make a better living or to get a better education it has become evident that our small successes only blind us to how little or negative the effect is, in the face of present realities in Vietnam. Thus to stay in Vietnam and remain silent is to fail to respond to the first need of the Vietnamese people—peace.

While working in Vietnam we have gained a genuine respect for the Vietnamese. They are strong. They are hard working. They endure. And they have proved over and over their ability to deal with foreign interference. But they suffer in the process, a suffering greatly intensified by today's American presence. This suffering will continue and increase until Americans act to ease their suffering. It is to you, Mr. President, that we address ourselves.

Our testimony:

The effects: We do not accuse anyone of deliberate cruelty. Perhaps if you accept the war, all can be justified—the free strike zones, the refugees, the spraying of herbicide on crops, the napalm. But the Vietnam war is in itself an overwhelming atrocity. Its every victim—the dead, the bereaved, the deprived—is a victim of this atrocity. We are usually far from the scenes of the worst brutality, however more than enough still comes to our attention. Viet Cong terrorism is real; so are the innocent victims of U.S. bombing, strafing, and shelling.

What we have seen: We have all seen or known about the human results of this war. Therefore we do not need to list an awful tally of atrocities. How Vietnamese react to these atrocities, however, is little known.

One week before the election, Viet Cong indiscriminately sprayed mortars on the Delta city of Can Tho, hitting hospital wards, and demolishing poorly constructed houses; the toll: thirty Vietnamese dead, three hundred wounded (the more solidly built houses of Americans prevented any American casualties). A small anti-Viet Cong rally was held the next day, but according to one resident, "Many of the people here place the ultimate blame on the Americans. . . . If the Americans weren't here in the first place this wouldn't have happened."

One day after the elections a Saigon paper (*Than Chung*—banned the next day) ran two pictures of bomb destruction in North Vietnam with the following comment (translation): "We can never accept the one-party system in North Vietnam but neither are we able to forget our blood ties with our fellow Vietnamese there, just as we are unable to forget the Vietnamese caught in the mortar attacks on Can Tho and Thang Binh. . . ."

For the Vietnamese, victory at any price is no longer acceptable.

We have flown at a safe height over the deserted villages, the sterile valleys, the forests with the huge swaths cut out, and the long-abandoned rice checks. We have had intimate contact with the refugees. Some of them get jobs at American military establishments and do fairly well. Others are forcibly resettled, landless, in isolated, desolate places which are turned into colonies of mendicants. Others go to the Saigon slums, secure but ridden with disease and the compulsion towards crime. These are refugees generated not by Viet Cong terrorism, but by a policy of the war, an American policy.

One volunteer wrote, "Cai Be (in the Mekong Delta) has a very successful refugee program as measured by the criteria of the government, but when measured by any human criteria it stinks. We have neatly arranged hamlets, good canals, military security, elections and dozens of other assets which win points in Saigon, but we don't have people living decent lives. . . . These refugees are, with few exceptions, farmers but they have been settled on plots of land so small that only the ingenious manage anything like a decent life. I say that the most ingenious can do this without knowing a single person who is that ingenious. . . . Not only do (refugee camps) force these people into an existence which is marginal at best, they do incalculable violence to the customs and traditions of the Vietnamese people. . . . The government has not offered a new and better life, it has only exchanged one form of terrorism for another." This is a situation created by a policy of war. But as one ranking American officer has said, "Refugees are a GVN problem."

What we've heard: Just as in the United States, in Vietnam there is no consensus about how the war should be stopped. But there is consensus on one issue: it *must* be stopped. To relate what the Vietnamese think is difficult, but we can relate what they say.

In a refugee village one of us heard an old woman say these words (translation): "These days of sorrow are filled with napalm, hate, and death. The rice fields turn brown. The new year brings a cold, clutching fear."

A young Buddhist teacher, on the eve of her self-immolation, made her last attempt to express the anguish of the Vietnamese people: "You Americans come to help the Vietnamese people, but have brought only death and destruction. Most of us Vietnamese hate, from the bottom of our hearts, the Americans who have brought the suffering of this war. . . . The tons of bombs and money you have poured on our people have shattered our bodies and sense of nation." A Saigon Catholic youth leader, active for over ten years in the youth movement, said: "We are caught in a struggle between two power blocs, and we can never forget that. Many people told me you cannot trust Americans, but I never accepted it. Now I am beginning to believe it. You come to help my people, but they will hate you for it." At the Ong Ich Khiem Pagoda in Danang, the broken heart of last year's Struggle Movement, a Vietnamese friend paused at a shrine, by a wall covered with photographs of young boys and girls. "Killed by Ky's Saigon troops during the Struggle," he explained in restrained English, by soldiers brought up to Danang by hastily-loaned American C-130's in the interests of "stability." A Vietnamese who teaches English scribbled out a poem over beers in a tiny dirt-floor restaurant:

> Monsoon laughters, peace for this shattered land
> of troubled minds of corrupted men
> of human pyramids of blood-soaked rice
> of hungry faces of pitiless barb wire.

The tide of the war: As volunteers in Vietnam, we work with people, not statistics. War reported in statistics gives a false picture. We read the monthly totals of Hoi Chanh (Open-Arms returnees), and then ask who these people are. Hard-core Viet Cong, suddenly disillusioned with a philosophy that has been their life and bread for years? No. They are marginal Viet Cong at best, if Viet Cong at all, looking for a little rest from this tired war and attracted by the dollar signs of the program. People who can be bought are not going to effect change in Vietnam. We read with anguish the daily body count of "enemy" dead. We know that these "enemy" are not all combat soldiers committed to one side. Many are old men, women, and young boys who ran when a helicopter hovered, who were hiding from the bombs in an enemy bunker, or who refused to leave their farms. We watch the development of the pacification program, from "strategic hamlet" to "revolutionary development" (an American term; in Vietnamese it is called "rural building"), and see teams of cadre operating in the villages. Who are these cadre? Young men and women, often motivated by draft exemption and the security of a government job, with three months' training in concepts that take several years to master. To the villagers, these black-pajamaed "imitation Viet Cong" are more interference from the government, perhaps the source of another handout. Certainly they are not a step towards "capturing the hearts and minds" of the villagers. Yet, RD cadre have also lost their lives in this war.

A road opens up, another closes. While working in Vietnam, we must travel these roads. We have not seen any increase in security in the past year. In Saigon and in other cities, roads are secure but they are full of holes from the steady flow of American tanks and trucks.

A village lives peacefully under Viet Cong control. Government or American troops arrive to "liberate" the population. Violence ensues, refugees are created, but the Viet Cong vanish. If the military decides not to plow the village under (as was Ben Suc in Operation Cedar Falls), the Viet Cong will come back and resume their authority.

Prostitution increases, corruption increases, crime in the streets increases, and more and more capable people join their compatriots —either the Viet Cong or those on the American payroll. The former have dedicated themselves to a difficult and uncomfortable struggle, with no end in sight. The latter have sought the easier road: the American dollar, a comfortable life, outwardly compromising their own culture. Inwardly they have not. In their eyes the U.S. is the exploiter to be exploited.

An election is held to legitimize a government generally detested by the Vietnamese. Cries of fraudulence are everywhere, but the U.S. ignores these cries in the person of Henry Cabot Lodge: "I think these elections were as good and orderly and wholesome as our own elections," he said after less than a week of observation.

Some results: the banning of two Saigon papers (*Than Chung, Sang*) on the day after the election, the two papers which were the most outspoken against the government and for peace during the campaign. "The elections are over," announced Vice President-elect Ky, after banning all press conferences without government approval. Repression continues.

While the U.S. has announced its dedication to the building of democracy in South Vietnam, it continues to support a government which jails pacifists and neutralists. The U.S. has repeatedly announced its support for self-determination, and yet assigns advisors to everyone from the top military command to the Department of Waterworks in Saigon. Credibility of leaders is a problem in the United States; in Vietnam there is no credibility. Rumors say that the United States has a 99-year lease on Cam Ranh Bay. True? That is not important. It is what the Vietnamese think that is important. They have no illusions about why the U.S. is in Vietnam. Many feel that America is in Vietnam to stop communism—at all costs. In some ways defeating communism fits Vietnamese interests *vis-à-vis* China, whom these people have fought for a thousand years. There is no love for China, even in the North. "A unified Vietnam," said a Saigon youth, "under Ho Chi Minh would not succumb to China." But they shudder when they see North Vietnam's being forced to accept her support. Self-determination in the North, as well as in the South, is being compromised by the American policy.

Conclusions: The war as it is presently being waged is self-defeating in approach. U.S. programs are meant to gain the confidence and admiration of the Vietnamese people through the Vietnamese government. "There is more anti-Americanism here today than there was before," said an IVS volunteer returning to Vietnam again after having spent three years here from 1963 to 1966.

The U.S. continues to support a power group which has proven for five years that it is unable to bring about unity and peace in South Vietnam. "When the Americans learn to respect the true aspirations in Vietnam," said a youth leader recently, "true nationalism will come to power. Only true nationalists can bring peace to the South, talk to the North, and bring reunification." Cried another youth leader, "Who is Nguyen Cao Ky? Ho Chi Minh and Vo

Nguyen Giap have been fighting for Vietnam since before Ky was born. Why should they talk to him?"

What we recommend:

1. Even in our situation, normally far from the fighting, we have seen enough to say that the only monuments to this war will be the dead, the maimed, the despairing and the forlorn. The trend has been escalation of the war. We say the trend should be de-escalation.

2. Children, old people, and the sick—not organized groups of armed men—are the most likely victims of defoliation. We say stop the spraying of herbicides.

3. Bombing stands in the way of negotiations. We have seen the results of bombing in South Vietnam, and can imagine what it has done to the North. We say stop the bombing.

4. No satisfactory conclusion of this war will come until all parties are represented in peace parleys. A movement in South Vietnam calls for the recognition of the National Liberation Front to be included in peace talks. We say recognize the National Liberation Front.

5. The United States continues to let self-interests stand in the way of self-determination in Vietnam. The U.S. must prove its commitment to compromise instead of waging an endless war of attrition. We say turn the question over to an international peace commission and be prepared to accept its recommendations.

By speaking to these questions, we have seriously jeopardized our positions in Vietnam. Some of us feel that we can no longer justify our staying, for often we are misinterpreted as representatives of American policy. Others of us wish to stay and to continue to serve the Vietnamese. It is with sadness, therefore, that we make our view known. But because above all our first concern is for the Vietnamese, there is no alternative. It is their cry and ours: End this war.

DEST	CARRIER
LAX	THAI AIRWAYS INTL.

FLIGHT		NAME
TG 770	30JAN	BILOFSKY, HOWARD

BOARDING		SEAT			
TIME	GATE		FIRST	BUSINESS	ECONOMY
0630	11				47F

Thai

Note

ABOUT THE AUTHORS

Don Luce, a native of East Calais, Vermont, received a bachelor's degree in agricultural economics from the University of Vermont in 1957 and a master's degree in agricultural development and farm management from Cornell University one year later. He joined International Voluntary Services in 1958 as an agricultural team member in the Highlands of South Viet Nam and in 1961 was named IVS director for the country, a post he held until his resignation in 1967. During his last year there he was chairman of the Council of Voluntary Agencies. On his return to the United States he was appointed a research associate in the Center for International Studies, Cornell University. He also wrote several articles about Viet Nam, lectured all over the United States, and was a guest on numerous television and radio programs. After completing his work on this book he returned to Viet Nam for a fresh look at the country under the joint auspices of the Board of Social Concerns of the United Methodist Church and Cornell University.

John Sommer, raised in Montclair, New Jersey, majored in comparative literature at Wesleyan University in Middletown, Connecticut, and studied for short periods in France and Germany. Receiving a bachelor's degree with distinction in 1963, he volunteered for IVS service in South Viet Nam. He worked for two years on education projects in the Highlands and then was named a team leader for IVS, working primarily in Hue and Central Viet Nam but also in other areas. Completing his most recent IVS service in 1967, he has lectured on Viet Nam in several countries under U.S. Information Agency auspices, pursued a master's degree which he received in 1968 from the Johns Hopkins School of Advanced International

Studies in Washington, and successfully completed the U.S. Foreign Service Officer examinations. He returned to Viet Nam briefly in early 1968 with Senator Edward M. Kennedy, as a consultant to the Senate Judiciary Subcommittee on Refugees, and he has also served as newsletter editor for the Viet Nam Education Project sponsored by the United Methodists' Board of Social Concerns. He is currently associated with the Ford Foundation in New York City.

INDEX